WAR,

EVIL,

AND THE
END OF
HISTORY

bernard-henri lévy

war,
evil,
and the end of history

TRANSLATED BY CHARLOTTE MANDELL

 MELVILLE HOUSE PUBLISHING
HOBOKEN, NEW JERSEY

© 2004 MELVILLE HOUSE PUBLISHING

ORIGINALLY PUBLISHED IN FRENCH AS
RÉFLEXIONS SUR LA GUERRE, LE MAL ET LA FIN DE L'HISTOIRE

© 2001 EDITIONS GRASSET & FASQUELLE

THANKS TO THE FRENCH MINISTRY OF CULTURE
FOR THEIR ASSISTANCE TOWARD THE TRANSLATION.

MELVILLE HOUSE PUBLISHING
P.O. BOX 3278
HOBOKEN, NJ 07030

BOOK DESIGN: DAVID KONOPKA

ISBN: 0-9718659-5-7
FIRST EDITION

LIBRARY OF CONGRESS CATALOGING-IN-PUBLICATION DATA

LÉVY, BERNARD HENRI.
  [RÉFLEXIONS SUR LA GUERRE, LE MAL ET LA FIN DE L'HISTOIRE. ENGLISH]
  WAR, EVIL, AND THE END OF HISTORY / BERNARD-HENRI LÉVY ; TRANSLATED
BY
CHARLOTTE MANDELL.
    P. CM.
  INCLUDES BIBLIOGRAPHICAL REFERENCES.
  ISBN 0-9718659-5-7
  1. POLITICAL VIOLENCE--AFRICA. 2. LOW-INTENSITY CONFLICTS (MILITARY
SCIENCE)--AFRICA. 3. AFRICA--POLITICS AND GOVERNMENT--1960- 4. SRI
LANKA--HISTORY--CIVIL WAR, 1983- 5. POLITICAL VIOLENCE--COLOMBIA. 6.
INSURGENCY--COLOMBIA. 7. COLOMBIA--POLITICS AND GOVERNMENT--1974-
I.
TITLE.
  DT30.5.L48513 2004
  303.6'4--DC22
                    2004003657

Contents

When September 11 happened my first reaction was, like every-one else, fear and astonishment.

Never, in the long history of terror, had an attack produced so many victims.

Never had a terrorist group so impeccably defined, in the same gesture, its military and symbolic targets.

Never had we felt so overwhelmingly the vulnerability of democracies faced with a threat, the scale of which, we all felt, had just changed, and we felt too that this was far from being the last word on this new scale.

I remembered what President Izetbegovic had confided in me, at the end of the Bosnian war: Iraq, as he knew from his intelligence services, had launched a vast program to build missile warheads equipped for long-range transport of bacteriological substances.

I remembered my last conversation with Massoud, that other enlightened Muslim, sworn enemy of the Taliban, who was assassinated just a few hours before the attack—as if his elimination was also part of the plan: according to him, Pakistan had, for several years, provided itself with weapons of mass destruction which, if its vital interests were at stake, it would not hesitate to use.

We hadn't reached that point, of course.

Especially since one of the peculiarities of this terrorism was exactly that it seemed to elude the old logic of "rogue states" as we had known it in previous decades: now it was a trans-governmental network; an international federation of organizations based in London or New Jersey as well as in Iraq or Pakistan; a NGO of crime; a cold-blooded monster without a state; a private army, without a country; an opponent intent on bringing us down, but all the more elusive since it couldn't be reduced to any of the public enemies that the United States of America had thought it was keeping at bay at the very moment when, from within, the greatest terrorist attack of all time was being hatched. . .

Still. That this terrorism was raised, that day, to a higher scale and a higher speed, that it began to feed on almost limitless scenarios of destruction, that we could feel it heading towards giant operations next to which all we had known till then (including, perhaps, the attack against the World Trade Center) would one day seem linked with the old world, that the worst, in other words, was yet to come—that is what, in the confusion of those days, in our grief, pity, and rage, seemed clear to many of us.

"War," ran the headlines of most of the major Western newspapers.

Well, yes, war. Many were those who, in the emotion of the time, thought the Western world was in fact at war. Many thought it would be a long war, very long, with victories, retreats, convulsive crises, periods of cooling down or cold war. Carrying to the end the notion of a fundamentalism that was taking the place of Communism on the stage of History on which the West had believed, wrongly, it could reign without opponent, I myself wrote that it was like a return to the 1920's, and that we had to stand together.

We saw the return, here and there, of a few whiffs of simplistic anti-Americanism. That seemed to me despicable.

The second reaction, which came almost right away: annoyance and then, very quickly, rage against the ignoramuses who, under pretext that the authors of these attacks had been raised in the shadow of Pakistani *madrasas*, and under pretext, too, that part of the mob, in Gaza, Baghdad, Damascus, or Islamabad, saw these kamikazes as new martyrs who had gone to avenge, with blood, the wrongs done to the "Muslim nation," fell for the idea of an alleged war of civilizations between Islam and the West.

The cleverest people quoted Nietzsche announcing that the wars of the future would be wars of ideas and world visions.

Others exhumed Samuel Huntington, author of a little work in which, in reply to the Neo-Kojevians (who, on the eve of the fall of the Berlin Wall, thought they saw passing beneath their windows, not History, but its end) he foresaw a war of the West against the rest of the world — "the West" versus "the rest," and, in the heart of this "rest," Islam.

There were even observers who noted that literature, as usual, had said everything before everyone else, since a French novelist, playing new notes on the old octaves of Céline, thought it a good thing, a few days before the tragedy, to lambaste the Muslim religion and its sacred book.*

In short, the same old tune kept being repeated everywhere to explain that there was "a problem with Islam": at best, Islam

---

*A reference to *Plateforme* by Michel Houellebecq.

was an obscurantist vision of the world that couldn't mix with modernity, was incompatible with the rights of man, democracy, secularity, the Enlightenment; at worst, Islam was a murderous, conquering religion, which carries massacres along with it as a cloud carries rain, and which had declared total war on the United States and on Europe.

I was not—far from it—a specialist in Islam.

But, like everyone else, I knew the story of the abolition of the Caliphate by Ataturk, or the history of Nasser's Pan-Arabism—proofs that Islam was not as incompatible as all that with the secular.

I knew, pretty intimately, the situation of Islam in Bosnia, and even, though not as well, that of the Senegalese brotherhoods—proof that Islam was foreign neither to democratic tradition nor to the law.

I knew, from my friend Christian Jambet, that the very word "jihad," quoted everywhere as signifying Islam's holy war against the world of the infidel, is a word that has taken on this meaning only recently and that, before that, before the Muslim Brothers, before the Wahhabites, before the Hanbalite school of Ibn Taymiyya, in short, before the end of the eighteenth century, it had always meant, literally, and for all the Muslims in the world, "effort on the path of God": a word of morality, not of politics; a word that expresses the spiritual tension of the faithful working, through prayer or asceticism, to get closer to God; a war, yes, if one insists, but an inner war, between self and self, a war of self against self.

I knew enough about Islam, in other words, to suspect that, at the very least, two Islams exist. The new war, if there had to be a war, would be waged between these two Islams as well as between Islam and the West; and that to accept his idea of an Islam entirely set against a Satanized West was truly too handsome a gift to give Bin Laden and those who resemble him, and for whom he was perhaps only the front man.

That there was also an obscurantist Islam was obvious.

That one could, in the beginning of the twenty-first century, in a Muslim country like the Sudan, be killed because one was Christian or animist, I knew something about that, since I had just returned from there.

That one could, in Pakistan—another country I knew a little (from the war of Bangladesh in the 1970's)—be condemned to death because one wore a Christian cross, or because one owned a rosary or a Jewish bible, or because one had said, in a low voice, to a friend, "If you want to know the truth about Islam, read Salman Rushdie." that was also a fact.

No doubt the time had come to denounce this fact, and these other self-evidences, loudly and vociferously. There was, there still is, an urgency to undertake an *aggiornamento*, a stock-taking, a general declaration, not of dogmas, but of the ideological formations to which these dogmas have given rise: can't the Islam that adapted to so many historical and geographical situations, the Islam that is so good at playing the game of modernity when it involves new technologies or world financial markets, can't that Islam disown the sects (the fundamentalists, the Wahhabites, the diverse disciples of the eleventh-century sect of the Assassins, the Taliban) that persist in distorting its ancestral message of mercy and peace? Isn't the world justified in urging Islam's political, moral, and spiritual authorities to appeal to the kamikaze trainees, from Cairo to Lahore, and from Samarkand to the French suburbs, to tell them in the most solemn way possible that it is not true, they will not go to paradise, martyrdom is in no way a means to win divine grace and blessing?

But from that to casting opprobrium on more than a billion human beings and on the faith that animates them, to identifying these billion human beings with the evil masters of whom, just after the World Trade Center deaths, they too will sooner or later be the designated victims, from that to falling in step with those who proclaim to us the clash of cultures but who actually do nothing but mount racial attacks, from all that is a step that I, for my part, categorically refused to make: I refused to respond to those who satanize the West with an opposite but equal satanizing of Islam.

The essential thing, for me, was not that.

I participated in those debates, of course; I gave my opinion on the future of Islam, Huntington, the risks and opportunities of an American military response, and so on, but I had my mind, literally, on something else.

I had my mind on this book, in fact; on the people, scenes, and climate of this book—I could not prevent myself from seeing what I was seeing in the persistent light of what I had just experienced, for months, of which this book was the fruit.

Kamikazes, for instance. In Sri Lanka, I had met a repentant kamikaze, a woman whose words, and even whose face, haunted me and kept appearing to me superimposed over what we learned, in the ensuing hours, about the World Trade Center murderers. I returned to my notes. I went over everything she had told me, and everything I hadn't used, about the enigma of this action in which one chooses to die in order to kill, to mingle one's holy death with the unclean death of one's victims. Didn't the killers have another way, after all? Weren't there solutions—bacteriological attack, missiles, Sarin gas as in Tokyo—other than this sacrificial solution? What is going on, in other words, in the head of a man or a woman who, from among all possible solutions, chooses the one that will allow him to accompany his victims in their death? I spent hours scrutinizing the pictures of Mohammed Atta and Ziad Jarrahi. I tried to imagine their life; their death; the last instants in the cockpit; the final questions, when they veered toward the towers; the way they watched each other's every move; the pressure of the group making sure each one was at the same stage of voluntary death as his companions; the morbid diminishing of their will, always subject, on the verge of a suicidal act, to a last-minute about-face; the immediate punishment of the defaulter; and then, before all that, well before it, the preparation they must have had for them to be capable, at the finish, of this insane action. Everyone has said so: it was a preparation that must have been spread out over years. But what, exactly, happened during these years? What kind of apprenticeship was needed—not just technical, but intellectual, moral, even, dare we say it, spiritual—to be absolutely certain that you would go to the very end, that you wouldn't break down, and that you would violate everything that attached you to your own life, to the passions of existence? My Sri Lankan had described her training camp in the Wanni to me as a place of ideological, as well as military, work. She had described the camp leader to me as a kind of master, endowed with a demoniac influence. Shouldn't we assume the existence, somewhere in Afghanistan or elsewhere, of a sort of academy of crime, a West Point of terrorism, a sect of murderous excellence devoted to this double schooling, mercilessly selecting its recruits?

The ruins. That landscape of ruins to which, in the images shown by all the televisions in the world, the lower part of Manhattan seemed reduced. Faced with these images of desolation, faced with the staggering spectacle of American power temporarily reduced to rubble, faced with this dead city of New York where, for those few days, one passed only shadows, wandering in the debris of steel and concrete, covered with ash and gray powder, some thought of a scene from a science-fiction film; others, of a page from a Tom Clancy novel; I couldn't prevent myself from thinking of those other dead cities, also in ruins, where I had been a few months earlier, and which I had just finished describing for this book. Kuito and Huambo, in Angola... Gogrial in the South-Sudan... All those ghost cities, inhabited by ghosts, which presented exactly the same spectacle... All those pages I had written, and that seemed to me now so strange, on ruin according to Hegel and according to Walter Benjamin... And then, before that, the shock of Sarajevo devastated—that day in 1994, especially, when I had gone to Washington to present *Bosna!* to Hillary Clinton and a panel of incredulous congressmen: "Imagine," I said to them, "a European city reduced to ashes... imagine a large American city reduced to the state of a black hole by a bomb..."; I didn't think I had conveyed the idea well; I didn't think, no one could have thought, that the great urbicidal madness that would be one of the marks, in the twentieth century, of all fascisms without exception, would one day hit here, in Washington, in New York, reducing them to the state of Angolan cities....

BERNARD-HENRI LÉVY

The disappeared. Those thousands of men and women buried in a million tons of rubble, perhaps crushed to death, whose bodies, at the time I write this, have not been found. No way I could fail to think of the black holes which were everyday life in the places from which I had just returned. No way could I not have in mind, now more than ever, those thousands of other men and women, buried in the Angolan diamond mines, swallowed up by the Burundian brush, scattered, forgotten. I couldn't prevent myself from thinking again of all I had just reported, a few weeks earlier, on the grief of the absent grave and the impossible mourning that ensues from it. Not, of course, that one erases the other or puts it into perspective. Or that my impressions of Africa or Asia were apt to weaken, in some way, the feeling of revulsion that flooded me. Or even that I gave in to facile, conventional indignation, full of nauseating ulterior motives, at the famous double-standards: "an unending array of images for Manhattan's disappeared—no images at all, scarcely a trace, for those of Burundi, Sri Lanka, the Nuba mountains." No. The resemblance, simply. A kind of contagion, proliferation of disaster. A company of ghosts that began, suddenly, to recruit from among the prosperous. The feeling of belonging to a world that had believed it could banish the Tragic, zap Evil, give notice to the very reality of things replaced by sweet and inoffensive holograms but that then saw them reappear, the Tragic, this Evil, this Reality, along with the meteoric violence of the return of the repressed. We were all Americans? Yes. But we were also all Burundians. All Angolans, Sudanese, Colombians, Sri Lankans. I saw Western humanity being caught up with by all those living-dead that it had wanted neither to know nor to hear.

And then the End of History. I never believed much in this business of the End of History. I even devoted another book, *La Pureté dangereuse* (Dangerous Purity), to pleading that History, as Marx says, has more imagination than men do, including the disciples of Kojeve, and that, just as the devil's greatest trick was, according to Baudelaire, to make us think he doesn't exist, so History's greatest trick is perhaps to play the comedy of its own exhaustion. But it is here, or rather today, that I have the feeling of seeing it most clearly. It is here, in the pages you are about to read, that I tried to think, especially, of the forms the confrontation could take place between, on one hand, historic countries, the metropolises of "world history"—and then the "provinces of the empire" on the other, the peripheral lands we have condemned to exit from the contemporary era very quietly. Well, here we are again. History was back. It was starting up again. The stock of possible barbarisms, which we had thought exhausted, had just been increased with an unprecedented variant. As always, as it is every time we thought it lifeless or dormant, it's when no one expected it that it woke up with the greatest fury and, especially, invention: other theaters, new front lines and new opponents, all the more formidable since no one had seen them coming.

And then there was, once again, the "damned." There were those crowds of poor people who were, for months, in the heart of my life and from whom I could not manage to detach my thoughts. What would be their place in the world that was being planned? Forgotten forever? Denied, more than ever? Witnesses, absolutely mute, of a confrontation that will in no way concern them and that will ignore them in every way? A third party resolutely excluded from a new war of the prosperous—for the

Islamists also, in their way, are prosperous—that will throw them back, for good, into the world of yesterday? Or, on the contrary, will they be sought out? Mobilized? Through ways that are for the moment impenetrable, reintroduced as factors in a game where no one knows the rules? A schema, at bottom, similar to that of the cold war, that time ("blessed" or "wretched," that is one of the questions of this book...) when their wars "had a meaning" and "participated in a worldwide struggle"? Could it be, to put it simply, that certain Tamil kamikazes, or a certain group of Sudanese guerillas, or a certain sect of Colombian drug-traffickers, was providing one of the two camps with auxiliaries? Can't we see the new army of crime importing child-soldiers, as slaves used to be imported? Still another hypothesis, the worst one: is it unthinkable that some, from among those excluded from meaning and historicity, had the terrible temptation, schooled by terrorism, to bring vividly back to mind those who condemn them, and who will continue to condemn them, to the role of voiceless torture victims? Among all those damned who listened to us declaring the ceremony of History over, won't there be other kamikazes who will say to the nations, "You ignored us alive, here we are dead; you wanted to know nothing about this death as long as it occurred in our homes, but now we throw it at your feet, in the inferno that consumes you; we were invisible alive, but now we suicides will become visible in death"? Some questions. I don't know.

The reader will find below, making up the first third of this book, a series of narratives of journeys that appeared in *Le Monde*, in somewhat shorter versions, from May 30 to June 4, 2001. He will also find, punctuating these narratives, fifty or so references to notes that refer to the same number of "Reflections," retrospective and in no particular order. Is it a question, strictly speaking, of notes? Or of philosophical and political afterthoughts? Or of the tatters of an older memory? Or offshoots? Or developments that didn't find their place in the articles but that suggested themselves afterwards? What is certain is that the ordered series of these digressions constitutes, ultimately, the main part of this work. As if, in this sort of business, it's up to remorse to gain the upper hand. As if the follow-up of an idea, or of a vision, is more important than its beginning.

The Damned

For a long time, wars used to have meaning. Just wars and unjust wars. Barbaric wars or wars of resistance. Wars of religion. Wars of national liberation. Revolutionary wars where we attacked heaven to build a new world there. Or other wars, all the wars, contemporaneous with a Marxism that had, among other virtues, the virtue of giving some guerilla from the Moluccas, from southern India or from Peru, the so-to-speak providential self-assurance that he was not fighting without reason since he was, even without knowing it, actively involved in a worldwide battle. Those days are over. The decline of Marxism, along with all the great narratives that conspired, with it, to give a meaning to what had none, namely to the infinite pain of men, has shattered that dogma. And it's like a great tide that has withdrawn, leaving behind it men and women, who continue to fight, who do so even, sometimes, with redoubled ferocity, but without our being able to read in their confrontation any trace of the promises, the coherences, or the epiphanies of former days. There still exist, of course, serious wars, which have a meaning. There still exist, in the Near East, for instance, wars where everyone can see that the fate of the world is at stake. But other conflicts are becoming more and more common, which have seemingly let go of the cord that tied them to the Universal, and about which one has the feeling, rightly or wrongly, that their outcome can no longer change anything in the planet's fate.

One could express this differently. For a long time, in our countries, the feeling of the Absurd, or of the Tragic, was conjugated in the singular. One believed in the Absurd, but only in private life. One wanted to think of the senseless, the being-for-death, but only in terms of individual destinies. But when the great temper-tantrums of our species occurred, when Humanity entered the scene in splendor or convulsion, then one changed one's tune and launched into the other kind of music, the other fanfare—the same people who had sworn only by Sartrean "nausea" now found it hard to imagine pure barbarities, naked violence; they explained to us that the collective, dark as it was, is necessarily the place for rational schemes and their obligatory fulfillment. Well it's for that attitude, too, that the forgotten wars of the twenty-first century sound the death knell. It is this naïve and, essentially, reassuring metaphysics that, from the depths of the night, the Angolans, Burundians, Sri Lankans, Sudanese, and Colombians force us to relinquish. With them comes a world where, for the first time in the modern era, and because the great narratives that provided meaning have fallen silent, great masses of men are caught in wars without aim, without clear ideological stakes, without memory, as the wars last for decades, perhaps without outcome—and where it is sometimes difficult indeed to tell, between protagonists who are drunk with equal parts of power, money, and blood, where lies the true, the good, the least evil, the desirable. It is the triumph, if you like, of Céline over Sartre. Or of the Sartre of *Nausea* over the one of

The Critique. It is a new world that is appearing where Job has the face, not of one suffering Just Man, but of entire peoples, continents, abandoned to this radical desolation—the same useless suffering, the same emptiness of heaven and of meaning and, in our midst, the same professors of distress who, like the "friends of Job" in the Bible, but with a background in ethnic studies or neo-third-worldism, apply themselves to decoding an adversity that has become illegible.

I know, of course, the dangerous aspect this comparison can have. But in the end something tells me that the fate of the Nuban mountain-dweller dying in the mud of his village, the fate of the Angolan diamond-seeker buried in a mine that has no other reason for existence but to enrich the new warlords, the fate of some Sri Lankan recruited at eight years of age into an army where no one knows for what cause it's fighting, something tells me that the fate of those who die without witness, thus, literally, without martyrdom* , is even more moving than that of a Guy Môquet dying in the splendor of his heroism or of that little Sarajevan who, a few minutes before climbing into his last trench, had told me that, whatever happens, he would have defended a certain idea of Bosnia and of Europe. To the horror of dying is added, I imagine, that of dying for nothing. And to that, that of dying in front of the indifferent spontaneous Hegelians that we are, we who, from the irrationality of a situation, soon concluded it was as if unreal and, thus, that it was useless to get mixed up in it. For the whole problem lies there. Isn't it because the confrontation that heralded it was unintelligible to us that, skilled as we were in genocidal logic, we still didn't see the Rwandan genocide coming? And, since the same causes produce the same effects, the same type of prejudice,

---

*"Martyr" is Greek for "witness"—Trans.

the same taste for the Idea incarnate, aren't they already in the process of making us blind to the progress of genocide in Burundi, or in the Nuban mountains in the Sudan?

So I went there to see. For a few months, with the assistance either of a French NGO in one place, or of a Burundian bishop appalled by the eclipse of God in his country, or, among the Nuba, with the consent of their exiled leader, dying in a London clinic, I wanted to take a step toward the other side, to the other shore, the regions of those untouchable wars hidden by other wars, the noble wars, the great Brahmanic wars in the trace of which a whiff of world-history continues to float. No doubt I never really abandoned our old reflexes: where are the good people? the bad ones? where is the border? Perhaps I didn't always know, either, how to go to the end of this new and, in our eyes, almost unthinkable reality: terrible wars, without faith or law, no less foreign to the logic of Clausewitz than to that of Hegel, and whose victims seem doubly damned because they no longer have even the feeble resource of telling themselves that they are struggling for a new Enlightenment, the triumph of democracy and the rights of mankind, or for the defeat of imperialism. But I tried. I tried at least to report, as faithfully as I could, what I saw in those grey zones where, contrary to conventional wisdom, they kill all the more, and with all the more savagery, when they do it seemingly without reason or plan. An engaged traveler. A report on the banality of the worst. Can one, under the pretext that they tell us nothing, choose to wash one's hands of these silent killings?

Old Holden Roberto can't get over it (1). Tonight, in Luanda, he has seen, with his own eyes, a truck full of Cubans and Soviets pass by beneath the windows of his house. My obvious surprise, my exclamations, are of no use. In vain I explain to him that the Cubans left Angola ten years ago and that the rare few that stayed have become dentists on the Marginal.* He insists. Almost gets angry. And now this former fighter for the war of independence, this party leader, who has become, with time, this little gentle-looking man, with the cautious and conciliatory manners, with impeccably coiffed white hair, launches into a strange speech in which his glorious past is mixed up with hallucinations of the present: a jumbled confusion of insurrection against the Portuguese; the war, almost immediately afterwards, against the Marxists of the Popular Movement for the Liberation of Angola (MPLA), who are victorious and oust him from power; Sartre on Capri; Fanon, who was a friend of his; and then that dark story of the Cubans, his enemies from long ago, he is sure he sees them returning, on certain nights, like ghosts, to the city.

"Go see," he insists. "Go into the *muceques*.* You'll see." And the old lion repeats, in a voice that's suddenly more high-pitched, that, yes, it's not unusual, some nights, to see the crazy people of

---

*A main avenue in Luanda.
*Shantytowns—literally, 'sandy places'—Trans.

Luanda escaping from the psychiatric hospital. They aren't given anything to eat. Nothing to drink. So they climb over the wall, the poor madmen. They pass through the camp's barbed wire. They turn up in the middle of the city, naked, incoherent, rummaging through trashcans. And that's what the Cubans are doing. And that's why they're combing the neighborhoods. They're hunting down the madmen of Futungo and killing them with a bullet in the head from a silencer. At which point he again changes register and, quite calmly, solemnly, with a trace of pride, takes out of his pocket that day's edition of the *Journal of Angola* where he shows me, in a corner of an inside page, a tiny article entitled "*El grido des vielho*"—"The Cry of the Old Man"— which calls for an end to hostilities. I am the "old man," he says apologetically. There are two of us "old men" in Angola: Jonas Savimbi, my ally from long ago, whom they call "o Mas-Velho," the oldest man, and me. Do you want me to tell you about the war in Angola? Do you want me to tell you about the fifteen years of the war of liberation, then the twenty-five years of the war between the Angolans—on one side the MPLA and, on the other, Savimbi's UNITA (National Union for the Total Independence of Angola,) which refuses to admit defeat and continues the fight from the bush? Fifteen plus twenty-five, that makes forty: isn't that the longest war in the history of humanity?

I went, of course, into the *muceques* of Luanda. I went, near the Roque Santeiro market, into the leprous slums of the city where I saw, not madmen, but men with one leg, the disabled, the ten-year-old prostitutes, the packs of children with nothing to do who sleep in cardboard shacks, women with gargoyle heads, men who no longer have any face at all. I saw, in this rich city, weighed down by the manna of oil and diamonds, buildings so dilapidated that they no longer have running water, so their stairwells are used as toilets. And I even saw, in front of these buildings, elite policemen, the *"anti-motims,"* armed with assault rifles, giving chase to "anti-social elements." But no sign, of course, of Cubans, or of Soviets, those ghosts who haunt the imagination of the "old man" of the war of Angola. Light from dead stars. Inertia of past battles. This very old war. The oldest, and, along with the war of Sudan, the bloodiest of all of today's wars. And this feeling, straight away, that the dead command the living, and that it's the ghosts who program and manufacture corpses. Five hundred thousand dead. Four million displaced. Why?

Huambo. I remember Dominique de Roux, at the Avenida Palace Hotel in Lisbon, then in the control tower of the Lusaka airport, in Zambia, where he spent entire days scanning the African sky, waiting for the plane of Savimbi, his hero: Huambo... Huambo... the President is coming from Huambo... the President is leaving for Huambo... he kept repeating this word, Huambo... it was the capital of his African Mao... it was his Yenan, his red base... and he could not utter the name without a visible and incantatory joy (2)... Of this Huambo, heart of the country of the Ovimbundu, Savimbi's ethnic group, of this former Nova Lisboa, which, in the end, he almost immediately lost and which, with the exception of a brief interlude in 1993 and 1994, never left the bosom of the MPLA, there remains an abandoned train station with steam-engine trains from the beginning of the century; the building of the "Compania do Ferrocaril," also abandoned—twenty years since a train has entered this besieged city! twenty years since one has left it!—and they even discovered, last month, the existence of seven hundred forgotten employees who went on strike because they hadn't been paid, now, for twenty years; there are some colonial houses, pink and decorated with flowers, including the house of Savimbi himself, shattered by a bomb, the central staircase still standing, untrained bougainvilleas tumbling into the ruins; and then there are the amputees; ruins and amputees; how many amputees, in twenty years, in Angola? How many of these badly made stumps, impossible to fit with artificial limbs, ulcerous? How many of these bodies reduced to a pulp, poorly mended, terrifying, for which Huambo, like Luanda, will be the shroud? No one knows; the government doesn't care, and no one knows anything about them (3).

Since the city is completely landlocked, with the UNITA forces still camped at its gates, I arrived by plane. Not a flight on SAL, the national airline, which are cancelled every other day. But one of those Beechcraft planes, run by private companies, piloted by Russians, South Africans or Ukrainians, and which, even if their cabins are decaying, their doors bent and their navigational instruments half broken, even if they are the ones that transport all the country has in the way of traffickers, vultures, real and counterfeit prospectors for oil and diamonds, do at least have the advantage of taking off every day. The real difficulty is landing. The Stingers of the UNITA have to be avoided, they're there, in the forest, on the edge of the security perimeter; last year they shot down, one after the other, two Hercules C-130's from the United Nations. But Joe, the pilot, is used to it.

The idea is to climb very quickly, to 20,000 feet, into the clouds. The idea is, above all, to stay there as long as possible, until you're absolutely positive you're exactly above the city of destination, and then to descend suddenly, in a spiral dive, while still remaining perpendicular to the runway and waiting till the last minute to level out the craft—all done instinctually, since the airport in Huambo, like all Angolan airports, no longer has a control tower. "Listen to that," the pilot says, a fierce smile on his lips as he cuts his engines. I listen, but I don't hear anything, deafened by the suddenness of the descent. "I think there's an attack on the airport." And, in fact, he is not mistaken. Like all the people of his kind, like all the mercenaries of the air who spend their time flying to and fro across the Angolan sky, he is an ear, a nose, a news agency all on his own. And I learn, upon my arrival, that there has just been, in the Santa Ngoti district, a raid by the UNITA, or by the dissidents of the UNITA, or by the starving soldiers who pass for militants or dissidents of the UNITA—the only thing certain is that the assailants rose up and united the village, that their leader made a speech, and that the inhabitants brought bowls of food.

In Huambo itself, everything is in turmoil. Not so much because of the raid on the Santa Ngoti district. But because of the presence in the city of another detachment of soldiers, these from the government, who arrived the night before on their way to "re-establish order" further south, on the side of the Serra do Chilengue, where the UNITA had attacked another village. They too are strange, these soldiers. They say they are there to establish order. But they wander about in a conquered land. They drive their machinery on the former General Norton de

Matos square, across from the government's "Palacio." And one of them, the best-dressed, their leader no doubt, shouts out for all to hear that he's thirsty, serves himself at the stall of a vegetable and soda merchant, takes me for a humanitarian aid worker and shouts: "Why this aid for the rebels? What about us? Why aren't there any standards? Don't our children have malaria?" and then, half undressing himself, brandishing his weapon, he says that it's rained, he's soaked, and someone should dry his clothes. "Excuse him," says the soda merchant, "he's not Angolan, he's a South African." A South African in the service of Luanda and the government? For an instant, like Holden Roberto, I think back to the time when the South Africans were on the side of Savimbi, trained him in night combat and formed his best battalions. And then, yes, of course: that was the other South Africa, the one of apartheid and death squads in the townships of Johannesburg; that was the other time, the era of the cold war and of the great planetary confrontation for which Angola was one of the theaters; how time passes. . . .

Kuito. I wanted to go to Kuito by road, from Huambo. So I took advantage of a convoy of trucks that was returning from Lobito, on the coast, with a cargo of logs and water stored in plastic bags. "It's not bad," the driver of the lead truck told me. "If they pay me for the risks I run, and if they don't ask me to drive at night, it's not too bad." We waited for an hour, north of the city, for the Sonangol oil depot to open (in Angola, the fourth largest oil producer in Africa, there are no gas pumps). It took us two more hours to get to Vila Nova, thirty kilometers to the east—a good road on the map but full of potholes, endless detours through fields that stank from the bad smell of unharvested crops rotting in the field , unharvested in all likelihood, because of the landmines (Angola holds the world record for its number of landmines—one per inhabitant, at least ten million...). More nervousness, again, when the convoy slows down too much, for that's the easiest time, as I know, for looters to attack the cargo. "You're afraid?" says the driver. "Don't worry. You have a nice jacket. They'll take your jacket, not your life." Then one more hour to arrive, ten kilometers later, at Bela Vista where we are stopped, this time for good, by an officer claiming that they're fighting, further east, in Chingar, and that, in any case, the bridge is broken. How long do we have to wait? He doesn't know. So I had to drive back in my hired car, which had been in back of the convoy. And once again it was a plane that would take me to Kuito.

They had warned me. My old friend, the journalist Tamar Golan, who had become the Israeli ambassador and who had fallen in love with Angola, had told me clearly: "Kuito is Sarajevo; it's Mostar; it's the martyred city par excellence, the most destroyed city in Africa; you'll see, it's atrocious." But there's a big difference between what you're told and what you see; a world of difference separates numbers (two wars; twenty-one months of siege; up to a thousand shells per day) and the shock of these walls blackened by fire, these piles of rubble, these sad landscapes, these poor people who have come back home to Joachin-Kapango Street where the front line passed through, but who live there now crammed into sheet-metal houses or under tarpaulins; and there's a huge difference between *the idea*—that in the middle of the Bosnian war, when my eyes, like those of so many others, were glued to the ordeal of Sarajevo, another city was dying, whose most beautiful buildings are reduced, like the Kuito Hotel, or the Bishop's Palace, or the five floors of the Gabiconta building, to their concrete skeletons (4)—and *the image* of these devastated streets, sometimes without water, at some times of the day without electricity, visited only by military vehicles, humanitarian 4 X 4's, and, at night, after curfew, starving, drunken policemen, who seem as if they'll do anything to get away from what, in their eyes, has become the seat of hell itself. "Hi boss," one of them says to me, a glimmer of hope in his eyes. "Can you give me a gazosa? A cigarette?" Then, acting friendly: "You know people in Huambo? In Benguela? Can you get me transferred? It's too hot here."

A lot of energy was required to achieve this disaster. Not just energy, bad will and murderous intentions, but also a lot of weapons, a lot of shells, a lot of tanks firing point blank, for a lot of days, over the principal avenue. This war may be a war of the poor. It is definitely a war of the squalid, of the seamy, since I've seen only sleazy, squalid people since I've been here. But it is also a war of the rich. It's a war that, in any case, smells of the money of traffickers in tanks and guns. They say that the operation of the oil reserves of Cabinda, in the north of the country, alone brings President Dos Santos between 3 and 4 billion dollars per year. They also say that the diamonds of the Lundas bring Savimbi a half-billion. And above all they say that this money is reinvested, at 60% for the one, 80% for the other, in military equipment. How can we not guess that it's this money that gives the ruins of Kuito their smell? Back again in Luanda, I learn that, in Paris, everyone's talking about the possible involvement of

Mitterand's son, and a few others, in an enormous arms sale bound for blasted and profitable Angola: why don't they all come, as penance, to Kuito, to contemplate the fruits of their business?

Porto Amboim. By road, this time. All the way. I've been told about a detachment of the UNITA that's been operating in the north, around Calulo. I've also been told about population movements of undetermined origin in the region of Ebo, more to the south. But about this road, the road that runs alongside the sea and, after Porto Amboim, goes as far as Benguela—a Dominican priest who uses it fairly frequently has told me it's reliable. The bridge over the Cuanze is being worked on, but it's passable. One checkpoint—this will be the only one—where I have to negotiate a little but where they just take down my license number. The Perdizes River. The Muengueje. A nature park, stocked with lions and elephants, which the President offered as a gift to his Chief of Staff. Another river, the Longa, with, in its loops, a jungle zone held by the UNITA but where I still don't meet anyone. And then, finally, Porto Amboim, a pretty colonial town, shaded by flame trees, but still somehow oppressive, with that smell of filth and bad heating oil that floats over the abandoned cities of Angola: "It's too late," the hotel manager tells me, an old white-haired Portuguese, with the hoarse voice of cancer and with a musketeer's goatee (5), who was, in the 1970's, one of the first white progressives won over to the MPLA; "it's too late; you should have come fifteen years ago, when the border between two worlds was here, at Porto Amboim; we were happy to be in the vanguard; we were proud; when you went inland, to the city of Amboim, you know you were risking your life but it was for a good cause; whereas, today..." He sighs, lowers his voice and, with his fingers deformed by rheumatism, makes the gesture of the magician showing the disappearance of the rabbit: "today, there isn't even a road anymore, to the city of Amboim..."

So to find traces of the road to the city of Amboim. Find, and follow, the old railroad track, it too abandoned, as in Huambo, which penetrates inland. Carcass of a car picked bare. Another, where one can make out, almost worn away: "*ano de construçao 1938.*" A piece of cement wall: "*prohibido urinar aqui.*" Tracks, but so rusty they've taken on the color of the trail's red laterite. Others, which have been looted, only the ties are left, already swallowed up by earth and grass—why on earth looted? What earthly use could there be for lengths of track stolen from the Porto Amboim railway? Weapons? Construction materials? Cooking utensils? Tools?

Stucco houses. Another village where half a dozen old men, busy watching a hut burn, assure me that I'm in a UNITA zone—then another half-dozen, further on, who say no, not at all, it's a government zone. And so on for fifteen kilometers or so. I stop there. First of all because it's getting harder and harder to distinguish the trail from the surrounding brush. But also because I have a strong feeling it will be the same further on, the same as usual: the same devastation, the same impression of a country in tatters—a dismembered, devitalized, lunar space, where everywhere you see traces of war but nowhere its logic, its meaning, or any sign of its end (6).

Back once more in Port Amboim, I see the old musketeer again, sitting on the veranda of his hotel, lost in his anger and his nostalgia. I see the flame trees that had enchanted me that very morning. But the city seems dead to me now. Not just melancholy, funereal, or the like, but dead, actually dead—residual humanity, tomb for the last lost soldiers of two ragged armies, end of the game. Is that why I came all this way here? For this spectacle of looming death (7)? Maybe, after all. Maybe there are many ways, for a city to die, and the war of Angola tells how. The Kuito way, which is Sarajevo's too. But also the Porto Amboim way—gentle disaster, slow agony without death throes, life seized by death, the living tied to the dead who devour them. A city is a center. This center has, in principle, a periphery that lives on it and that it feeds on. If this periphery is consumed, or if the center gets cut off and withdrawn (which amounts to the same thing), or if the links between them are undone because a railroad stops and its tracks have been looted, then all the balance, the charm, is broken. The city looks alive, but is no longer. The city increases, develops, even swells, like Porto Amboim, with tens of thousands of refugees crammed into the old Portuguese apartment buildings—but swells as cysts do, fat only with a malignant vitality. The Angolan cities are no longer cities, but cysts in dead bodies. The UNITA and the MPLA reign over cysts and dead bodies (9).

I've just noticed a strange thing. Since I've been here, I haven't once run into a UNITA checkpoint. Checkpoints are, as a rule, important. They are the real markers of African wars. In Croatian Bosnia, for instance, checkpoints were the main way power was asserted, territory defined, and money taken. But the fact is that, on the roads around Porto Amboim, Huambo, and Luanda, I didn't find any.

Of course I can always tell myself that I didn't go far enough and that if I had gone as far as the city of Amboim... or if I had gone into Mexico, at the border between Zambia and the Congo... or if I had kept going, the other day, with my convoy of water and logs...

But perhaps this too is the peculiarity of this guerilla warfare, its style. Perhaps this is the great tactical skill of Savimbi's men, to be nowhere the better to be everywhere, never be visible hence always be threatening. "Why would you want there to be control posts?" Abel Chivukuvuku, a longtime companion of Savimbi, teases (that's another strange thing about this war: there are people from the UNITA, real ones, not traitors or people won over later, who, since 1994 and the Lusaka agreements, have been living openly in Luanda...). "Why get pinned down in that trap when it's so much more profitable to be as we are, elusive?"

Better still: perhaps we are touching here, beyond even the UNITA, on one of the characteristics of this war and of African wars in general. They say, "The UNITA holds this." Or, "The government holds that." But what, after all, does "hold" mean? Who holds what and why? What if the rule is that none of the warring parties "holds" anything at all? And what if it's a question of a war of a new kind—or, on the contrary, very old—that has other stakes than those of the mere appropriation, control, and governing of territories? The destabilization of the opponent, for instance. Or the perseverance of everyone in a warlike existence whose first driving force, whose original motive, he himself has wound up forgetting (10). Or the enrichment, through oil and diamonds, of twin cliques—one in the State, the other outside the State—of warlords who with all that already, would surely ridicule the idea of holding some road or some village...

One sign that does not mislead: the style of the operations carried out by the UNITA. The occupation, the other day, just before I passed through it, of the Benguela airport: three hours and then they're gone. Or the raid, in the Chihongo district, twelve kilometers north of Menongue: strike a blow that shows they are indeed there, ransack the clinic, but above all don't stay, don't try to establish a bridgehead or a base, return quickly to the brush.

Another sign: the way the government itself administers the zones it conquers and claims to control. "90%," says this morning's press... "The government controls 90% of the territory..." Perhaps. But what exactly does it control? The provinces or their capitals? And what kind of "controlling" is this, waiting six months to send administrators to Bailundo and Andulo, the two mainly rebel places, recaptured from Savimbi? Or, worse, of what "control" are they speaking when they have forgotten, for almost twenty years, to rebuild Ngiva, the capital of Cunene, devastated by fighting? They say, in Luanda, "Luanda is the capital, Angola is a landscape." They also say, "President Dos Santos, in ten years, has never left his palace in Funtungo." A way of saying that, for this ex-champion of revolutionary progressivism, this Marxist, this inheritor of the great fights and ideologies of the century, he now has two countries: a usable country that is limited to Luanda, a few sections of the coast, the oil zones, which form a kind of "offshore" country, leased out to Elf, Exxon and BP-Amoco; and then all the rest of Angola, which has, in his own opinion, only the uncertain existence of shadows.

An odd kind of war, decidedly. Odd in its relationship to the land, to the battlefields, to places. No longer is it this region for one person, that region for another. But an immense space, almost undifferentiated, overcome by a slow leprosy, where armies of lost soldiers keep clashing, whose real objective is less to win than to survive and kill (12).

Still, all the same, there is a position. Still there's a city, a village, a zone that the government insists on controlling. In all the wars in the world, it's very simple, you establish an army there, you build a garrison. In Angola, not so. Armies are too expensive. Too costly. This is true even in the literal sense, since the best soldiers are often mercenaries—they prefer to say, here, "technicians"—bought at the price of gold from companies like the South African Executive Outcomes, officially dissolved at the end of 1998, and led by a man who used to be responsible for Special Services during Apartheid. So they proceed in other ways. And they mobilize civilians who will do, in their place, the work the soldiers have been spared.

I saw this in Menongue, further south, on the outskirts of what the Angolans call "the land at the end of the world," so terrible it seems to them.

There, in fact, in Menongue, there is a refugee camp. Not much of one. But a normal camp. Normal sanitation. With good huts of stone and wood. And this camp is installed in a zone that has been stripped of grass, stripped of trees, and, thus, cleared on the whole of landmines.

And then there is another camp, twenty kilometers further, on the other side of the Cuebe river, in Japeka, at the end of an impossible track, surrounded by tall grasses, thorny shrubs, and, necessarily, by landmines, where they have resettled several hundred refugees, in huts that are far worse, with roofs made of sheet metal supported by stones.

So I try to find out why.

I try to find out what strange reasoning they used to decide to transport people from a good camp to a bad one.

"The first one was overpopulated," they tell me, "it had to be relieved." Untrue. I visited it. It was empty.

"The zone of the second one was a good zone," they assure me in the office of the governor who, let it be said in passing, is not visible, for he is doing business—*sic*—in Luanda. "We knew the refugees would be peaceful there." Untrue. I went there too. I questioned the farmers. They all confirmed that the zone is on the contrary quite dangerous, that no one lives there of his own free will, that it is infested with landmines and under fire from UNITA.

No. The real reason is elsewhere. A camp is not just refugees. It is also humanitarian aid. Food supplies. A millwheel of trucks and cars flying pennants. So that by creating this second camp, by placing their refugees and the whole humanitarian system that goes with it, at the outpost of these newly conquered and thus precarious and dangerous lands, the government was creating a human shield, or a sanctuary, more effective than an army.

I saw the same kind of situation in the outskirts of Huambo, at the edge of the security perimeter.

I saw the same system on the hilltops north of Kuito, in Cunje, a little railroad town that has long been one of the bases from which UNITA bombarded the city and where the MPLA established a center for malnourished children.

It has to be one or the other. Either the logic of Porto Amboim: do nothing; laissez-faire; just let Angola (except the useful areas) give in to its slow leprosy. Or, as here, the Menongue logic: hold the position; yes, this time, hold it; but with civilians as hostages and humanitarians as the sentries.

Between the two attitudes, one point in common: two spectral armies that spend as much time avoiding each other as they do confronting each other, and have chosen to fight each other by means of interposed populations.

Cuango. Province of Lunda Norte. That famous diamond-bearing zone that the two rival armies of the UNITA and the MPLA are supposed to fight over.

The first surprise is the plane. Whereas the arrival in Huambo, but also in Kuito and Menongue, had been so rough, and, like everywhere else in Angola, the law of the spiral descent prevails, this plane approaches and lands with no problem: as if, for the first time, enemy missiles were no longer to be feared.

The second surprise is, in Cuango itself, the city's main street. It is alive. Noisy. Bustling with a crowd of blacks and whites mingled together, Belgian traffickers, Israeli or Lebanese intermediaries, Ukrainian pilots, agents from De Beers or from Endiama, the national company, mercenaries, sellers of video-cassettes or shirts, passersby. And now, suddenly, in this Wild West setting, standing in front of my "boarding house," I see, at one end of the street, a company of disarmed, idle, ragged government soldiers approaching, and at the other end, another troop, almost identical, their uniforms similarly ragged, but these belong to the UNITA, MPLA and UNITA, on the same street? Why not in the same fight, as long as they're there?

And then, third surprise: the diamond mines themselves. Except "mines" is a fancy name for this group of half-naked men, standing in the river's current, a rope between their teeth, their hands scorched, their eyes blinking in the sun, who are, under guard of a detachment of the UNITA, in the process of digging the red sand mixed with gravel and sifting it—and then, a little further on, two or three kilometers away, the company of the "mining brigade," or in other words the army and the MPLA, watching over another group of diggers who take turns on a beam thrown across the river, from which they plunge a little hand spade into the muddy water, a rope tied around their waist. "It's your surprise that surprises me," jokes Pierre, a Belgian businessman who chartered the Antonov plane in which we arrived and whose job consists of "representing" the independent diggers to a "purchasing office," linked to an international company. "No, there's nothing surprising. It's the same all along the river. Why would you expect the MPLA and the UNITA to make war here? What benefit would they get from that? Just imagine the army attacking this group of *garimpeiros* protected by the UNITA, what an uproar that would cause! All the searchlights pointed at the area! Not to speak of the UNITA's retaliations, which would, in turn, keep them from working! In fact, their interests are linked, if only when it comes to foreign companies."

In short, a strangely peaceful zone. The only one where I can find no trace of confrontation. That's the final paradox of this war. They fight each other, and with an incredible perseverance, wherever there's nothing but poverty, desert, villages plundered over and over, dead cities, lifeless landscapes. But wherever there are riches, in the horn of plenty that the Lundas are, a non-war is imposed, a gentleman's agreement, and, effectively, another kind of sharing, which contains perhaps the only logic of this war.

On one hand, the diggers. They should be called slaves. A group of people of no account, who have come, by the truckloads, from Zaire. They start by taking away their shoes. Then their papers. And when they've lost both shoes and papers, when they're nothing but nameless and identity-less tramps, when they know they can starve, drown, have their eardrums exploded, not climb back up from the quarries dug into the riverbanks and who, most of the time, collapse, when they're quite certain the earth can bury them without anyone, any-where, caring anymore about their existence, then the devil's pact is sealed: for the luckiest, each week, the equivalent of one or two days of miraculous catch; for the others, most of them, who got into debt to set up what they call their "stake," a gem-stone from time to time that will serve as payoff—if that! Not the most beautiful or the most transparent stones, since they return by right to the "protectors"! And if some unfortunate man decides to cheat, if he has the temptation to stick one up his ass, then watch out for the reaction—everyone on the bucket, in the enema shack, and punishment, sometimes death, for the thieves.

And on the other hand, the slave-labor guards. But guards with a double, imperceptible face. Some are from the UNITA. Others from the MPLA. Still others are members of the MPLA who have profited from their posting to set up their own busi-ness, to set up their own "stake" or to create, with the complic-ity of the generals, their own security company or aviation company. For a soldier, to be transferred to the Lundas is the chance of a lifetime, an opportunity that will never come again, the lottery. In Luanda, there is a whole game of influ-ences, elaborate networks, a traffic of false documents, a mafia, organizations, seedy hotels, that help them compel destiny. And there's talk of entire detachments of troops that, scarcely arrived, broke up, melted into countryside, vanished into thin air. The official version says, "died in combat." Or "taken by the UNITA." Or simply, "disappeared." And, in a way, that's true. For all those men swallowed up by the Lundas, engulfed in its Sargasso of crime and wretchedness, all those officers who grew up in Marxism and who end up thus, in the skin of penal colony guards and slave traffickers, aren't they the most lost of all the lost soldiers?

The slave guards against the slaves. The two sworn enemies united in one macabre embrace for which the war's damned would pay the terrible price: is that what the meaning of this war comes down to? Its ultimate, sordid truth? I think back to Holden Roberto. I think back to Dominique de Roux. I see him again, this activist, this dreamer, final avatar of the committed right-wing intellectual, who still found a way to inject a little dream, a little dawn, a little thought, into this quagmire. I see again the Portuguese captains of April, those reds (13), who also thought they saw a celestial light dawning in this mud. What would they say about this disarray, this chaos?

"The problem is the head (14). It's important, at the moment of the explosion, for it to break clean off, remain intact, and roll to the right place, decided in advance by the Leader."

Srilaya had been one of those volunteers for death, programmed by the Tamil independence-movement fighters, as one programs a prototype or a precision machine. She had been one of those living torpedoes, those asphalt kamikazes, who are crammed with explosives and then let loose in Colombo, mingling with the passersby, looking out for their target: a policeman, a soldier, a famous Sinhalese personality whom they will accost, then tackle, before setting off the blast-off system built into their suicide-vest.

These "Black Tigers" are the city's nightmare. Its constant obsession. Its psychosis. Who is a Black Tiger? Who isn't? How can they be recognized, these maniacs? How should you react if, by chance, fate places one in your path? Struggle? Beg? Cry out to him, while he's clutching you, in the few seconds remaining to you before the bomb in the vest goes off, that you are innocent, that you want to live? How many are there, anyway? How many have infiltrated, have succeeded in foiling the security systems installed in the train stations, on the major roads, at the intersections, at the airport, and who are ready to pay with their lives for the dream of a separate Tamil state, in the north of Sri Lanka? "Hotline," the website of the LTTE (Liberation Tigers of Tamil Eelam), the army of the Tigers, says over a hundred. The *Island* and the *Daily News*, the Colombo newspapers that actually hardly speak of it at all or, when they do, appear with entire columns, sometimes pages, covered by enormous "Censored," in capital letters, put there by the administrative staff headquarters—the Sinhalese press, then, says on the contrary just a few dozen. I wanted to approach one of them. I wanted to know what a man, or a woman, looked like who had chosen to act under the influence of a pure death wish. So here is one. A repentant one, indeed. Living for several months, hunted by her former companions, in hiding in a working-class neighborhood in Colombo. But originally from deep within the movement. And she had stayed there long enough to be able to tell about its rules and rituals.

She is thirty years old. She is pretty. She has the physical appearance of a sober intellectual, a little austere, Zen-like. She speaks thoughtfully. In perfect English. In a monotone. In one breath. Interrupting herself only at the approach of the waiter in the capital's hotel restaurant where we had arranged to meet. The Catholic priest who organized the contact lingers during the first few minutes of the interview and then, feeling she is being distracted by him, he slips away. She thinks it would be amusing for me to give her true name but asks me, on reflection, not to do so. She also says she wants nothing more from life than a visa for London or Paris (15). She talks.

"It all started four years ago. The army had kidnapped my father and later his dead body was found. One day, some men arrived, in a truck, at the village. I knew one of them. He was a friend of my father's and we had seen each other frequently when we were children. He said to me, Do you want to avenge your father? I said, Yes. He asked me, Are you still a virgin? I said, No. He replied, That's too bad, virgins are more suitable, but no matter, make a written request and put it in the suggestion box, the yellow box, in your village. Three months later, he came back. The request was accepted, he told me. The Supreme Leader, Velupillai Prabhakaran, has deemed you worthy to apply. And they led me into a camp in the Wanni, in the jungle, near Mallawi.

"That was the first camp. The Organization couldn't know if we were going to hold out, if we were going to change our minds, so it put us in a preliminary camp that was a testing camp. They gave me trousers, boots, shirts. They cut my hair. In our country, Sri Lankan women wear their hair very long. But that gets in the way if you have to fight. So there is a special decree from the Supreme Leader that says one has the right to cut one's hair, and I did. And then they gave us political training: the Buddhists have been the enemies of our race for two thousand years... we Tamils, Hindus, have a right to self-determination... it is right to die for that... it's a way, too, to go to heaven more quickly, shortening the chain of reincarnations—a short cut to Nirvana! An offering that allows you to be reborn in the body of a high-caste woman!... I believed all that. They repeated it to me so much that I ended up believing it (16).

"The second camp came after a year. It was a training camp, still in the Wanni. They taught the women who, like me, were not virgins to spend a day with a grenade in our vagina. They put replicas of the suicide-vest on our backs—those big heavy vests, stuffed with dynamite, with a detonator, a cable, and steel balls, which the Leader himself had conceived of after seeing them at the cinema in a Rambo movie. We had to live with that. We had to prepare ourselves for the day when we would throw ourselves on a target, or pin them to the ground, and then we would activate the detonator to explode it. Sometimes they were real vests and we slipped them onto the trunk of a coconut palm, or on an iron or wooden effigy, and we made them explode. It was becoming serious. There was no longer a question of turning back, of regaining one's freedom. I had a friend who, one day, had her doubts. She said that she missed her family and that she had no private life. One night, she disappeared. They told us she had deserted. I think that wasn't true. I think, in fact, they liquidated her.

"One day, at the end of another year, they put me in a truck to take me into town. On one hand, I was content. Because I had been in the jungle too long. I was thin. I was eaten alive by mosquitoes. But on the other hand, they still hadn't given me an objective. We'll contact you, they told me, we'll contact you. But, for now, they took away my identity papers. They asked me to rent a room in Colombo, to try to lose my Wanni accent, to erase all the traces that could, if I were arrested, lead back to my village, to take a normal job—making tea in a restaurant. And I waited. That's maybe what saved me. For if I work it out, if I put end to end the time that I waited, it makes one year in the jungle, then one year in Colombo, and I think that was too much.

"As long as I was in the jungle, I didn't ask myself questions. I knew that the day would come when I would put on the vest, when I would take my last bus, when I would give my last coin to my last rickshaw and would wait, in the middle of passersby whom I would have tried hard to resemble, for the target I was going to sacrifice. And this idea did me good, I was happy.

But then, I don't know if it was the city, or the restaurant, or life. The day when they finally came to take me, the day when they came to ask me if I had any near relations whom I was going to leave in need and who needed to be taken care of, the day when they said to me, 'This is it, get ready,' I was no longer ready. They gave me the cyanide pill that allows you not to fall into the enemy's hands alive. They told me I had a right to a last meal and a final salute from the Leader, that it was like a *prahuta*, a 'sacred meal' for the Hindus. And that's when I escaped."

I got to know the city of Batticaloa thirty years ago, during my first trip to Sri Lanka. As I remember it, it was a lake-dwelling city, built between the sea and the lagoon, with a maze of small intersecting streets that resembled the cities of the Ganges delta, at their most cheerful. I had come there to meet Sirimavo Bandaranaike, back from Bangladesh and its war (17), head of the government at the time, mother of today's President. She had become the talk of the town of the international ultra-left by appointing—a major first!—Trotskyite ministers from the LSSP (the Lanka Sama Samaja Party).

Now, it is Batticaloa that is in the midst of war. The zone of turbulence has moved, and it is here, in this pretty little city, pearl of the northern coast, paradise for tourists and for politicians on holiday, that the evil winds of hate and fear blow. The government workers are still there. But they know they are, along with the handful of ex-convicts they brought there to rebuild the irrigation system, the last Sinhalese in the city. They also know that the land, in a few hours, will belong to the Tigers and to their nighttime government.

Night, actually, has arrived. My contact has shown up, almost without concealing himself, in the house where I'm staying. And we have started out, along the lagoon, towards the south, in the direction of one of those mysterious bases of the Tigers who control the back country.

A few kilometers by car. A ferry where we find two boys, very young, nice-seeming, with walkie-talkies switched off. Half an hour by foot, in a landscape of paddy-fields lying fallow, where we pass two abandoned military posts, then a third, further on, near a fishing village that we avoid. Then the forest. A tangle of creepers, bamboo trees with serrated stalks, brambles, banana trees, breadfruit trees, where my guides, aided by flashlights, easily get their bearings. And then, at the bottom of a path where whiffs of the heavy scents of my walks from long ago, in the jungle of Bangladesh, reach me, along with a gleam of light, the sad sound of a tambourine, a gushing spring—and, finally, a clearing, at the edge of which I can make out, in the moonlight, a cannon mounted on a wagon, a flag flying on top of a mast, and, stretched between two trees, a fresco, painted on wood, that represents a young man in a black uniform, machine-gun at his shoulder.

In the clearing, bags of sand. Tires. A pile of wooden crates on which oil lamps have been placed. An altar with the elephant god. Bicycles. A little motorbike. And, surrounded by a bamboo fence, five mud huts. Then a sixth, set apart. Not the nicest one. But the newest. And the only one, above all, to have electricity, hooked up to a generator. This is the bungalow of the camp leader, who is lying on a hammock, conferring with his lieutenants while watching from the corner of his eye over bananas frying on a stove: a young giant, scarcely twenty years old, with a bare chest and a faded blue sarong, back of the neck shaved; except perhaps for the gold chain around his neck (the cyanide capsule?), he makes me think irresistibly of Akim Mukherjee, the young Bengali commander of the Mukti Bahini (Freedom Battalion) column with which, at the time, I had entered liberated Dhaka.

"You are in a liberated zone," he begins, without getting up, and gestures for me to sit down on a tin box opposite him. "Welcome to Eelam."

I ask him, while a child brings me a glass of tea, what he means by liberated zone.

"A zone from which the Sinhalese state has withdrawn. Here, you see…"

We see, on a television set on top of a cooler, a brigade of Tigers in the process of distributing food.

"Here, we do everything. Food. Police. Schools. Judges, who pledge allegiance to Prabhakaran. Everything."

I know that's not true. I know that it's even one of the paradoxes of this war: the irreproachable aspect of the government of Colombo which, in the zones it has lost, and even if it's only to avoid admitting defeat and having to recognize secession, continues to ensure public services and pay civil servants, even if they're chosen by the Tigers and under their heel. But I let him continue.

"How long are you staying here? Just the night? That's too bad. Otherwise you might have seen how popular we are. We are giving the people back its freedom, its dignity."

I point out that the business of "torpedo-women" doesn't seem to me to go far in the direction of this rediscovered dignity.

"On the contrary. Women had been servile. By becoming fighters, they are breaking their chains, they are freeing themselves."

And the children? Those schoolboys torn from their families to be made into soldiers?

"We don't tear anyone away. The families are proud to pay this tribute to Eelam."

Then, with a wink to his lieutenants who remain, standing, during the interview, their eyes dull and listless, their faces bleak, expressionless:

"Anyway, you know, children... Isn't that exaggerated, the stories about children? Often they're adults. But they don't look their age."

He laughs. The others start smiling and, on command, they laugh too.

"Your problem," I say to him, "is recruitment. There are only six thousand of you. Faced with an army of 120,000 men."

"That's true, but look at this."

He gets up, goes to turn the bananas, then, taking his time, with a studied air of nonchalance, approaches a large map, stuck to the wall.

"Look at what a few thousand men can do, ready to sacrifice themselves for the inalienable rights of the Tamil people on its historic homeland of the north and east of Sri Lanka."

He shows, on the map, marked by colored thumbtacks, the zones, around Batticaloa, that the LTTE controls.

"You need weapons for that," I say. "Where do you get them from?"

Another glance at the lieutenants. Another forced laugh.

"From the Sinhalese army. That is our supplier."

I know, here again, that he's not saying everything. I know that the Tamil guerilla movement, since it's supported, in Indian Tamil Nadu, but also in Europe, by a sizable diaspora, is the richest and best organized guerilla movement in the world. And I have read a Lloyd's report listing the quantity of equipment, including surface-to-air and surface-to-surface missiles, from the Ukraine, the Balkans, Central Asia, and Cambodia, shipped on boats belonging to companies that are indirectly controlled by the Tigers. But he sticks to his story. And I am treated to an alternating double portrait of an exhausted, despairing Sinhalese army, systematically avoiding combat, fleeing, and abandoning entire arsenals behind it: soldiers in full flight from Chundikuli, near Jaffna, begging farmers to take their Kalashnikovs in exchange for a coconut or a glass of water... crazy soldiers from north of the Wanni shooting at policemen who are trying to stop their flight... soldiers from Vavuniya, in the North, begging for civilian clothes and a bus ticket to get home...; and then, on the other side, a Tiger force, invincible, since it is gifted with a "correct way of thinking," that of Velupillai Prabhakaran, who seems, if you listen to him, a kind of cauldron (18) in which scraps of Maoism, rags of Pol-Potism, a zest of fascist populism, and a touch of fascination for the Japanese kamikazes of the Second World War marinate, all in a stock of militant and fanatic Hinduism.

Two political Hinduisms? The liberal, tolerant one, friend of democracy and the Enlightenment, of my Bengali friends from before, Akim Mukherjee and his Hindu Mukti Bahinis? And then this one; lugubrious, bloody, magnetizing like iron filings the debris of the worst the twentieth century has produced, vomited out?

There are many ways to get to Jaffna, the big city of the North, which was, for five years, the capital of a semi-state within a state, administered by the Tigers, and which the army recaptured, in December 1995, after fifty days of fighting.

There is the sea route, possible once every two weeks, up to Point Pedro, on the *Jaya Gold*, the Red Cross boat, which is reserved for the transport of either the sick and wounded or humanitarian aid and mail, but which was discontinued—I don't know if the reason was the war or the monsoon. And there are the Ukrainian Antonovs, which land at the military airport of Palali, eighteen kilometers north on the Peninsula, which carry humanitarian aid in one direction and soldiers on leave or dead soldiers in the other—and sometimes, like today, passengers.

They are fighting, on the morning of my arrival, around Jaffna. On the Kaithady bridge, in the lagoon, where the government claims to have killed fifty Tigers, including fifteen children, who have been gathered together, foam on their mouths, in seizures of endless convulsions—probably from expired cyanide. And on the Navatkuli bridge, even closer, where I try to go but don't manage to get beyond the Sinhalese line: the noise from the cannons, in the south, from the Tiger positions; sirens from the only ambulance bringing the wounded to the camp infirmary; men running and shooting in every direction; others, holed up beneath mountains of sandbags, covered with corrugated khaki metal sheeting; and an unkempt captain, typing with two fingers in the bottom of his bunker the triumphal communiqué he's going to phone in to the other branches in a few minutes (it's always like that, in Sri Lanka: the heavier the losses are, the more critical the situation is, the more triumphant the communiqués are!).

But the city itself seems calm. Traces of battles, of course, on the sea side. Streets, in the center of town, that are quite damaged. But those are old signs of destruction. And not as serious as I had imagined they'd be. They don't prevent a miraculously normal feeling of day-to-day life: the schoolgirl's pleated skirts and ties... the flowering mango trees... a movie theater... banks... electricity almost everywhere... rickshaws that weave in and out, at top speed, between the barricades... the Tamil, hence Hindu, temples, guarded by Buddhists soldiers... even the policemen, almost polite when they make a bicyclist dismount to make sure his seat isn't booby-trapped, or when, on Main Street, they make the bus passengers get out so they can search their bags...

It's there, near Main Street, where I had settled in, in the little hotel—one of the rare ones where the telephone was in good working order—whose impeccable façade, crammed in between two gutted houses, looked like a theater set, that I meet Dayaparan. The people of Jaffna don't speak much—perhaps because, deep inside themselves, they're not so sure the Tigers won't come back, and so, in their doubt, they remain prudent: what if the withdrawal of the LTTE were only a tactical withdrawal? What if it abandoned the city just to preserve its army? Doesn't it still hold Elephant Pass, which commands access to the Peninsula? And the sea... the four hundred "Sea Tigers," with their pirate ships, their suicide boats, aren't their enormous floating bombs (three meters long, with lateral pontoons, 25 kilos of plastic explosives, two-horsepower motors, long-distance propulsion systems) capable of cutting off the Navy routes at any instant and of attempting a landing, any day, at Thanankilappu?

The young Dayaparan has lost everything. So he talks. He is twenty years old. With real grace. Looks like an angel. Except when he begins to tell about his terrifying adventure. Then a look of conquered, fierce anger appears on his little adolescent face, crossed with a fine mustache, nodding continually from right to left as the Sri Lankans often do.

"I was nine years old (19). There are some who become child-soldiers because they've lost both parents and they only have two options left: either beg, or kill to earn something to eat. I wasn't like that. My father was alive. And when the Tigers came, when they set up the loudspeaker in the village and they exhibited the bodies of two orphans killed in combat, the principal of my school didn't agree, but my father did. Maybe because he was proud. Or because he felt guilty because of our neighbor whose son had died in combat. Or because there were too many of us in the house—there were eight of us—and that made one mouth less to feed; and because, besides, they promised him some land, in Chavakachcheri, in a subdivision for 'families of martyrs.' I don't know.

"In the beginning, when we reached a camp, we did little jobs. Cleaning. Digging trenches or shelters. Selling coconuts in town. Crawling behind enemy lines to set landmines or to spy. And learning how to kill with a knife dipped in cyanide. When I turned twelve, they put me in a unit that was going into villages for fresh supplies: we had weapons, we shot in every direction, which made people afraid, and we took the animals, the chickens that were there. And then they must have thought my training was complete: the *Iyakkam*, the 'movement,' had become my real family, and I was assigned to an attack group of 145 children, all my age, plus some adults for supervision.

"I know there are units of child-soldiers that the LTTE sends routinely to the front line to spare its good regiments. Sometimes they're drugged. Sometimes they don't even need to be drugged: they're just more unthinking, and they have no limits. That's why they use them and put them in the first circle, either to break through enemy lines, or, when the enemy is attacking, to cushion the shock. I didn't have that experience. I know it exists, but I didn't experience it. In my unit, we always began with photos, videos, or a sketch of the target we were going to attack, and, because of that, the losses weren't as great. Did we have courses in political training? No. They spared us the politics. Maybe because we were children and we were probably just going to die. But maybe also because we had a very brutal, illiterate leader, who didn't believe in anything, except in war, in the 'Organization,' but also, like Prabhakaran, the supreme leader, in the *mentram*, in magic formulas, based on astrology.

"Five years ago, I was in Jaffna when the city fell, and the LTTE told all the Tamils to withdraw under its protection into the jungles of the Wanni. It was all by chance. I was on a mission for the leader, who had been told to send in child spies to steal the map of an enemy base on the Northern front. But I think that's what saved me. I spoke to him one last time, on the telephone. I saw, that day, that he didn't even know how to read a map, that he had no memory. And I took advantage of the confusion everywhere—some were obeying the LTTE, others refusing to climb into the tractors and choosing to stay—to cut contact and hide. Since then, I've been living in fear: I know that, one day, someone will come; he'll just make a sign for me to follow him; and they'll kill me—that's all."

This pair, the child-soldier and the illiterate leader... The double face of this leader and of the other one, the one in Batticaloa, who seemed to know so much, on the contrary, about twentieth-century history... And if, at bottom, it's the same thing? If they are the twin faces of the same mortifying hatred? On one hand, a *tabula rasa*, zero degree of knowledge and thought—the childhood of leaders, of suicide bombers, of people restored to their purity. And then on the other, the farandole, the finale, the great supermarket of identities, the last parade of ghosts in the ruins of an abolished future—final summer of ideas, the smell of the last judgment, the apocalypse as usual.

To understand a country at war, especially to grasp its complexity, there is nothing better than the channel of a non-governmental organization. This ancient conviction, which has been a fixture for me since the time long ago when we founded Action Contre la Faim (Action against hunger), is proved true once again here, with some friends from the ACF, in fact, whom I accompany into the "grey zones" of Trincomalee, the other coastal city in a state of siege, north of Batticaloa.

The market town of Kinnuya, on the other side of the ferry and the Air Force bases. Its long streets flooded by the monsoon. Its blue pennants, stretched between the houses, mementos of the last electoral campaign and of the town's support for President Chandrika. And that Muslim engineer who tells about the impossible situation of his community, the third group on the island and, perhaps, the most threatened: "We speak Tamil, but we are not Tamil, and even less are we Tigers—they see us as false friends, they hate us, rob us." Muslims as excluded outsiders?

Islam caught in the crossfire of Buddhism and Hinduism? Sri Lanka as a paradoxical epicenter where these three immense religions clash against each other, like tectonic plates—and there, in the epicenter, at this "central extremity," a Koran in a position that's not just in the minority, but median? That's an interesting piece of information.

The Tamil village of Kadaloor where we are received, on the threshold of his house, by the village leader—salt-and-pepper moustache, face pitted by hardship. The Tigers have passed through here, he says, in a wearily matter-of-fact tone. They blew up the generator. Is the village taxed? Does Kadaloor, like Kinnuya, suffer extortion by the LTTE? "Yes, of course. Like everywhere else, they demand a tax on black stones, since they are used for building houses. Another tax on herds and harvests. And then for a few years now, maybe four, a tax on wood. They want to preserve the jungle. So they tax green wood. That's normal." But there's something else, he adds, his voice suddenly lower. "We've had another visit... From the army... They didn't tax us—but it's worse than that..." He doesn't say any more about it. He gets up and, as if he regretted having said too much already, brings us to see how well his patch of banana trees has grown. Gérard R., from ACF, later tells me that Kadaloor is the last Tamil village in the region; that the army, yes, the Sinhalese governmental army, has destroyed dozens of villages like this one; and that Uppeveli for instance, you see Uppeveli, there on the map, five kilometers from Trincomalee? Well Uppeveli has disappeared, the army has razed Uppeveli. Another piece of information.

The road itself, or I should say the track, scarcely drivable, so waterlogged and muddy we have to stop to wedge the jeep's front wheels; the farther we advance the fewer people we meet. Empty brick houses. Isolated farms. Traces of a destroyed village. A cow, wandering free, who opens up the path for us. Bicyclists, rare, often in pairs, sheltered beneath large umbrellas, who take care not to stop. Flocks of crows. Women. Especially women. Don't they say, in Sri Lanka, that this war has produced so many dead or, in any case, disappeared people that sometimes, in the villages, there are five times more women than men (20)? They are afraid, these women, of the Tigers—there, quite close, on the left, in the villages of Uppuru and Iralkuli, with their anti-air-craft weapons and their cannons that only yesterday were bombarding the zone. But they are also afraid, I discover, of the Sinhalese "Air Force" which has been blindly bombing from its bases in Trincomalee. Another piece of information.

And then finally Sungankuli, "The Catfish-Pond," the last village at the end of the trail, on the edge of the inhabited jungle and realm of the Tigers. There used to be fifty-three Tamil families there. Now there are only nineteen. And where are they now, these nineteen families? Why don't we see them? There's no one in the little brand-new blue and orange school. No one in the area of the temple—a simple standing stone, beneath a tamarind tree, opposite which they (who?) have placed a piece of wavy sheet-metal, a saucer filled with yellow wax, and a little stone, smaller, sculpted in the shape of a rat. No one in the houses which, if their adobe weren't in such good shape, if their roofs of dried palm leaves and coconut palms weren't so obviously taken care of, would seem completely abandoned. Finally the village leader—he is there when we arrive but very quickly disappears, after telling us he's only the "resident leader" and that the real leader, the *grama talaivar*, or non-resident leader, is in the city, on the coast, in Alankerny. Everyone is afraid, that's obvious. Terribly afraid. But without, once again, being able to tell what terrifies them more, the Tigers who claim to liberate them or the army that is supposed to protect them. Without their being able to decide what was worse, for the owner of the tea-stall, for instance, near the school: the Tigers who, suspecting him of being an informer paid by the Navy, came to look for him, the other week, to take him into the jungle and interrogate him; or the Navy which, learning he had two sons with the Tigers and finding, upon reflection, his many trips to Alankerny suspicious, came to collect him, the month before, to take him to the Boosa camp, in the southern part of the country, where he had already spent three years of arbitrary detention...

The old woman, on the road going back; that poor old woman who is crying in front of her house, little dry sobs, without moving, almost without tears; that very beautiful and very old lady in the process of contemplating, overwhelmed, her tree, stripped by a passing elephant and, further on, on the path, enormous grey mounds of excrement—what is she afraid of, this woman? Of the Tigers and the Air Force. Of the Air Force as much as of the Tigers. Of this two-faced war, of this war without a face, eater of men, which has taken away her sons, her husband, her brothers, and which makes it so that tomorrow night, when the animal returns, and she is sure it will return, there will be no one, not even a *kavalalar*, a guard, to light torches and protect her garden.

Yashoda's story (21).

She is Tamil. She is another very old woman, her face dried out, her back bent. She knew we were coming, with Alexandra Morelli, the head of the UN mission. So she has pulled back her hair and put on a beautiful blue sari, dotted with gold. She has lived in camps for more than twenty years. In her home region, first, south of Kandy. Then in Wanni. And now here, in this Alles Garden camp, north of Trincomalee, with its huts of dried wood and palm leaves.

Her Kandy house? It was another kind of hut, in the workers' terraced houses of the tea plantations. One day, the Tigers came. After them, the army came too. The village was relocated. The entire population, deported. And that was the end of her house.

Her family? Her husband disappeared at the same time, arrested by the army, they never knew what became of him. Her eldest son also disappeared—some, in the camp, who are village elders, say that he went over to the side of the Tigers, but how can anybody be certain? She only has this son left. She shows a little man, old like her, with a sad smile, teeth reddened by betel nut, torso bare, his chest hollow, with a checkered loincloth, who takes a little step forward to present himself, outside of the circle that has formed, beneath the shed, around Yashoda. "He is my family. That's all the family I have left. My son."

Today, then? This camp? How is life, in a camp like this one?

"Oh! It's a good camp. With nice solid huts. We're content. The only problem..."

She hesitates. Then addresses the leader of the United Nations mission.

"The only problem is the WC's. They made us a nice row of WC's, from boards. But without doors. So we, especially the women, are exposed to the wind. You should go look. Opposite them, there is the monkey rock. And behind the monkeys, the soldiers. It's not normal to relieve oneself in front of monkeys and soldiers. Do you think they could have doors?"

The mission head takes note. Then asks:

"And the army? I had arranged it so that the army doesn't enter the camp any more. On condition, of course, that the Tigers do the same. Do they...?"

The old woman cuts her off.

"No, no. The Tigers don't come anymore. Never."

I know that, on this point, she is not telling the truth. Less than an hour ago, while I was loitering, alone, between the huts, I saw a Mercedes enter the central path and stop in front of the fried-dough stall. Two men. Obviously Tamil racketeers. Even in the camp, even in this place of humble misery, the law of extortion and violence!

"Yes, but the army?" insists the mission leader.

"There it is, the army," the old woman replies, pointing to the sky.

We hear, first far away, then quite close, a muffled rumbling, followed by a series of explosions. And we see great plumes of smoke that rise from the treetops and break up into the clouds. The woman counts.

"You hear? Twelve explosions. That means two planes. They sent two planes to drop twelve bombs. It's here, in the forest."

I think of the eight K-Fir bombers Israel has just delivered, which, they tell me in Colombo, have multiplied by five the firepower of the government air force. I think especially of the telephone call the mission leader made an hour ago, as she always does before taking to the road, to the major in charge of the Trinco air base: "I'm leaving; no bombing planned in the zone?" "No, no, there's nothing planned, you can go without fear"...

But the mission leader insists.

"Did the army keep their word? Did it stop coming and going in the camp?"

"Yes. But things, now, are happening outside. A young man, the other day. He passed through the checkpoint with a television remote in his pocket. What is that? said the soldiers. He didn't answer. So they thought it was a weapon. They were afraid. They shot him in the leg. And the young man is crippled for life."

She thinks. Then, dreamily:

"That's it, they're afraid. That's what makes them so mean. We too are afraid. But that doesn't make us mean..."

A discussion follows then, in Tamil, with the other refugees. Another story, apparently, that they want her to tell.

"There's another story," she continues, not as willingly. "It was a few days ago, near here, in Iqbal Nagar. Two young men with a moped. They blew a tire. So they were pushing the moped. But then. They came from the village of Gopalapuram, which is a bad village since the inhabitants, the week before, had had a demonstration that annoyed the Navy a lot. So, suddenly, they're suspicious. So they're arrested, they're brought into a windmill and then..."

Yashoda falls silent. I recognize this story, which I read on the website of the LTTE, and which I had confirmed through an independent source. I know that the two young men were tortured, disemboweled, that they tore out their eyes, and that they ended up killing them. And I know, above all, that stories like that, in which it's the army that kills, are generated every day, from one end of the country to the other, beginning, quite recently, with the pogrom started in the Bindunuwena camp, 200 kilometers from Colombo, south of Kandy: a rehabilitation camp where repentant Tigers, often child-soldiers, are penned in; a dark story of detainees who, behind their barbed wire, provoked their jailers by lifting their sarongs and showing their genitals; the hysteria of the jailers, of the village, of the neighboring villages, of Sinhalese extremist organizations, of the soldiers and policemen who were present, all of them getting worked up, all of them cursing the Tamil "dogmeat"—and a few days later, on the morning of November 24th, a crowd drunk with hatred and blood forces open the gates to the camp and cuts up half of its occupants with kitchen knives and machetes.

Yashoda has fallen silent. She has lowered her eyes and fallen silent—her mouth a little open, as if she were going to cry. It is true she has said the important thing. A civilian population caught in the stranglehold between a fanatical guerilla movement and a barbarous army without principles. Combatants who, perhaps because this conflict has lasted too long, or because it is unfolding, necessarily, to the indifference of the nations and of great international institutions, allow themselves the use of methods, and crimes, as unjustifiable in one camp as in another. In short, a daily massacre of innocent people who have become, worse than hostages, the stakes of an insane war. In Sri Lanka, for twenty years now, death has been recruiting wholesale.

Have arrived in Bujumbura. Sky white with heat. Muggy. That rather stifling smell so characteristic of African airports. And, right away, in front of the Novotel, in other words in the heart of the modern city, across from a group of "expats," in white Lacoste tee-shirt and shorts, straight out of the Belgian colonial era, there is a teenager, almost a child, who has just been stopped by a patrol. Papers? No papers. Or rather yes, a shapeless scrap of paper, dug out of the depths one of his jean pockets, which the soldier examines. "Who are you? Where do you live? The stamp is rubbed out!" He examines it again. Holds it out to a colleague. Repeats, calling to witness first his colleague, then the brigade, then, it seems to me, the group of expatriates: "The stamp is rubbed out! The stamp is rubbed out!" Then, to the child: "Hutu? Sympathizer of the Hutu killers? No? Then prove it! Come with us to clear the banana plantation in Tenga!" The child, strangely, doesn't seem so impressed. At first, he tries to explain something to the soldier. The stamp, probably... Says he sells fishing rods on the shore of Lake Tanganyika... And then he shrugs his shoulders and smiles—as if he's not so unhappy as all that, at bottom, to follow the Tutsis and go clear the banana plantation in Tenga. "He had no choice," one of the witnesses tells me later. "For the kids of Bujumbura, it's unemployment or the army. And they know that, in the army, at least they'll have something to eat, and a bed, and even a little money, since Burundi is the only country in the region that still pays its soldiers a salary." The child is in the truck. The truck has disappeared, at the end of the Avenue du Peuple-Murundi. Bujumbura, another country of child-soldiers?

It was in the Hutu district of Kamengué, north of the city, that I first began to inhale the atmosphere of the Burundi war. Half the houses are destroyed, seemingly by heavy artillery. The other half is rebuilt, but with a mixture of bits of wood, fragments of cloth and big boxes, tin or blue plastic strips still marked UNHCR; it has all been invaded by vegetation. A strange atmosphere reigns over the neighborhood, a mixture of fear, suspicion, abandoned hope, and weariness: long lines of men and women walking aimlessly, their gaze empty (22)—I knew, before I came here, that it is defenseless populations that are, as in Sri Lanka and Angola, the main victims of the merciless confrontation that sets the governmental Tutsi army against the rebel Hutu militia, but I hadn't imagined the desolation would be so palpable. This morning, rumor has it that a rebel unit has infiltrated the neighborhood and, last night, in front of the church of the Jehovah Witnesses, killed two women they took for Tutsis. So the paratroopers are here. They patrol. Guided by three *nyumbakumi*, the heads of housing blocks, they enter people's homes, empty out suspicious huts, interrogate some, line others up against the wall. But without a noise. Without a shout. For a second, I tell myself that it's the presence of a foreigner that keeps some of them from striking too hard, or the others from protesting too loudly. But no. It's just the way of life in the neighborhood. Violence and dailiness mixed together. The austere brutality of the soldiery on one hand. These women who, on the other, continue to crush cassava or sell charms or, like one woman sitting on the ground, almost naked, her breasts dry and flaccid, breast-feeding a child swollen with edema and shivering: this way the women of Bujumbura have of carrying their babies like little corpses; this unspeaking, worn-out despair, this end-of-the-world sadness that seems to have descended upon an entire population (23)—the opposite of the effervescence that characterizes all the African cities, even the poor ones, that I know.

Same feeling in Mubone, in the village of Mutimbuzi. This district isn't shown on any map. It isn't even a district, really, but a camp. And this camp was created recently, one day when the army, preparing for a "clean-up" operation in the hills that are mostly Hutu, informed the farmers, as it always does, that they had twenty-four hours to leave the zone and gather in the plain, near the barracks—after which it blocked the paths leading to the town, and whoever had chosen to remain on site despite the warning was considered an accomplice of the rebels and, like them, subject to being slaughtered at any instant. Some, of course, remained. Or weren't informed of the orders. Or feared that, by obeying, they would get on the wrong side of the other camp, which would never let them return to their houses. So they were declared effectively accomplices, legitimate military targets, and there were, on the two hills of Nyambuye and Kavumu, which are traditionally strongholds of the Hutu rebels of the National Liberation Forces, dozens of civilians killed at point-blank range. Silence again there. Reticence of the survivors to talk about it. And an infinite sadness in the eyes of the hundred or so able-bodied men in the process of digging, under threat of Kalashnikovs, a giant trench that will be used as open-air latrines. "There are no more relocation camps in Burundi," Eugène Nindorera, Minister of the Rights of the Human Individual, of Institutional Reforms, and of Relations with the National Assembly, had told me that very morning. Well, there are. Here is one, just outside the capital, covered in dust and filth, at the end of this track unsuitable for motor vehicles where I arrived by chance, looking for the route between Cibitoke and Kinama, and where a few thousand men, women, and children survive, caught once again in the crossfire: the Tutsi army, on one side, which regards all Hutus as potential enemies and targets; the Hutu rebels, on the other, who seem ready to do anything, including terrorizing their own civilians, destroying their houses, and forbidding them to return to them, to establish their hold over the country. "Who are you?" barks a sergeant, as thin as the diggers, as wretched as they, his uniform in tatters, his skull covered with scabs. "Who are you? You have no right to be here!" You can feel that he has nothing in the world, this sergeant, except for his new Kalashnikov, aimed at over-curious intruders. And you feel, above all, that it would be useless to insist: the relocated people would obviously not have the right to say any more, even if they wanted to. Are they, in fact, relocated people? Or hostages? Or forced slaves?

Kamengué, again. But at night. The soldiers have left. They have withdrawn to their quarters, on the outskirts of the neighborhood, and have, as they do every night, ceded the land to the

Hutus. And it's another neighborhood—another atmosphere, so another district, almost another city—which takes shape thanks to the night. Sounds, now. Gunshots, which come from the hills. But also raised voices. Transistor radios. A motorbike backfiring. A fistfight. A guy who offers me girls. Another who follows me to sell me a CD by Céline Dion. Another, shivering from fever, who is being brought in from the mountains to be cared for in the clinic. A group of "recuperators" who, with bare feet, straw caps or hats on their heads, go from house to house to collect either food supplies or the 2,000 francs due quarterly to the rebellion. Or "Chez Roméo," a quiet arbor made from sheet metal and logs where they spoke to me, the other morning, of nothing but soccer and food, where the only issue was knowing when fishing would be re-authorized on the lake and when the owner would start serving his succulent fried "*ndagala*" again—now it's transformed into a noisy forum where, seated in front of pitchers of banana beer, a dozen men discuss the way Hutus are treated in the army. One: "I hear the officers beat up Hutu soldiers." Another: "I saw men from a Tutsi troop kill their Hutu officer with a bayonet!" A third: "At night, when you pass by the garrison, you can hear cries, and blows, and soft, muffled thuds, like when you pound meat." It is midnight. The tone rises. Tempers flare. A gathering has formed, in the street, in front of "Chez Roméo." It's curfew-time, the priest who is accompanying me says. We have to get back.

Faustin is Tutsi. So he belongs to the other, minority ethnic group, which has held the levers of power since the Belgians left, and which lives in terror of Hutu revenge and violence: Rwanda is so close! The two countries are so similar, almost twins! How can one be Tutsi, here, in Bujumbura, without always having the precedent of Kigali in mind? His life, Faustin says, was turned upside-down five years ago, when they found his father's head, along with the heads of three soldiers from his unit, stuck on a lance, at the edge of a field of coffee trees, near Tenga. That day, he went off in search of the rest of the body. He scoured the whole region. Questioned the farmers. He even found the brother of one of the "assailants" who told him everything: the attack in the middle of the night; the massacre; that there was in the unit, as in most units, a Hutu noncommissioned officer, and that he's the one who betrayed them, and who led the killers to the isolated position, on the top of a rocky peak, where the unit was supposed to halt the infiltration of "intimidators." And he identified the body, finally, ten kilometers further on, in a garbage dump, naked, decomposing, with his dog tag slipped onto one of his feet. Since then, finding corpses has been his specialty. They even say, in Cibitoke, the Tutsi neighborhood where he lives and where I came to meet him, that it's like his profession. The neighbor whose wife was decapitated... The other one who is sure that this headless body, found, its testicles stuffed with pins, on the shore of the lake, near "Safari," the fashionable beach, is the body of one of his brothers... A third whose baby was strangled, then cut up, the pieces of its body found near Tenga... He, Faustin, is the one they come to see, every time. He is the one they turn to to reconstruct these mutilated bodies. His profession? He replies, solemn, almost proud: hunter of Tutsi corpses tortured by the Hutu demons.

Tenga, finally. For the three days I've been here, they keep telling me about Tenga, this labyrinth of coffee trees and forests, on the road to Bubanza, which the Hutu rebels and the National Liberation Forces seem to have succeeded in making into an inviolable fortress, at the edge of the capital, with trenches, bunkers, stores of defensive and offensive weapons, landmines. And so, this morning, I decided to go there to have a look. An all-terrain vehicle, armored, from the French embassy. A checkpoint in Kinama, the other great Hutu neighborhood of the city. A group of soldiers, torsos bare, Kalashnikovs slung over their shoulders, who kill time, under a banyan tree, playing dominos. Another barricade, in front of the coffee trees—a thin cord, almost a thread, stretched across the road, but from which hang, so that cars can't miss it, strips of multicolored plastic bags. And then suddenly, a few kilometers further on, on the now deserted road where we've been told to drive at high speed and not to stop on any account, an explosion; another, a little closer, which seems to come out of the ground; a machine gun in the ditch; soldiers, in the middle of the road, panic-stricken, shooting blind, straight in front of them; others, pinned to the ground, half hidden by the coffee plants, also shooting into the void; others, very young, breathless, leaving the underbrush, faces covered with mud, doubled over, carrying a stretcher; the crackle of a walkie-talkie; an officer's shouts; bursts from automatic weapons now coming from both sides (24); the image again—dreamed? hallucinated?—of a terrible head, as if daubed with paint, which no longer belongs to a soldier and which seems to gush, for a brief instant, on the reddened tip of the coffee trees; the truth is that everything is going very quickly and I have scarcely had time to realize what was happening, to close my window, to get down, and that the men with the stretcher are there, they make the driver get out, change their mind, force him back into the driver's seat and put the wounded man on the back seat of the car, next to me, stretched out. His complexion is grey. His breath short. He vomits out little clots of blood and groans. Let's go, let's go, drive quickly, you can see he's wounded. And the car does in fact move off again, the Congolese driver crouching over his wheel: ten minutes later, we have returned to the Kinama checkpoint, then to the Prince Régent Hospital, with the wounded soldier.

It wasn't very easy to get back out of Bujumbura. The embassy, put off by the Tenga episode, advised me against it. The Minister of the Interior straight out forbade me from leaving. My old friend, the French colonel Guy de Battista, formerly of Sarajevo, who had become responsible for the safety of the United Nations Mission for Human Rights in Burundi, explained to me that, since the murder, a few months ago, in a relocation camp in the province of Rutana, precisely where I want to go, of the Dutch leader of the World Food Program and of the Chilean representative of UNICEF, cars with the white pennant of the NGO are no longer a guarantee of safety. So that I ended up simply asking a taxi to drive me south, and the taxi-driver replied yes, okay, the roads are good in Burundi—but on one condition, and only one, which he clung to quite adamantly: that we make the journey on a Saturday and, for instance, today. Why Saturday? Because the "genocidal attackers," the Hutus of the FNL (National Liberation Front) the images of whose abominable crimes the entire country keep replaying over and over again—that priest whom they forced to eat his own penis before they crucified him... those babies buried alive... those children impaled, sprinkled with gas and burned, in their school, by the principal himself... —are also excellent Christians, generally of the Adventist persuasion, who don't smoke, don't drink, arrive in the villages singing hymns at the top of their voices, and they consider Saturday a sacred day, devoted to prayer, on which one must above all not shed blood. Those who are used to African wars say that the best time to travel is noon since it's suddenly so hot that even the combatants have a siesta. Here is another time, unique to Burundi: Saturday, all day, since it's the day of rest for the "genocidal attackers."

On the road, then, for Rutana. Highway 7 first, the most direct, which goes through the interior but where the soldiers, at the end of twenty or so kilometers, make cars turn back. Highway 3, then, which runs along Lake Tanganyika and will obviously be longer—but Burundi, once again, is so small! The distances are so short! The driver is certain, despite our setback, of arriving before six o'clock, which is when the army returns to its barracks and when the guerillas retake control of the major roads. Dark rock of the mountain, on the left. Grass and bushes, by the lake. Patrols of red berets all along the road and also, it seems to me, halfway up the slopes, in the mountains. Other patrols, civilian, armed with sticks, machetes, or hammers: are they going to prevent us from continuing? No, false alarm, they just wanted us to make room for two of them and drop them off in the next village. In short, a good road, it's true. Surprisingly smooth for a country put to fire and sword where one house out of two, when it is still standing, bears signs of gunshots on its façade. Up to Nyanza-Lac, the last lakeside town before entering the interior, where we are blocked for good—a barricade of dry branches, bags of sand, bunkers below and a sergeant who looks at me for several minutes, from afar, before deciding to approach. "War zone, you can't pass through." "I thought curfew was at six o'clock?" "Here, it's four o'clock; you can't get through." At which point a consultation is held, in Kurundi, between him and the driver from which emerges: first that the driver must immediately turn back; second that I myself can, if I wish, and for a fee of ten dollars, sleep there, in the unit's rest house, in the hope that tomorrow another car will pass by. Another endless discussion for permission to pay the ten dollars in French francs. Small problem of hurt feelings when I have to get him to understand that I have my sleeping bag and don't need the blanket he offers me. But finally, everything works out. I just have to wait.

Am awakened at five o'clock. It's the soldier from the night before. But in a good humor. Almost merry. "You're lucky. A convoy's arriving. Reinforcements for Rutana." "Why reinforcements?" "Because an infiltration of *intagoheka* (literally "those who never sleep," another name for the Hutu militia) has been reported coming back from Tanzania. And the garrison wants reinforcements." Just time enough to swallow a glass of boiled water with a dash of powdered milk. And the convoy is there. Two transports of troops. A tank. Many field guns, mounted on Toyotas. A machine gun, to open up the road. A half-covered truck in which I make out a loose jumble of rifles and handguns. And, right behind it, an uncovered truck where I climb in amongst a joyous band of young men, almost children: some are wearing uniforms; others not; the one who seems to be their leader, and who speaks French, is wearing a white wool hat over which he has placed his beret; another wears frayed khaki shorts, boots, and, over his bare skin, a grey flannel jacket that's too warm; among all of them, my arrival provokes a commotion: who am I... where do I come from... can they try on my glasses... my shoes... one even tries them on, his small feet floating in my large shoes, which makes the other laugh a lot; I find it difficult to make them understand they're my only pair, I can't give them away, and that makes them laugh twice as hard... Are these the "reinforcements"? Are they the ones being counted on to repel the advance of "those who never sleep"? And what a strange disproportion there is between those stocks of weapons (they say they come from all the lost armies of the Africa round the Great Lakes, the army of Mobutu, of Idi Amin Dada and Milton Obote, the Rwandan ex-FAR [Rwandan Armed Forces] of Habyarimana, all swallowed up by the tropical forest, the wreckage of which, as after a storm, fell in the guerilla zones of the Congo and of Burundi)—what a disproportion between that firepower and this troop of ragged, tousled, rowdy, badly trained kids! Half an hour later, we are in Rutana. And we haven't met a shadow of the rebel column that's supposed to be coming back from Tanzania. False alarm? Rumor? Or the mystery of a war in which, as in Angola, the front lines keep moving and slipping?

Same situation, and same surprise, after Rutana, in the hills, in the savannah, fifteen kilometers as the crow flies from the border, where they assured me the rebels had an outpost, but where I find instead yet another Tutsi unit. "The genocidals held the position," the officer explains to me, a kind of Hercules, all neck and shoulders, who brings to mind a buffalo and has all the physical characteristics that advocates of race-wars usually attribute to Hutus. "They were there, yes, for two months. But they left, yesterday. They had weapons, you can be sure of that. A lot of weapons." He shows a machine gun set next to a howitzer and, further on, in the brush, in the shelter of a rubberized tarpaulin, crates of ammunition and mortar shells. "But they didn't have enough to eat. So we were patient. We waited for them to have nothing left, either to eat or to drink. And then we just had to pick them off..." Prisoners? He laughs, an evil laughter, hard, insolent. "In this war, no one takes prisoners. When you have one..." Balancing both arms, he makes the gesture of throwing a parcel: "when you have one, when you have an attacker who falls into our hands, find the trash!" And, seeing my disapproval, he takes me to a mud hut where two of his men are sleeping, who get up when he arrives and stand to attention. "Look at that." He shows me, in a corner of the hut, a new foam mattress, still in its dust cover, and, with an accusatory finger, shouts: "They burned two of our men in mattresses like this one; so when we take one, well..." He looks for words, seems to question the two men with his gaze—but, when nothing comes, he repeats: "Trash! Trash!"

I go back, the same day, by the same road, in a taxi rented in Rutana, towards Bujumbura. This time I notice that all the people I pass on the edge of the road who are neither soldiers nor members of the militia are women: where are the men? Hidden? In the jungle? I also notice that a number of the women, especially the ones heading back towards the south, carry on their heads pieces of sheet metal piled up: the sheet metal from their houses, their last piece of wealth, that they'll sell in Tanzania?

Or from neighboring houses, abandoned by "attackers," or "accomplices of attackers," who have fled into the jungle? Back at the lake, after Nyanza, I am surprised to notice that the previous day's checkpoint, the one where I had to stop, has disappeared. It was there, I'm sure of it. I'm not dreaming, it was there. But I don't see it. No soldiers. No barricade. Not even the hut where I slept, and which has vanished. Ten kilometers further on, to the north, where there hadn't been anything, I'd swear it, absolutely nothing, yesterday morning, now I find the control point there: the same barrier of dry branches, the same block of sticks surmounted by sandbags painted camouflage color, the same lazy arrogance in the leader of the post who resembles the other one like a brother—and still the same mystery of the mobility of these fronts which move according to some unknown law. "But I know, boss," the driver tells me. "It's the air spirits. It's to divert evil spirits." Maybe so, after all. Maybe, under the circumstances, one has to take into account the devil and evil spirits. A war of ghosts, again. A war of phantoms. At the risk, I well realize, of making this war unreal. Of depoliticizing it. At the risk of making it such a perfectly ghostly war that it becomes ungraspable, blind, without clearly ascribable causes, without stakes, almost without effects: the old theme, which I have so much mistrusted, of the famous "End of History" (25)—these edges of the world, Kojeve said these "provinces of the empire," where only ersatz events occur, obscure, of no consequence.

Athlete's build. Black, military moustache. Hard gaze. The way he has, when he speaks, of tapping his foot in time. That singsong tone of voice, both gentle and slightly menacing, which could express authority but, in this gloomy building, its windows open onto the stormy night, has the opposite effect on me. Isn't President Buyoya much more alone and fragile than he says? Aren't they busy firing grenades, this very night, at the gates of his residence, on the hill of Sororezo? And that elite guard glimpsed, as I was arriving, under the parking lot awning taking cover from the rain, those soldiers, wrapped up in their overcoats, who scarcely bothered to inspect me—is it really with such as they that the safety of a threatened president is insured? "The stakes of this war, you say... The stakes..." He thinks. Taps his foot, but aimlessly, like an out of whack metronome. "My personal stake, in any case... I can tell you why, instead of continuing to lead my life as a researcher in the USA, I decided to resume this position that I had already occupied from 1987 to 1993." He closes his eyes. Taps again, both with his foot, and with his fist, as if he wanted to collect memories, take a running start and really convince me that Burundi is not this exhausted, absolutely twilight land, which has left world history, gone out of orbit. "First I want to shatter this myth of a racial war between Hutus and Tutsis; we are the same people; we are an old nation where ethnic groups have lived in harmony for centuries; first German, then Belgian colonizers were the ones who constructed this fable of a race of Batutsi breeders, closer to the Whites than the Blacks, who came from the high Ethiopian plateaus to oppress the Bahutus. And then..." Electricity outage. An aide-de-camp brings a lantern. His face, lit from below, now seems alive only in the jaw, and the mouth, which trembles a little. "And then, I don't want Burundi to experience the fate of Rwanda. I don't want, at any price, to let the advocates of Hutu Power do what they like—and you can be sure they have the same intentions here as in Kigali. Do you know how many Tutsis they've killed, just by the end of 1993 alone, when President Melchior Ndadaye was assassinated? 200,000! A quarter of the Rwandan deaths. Whether you like it or not, it's a genocide waiting to happen."

He asked me to call him Luc. He works for a European NGO during the day. He is a guerilla at night. And no one, in his daytime life, seems to suspect those other activities that, after many hours of conversation, I end up reconstructing: nighttime incursions into the hills; journeys, by way of the crocodile-infested lake, on the banks of the Kivu, in the Congo; the role he played, a few months ago, negotiating a right of way, for rival parties from the FDD, through the FNL-controlled jungle of rural Bujumbura; weapons, especially; the organization of the transport, to Tenga, of heavy weapons of the Rwandan ex-FAR; in short, an entire clandestine activity that makes this massive man in his fifties, with the overlarge intense eyes, the horseshoe-shaped beard plunging low onto his chest, one of the civilian executives of the Palipehutu, the *Parti Pour la Libération du Peuple Hutu* (Hutu People's Liberation Party). What does he say about this Hutu genocidal urge that Buyoya talks about? "A joke!" He calls to witness the priest who has organized our interview. "It's a sinister joke, to talk about a genocidal wish, when one holds, as he does, all the levers of power." Then, with a flash of hatred and cunning mixed in his look: "Did Buyoya tell you about the 400 civilians massacred by his army, last August, in the province of Cankuzo? And about the 150 dead in Muzuyé, who had to be buried in communal ditches before the NGO's made a scandal? And the Church of the Pentecost in Butaganza? Did he boast about those Tutsi soldiers who told the inhabitants of Butaganza to take shelter in the church and, when they were there, aimed at the church, threw grenades inside, set fire to it and finished off with bayonets the ones who tried to flee?" Horrors against horrors. Victims against victims. Still, there is a common wish, faced with the Kojevian hypothesis of a spectral, absurd (27) confrontation, without stakes, to anchor this Burundi war in the sure ground of a political rationality: the threat of genocide for one; the struggle, for the other, between the exploiting Tutsi and the exploited Hutu...

"Hutus shelled the airport. They hit a Sabena plane." When David Gakunzi, head of the Martin Luther King Center and one of the rare intellectuals in this country who gave me the feeling of never thinking in terms of ethnic groups, of always bringing everything into consideration to get beyond this false Hutu-Tutsi divide, and of dreaming of an authentically "citizen" future—when the young Gakunzi, with his misleading Bob Marley-like looks and his big round multicolored hat holding in his tied-back hair, appears suddenly in the breakfast-room of my hotel to tell me the news, the information is everywhere already, and the whole city is talking about nothing but this incredible feat. The last time was January 1st, 1998, when the genocidals swooped down on the airport garrison and killed a dozen soldiers. The general staff, at the time, had been categorical: we have driven them back beyond the hills; the city, we promise, is from now on absolutely safe from this kind of murderous raid. So now we have proof that was false. Now there's proof that the enemy can strike where it likes, when it likes, and as it likes. And even though this raid didn't produce any victims, the Brussels-Bujumbura service, already reduced to one single flight a week, was one of the country's last links to the outer world, and the attack is bound to have a considerable symbolic impact. So now there's turmoil in the city. A state of panic in the community of French and Belgian expatriates who had been living in the illusion of a war that didn't touch them. And an even greater confusion among the Burundians themselves who experience first the attack and then, almost immediately afterwards, Sabena's decision to suspend all flights, as one more blow, a punishment, night falling on the city, prison closing in, a quarantine: "Devil take Buyoya, Luc, and the rest of them," the Europeans seem to be saying, "we have decided to close the door, to throw away the key, and to disassociate ourselves once and for all from your incomprehensible conflict." I take to the road, the other road, leading north, which will let me leave the country through Rwanda, leaving behind me a shattered capital, in a state of shock, at the end of its tether.

Is it this business of the Sabena flight? Is it the idea, which is pursuing me, of that city momentarily cut off from the world, isolated, asphyxiated? Is it simply fatigue? I have the impression that a different atmosphere arose in this new setting, and that this northern part of the country is more desolate, even more disadvantaged, than the South. This broken fountain. This other one, five kilometers further on, where a hundred or so poor people stand in line, holding plastic cans, watering cans, gourds—patience of the blind, immobility of corpses (28). A Hutu cemetery. Another one, Tutsi, with its graves overturned. A destroyed school. Burned coffee fields (29). The road itself, the bridges, half broken. The enormous bellies of the children. The pervading stench of rotting corpses. Entire villages looted—one has to come here, yes, to this region, to learn what a looted village is, truly looted, when not a tile remains, not a piece of sheet metal or cinder block, not a post outside, when an antlike swarm of human activity has scraped off everything, down to the bone and beyond. Not a ruin, but a nothingness (30). Worse than war, the after-effects of war, when the war itself has run out of steam, when it has exhausted its last resources, when it has killed so much, burned so much, that it is like those forest fires whose incendiary rage finds nothing more, in its passing, than deserted land and that keep on burning, nonetheless. The image comes to me of a new kind of bomb that would leave things standing, and even men, but would empty them—how to say it?—of their positivity, of their substance (31). The image, too, of those black holes the astronomers speak of: perhaps there are black holes in history too; perhaps there is, in the life of peoples, the equivalent of those planets that are resorbed and whose density increases as they dwindle; perhaps Burundi is one of these black holes—a density of infinite suffering for a rarefied place, compacted in on itself, on the way to effacing itself (the "End of History" again!) from our real and imaginary landscapes, our political screens, our radars. In *Le Temps du mépris* (Days of Wrath), Malraux writes—it's Kassner, in his prison cell, on the eve of his death, who is speaking—"The worst suffering is that of the solitude by which it is accompanied."

Hutus? Tutsis? I am at the end of the trail. In front of me, the Rwandan border. In front of the customs-post, a traffic-jam of women, huge bundles on their heads, who are going to try to sell their possessions on the other side. Perhaps Luc was right, and this war is reducible to a particularly fierce form of class struggle. Perhaps it's Buyoya who was telling the truth—and even if there's just a suspicion, even if there's just a minute possibility that Burundi could one day be Rwanda, everything should be done to avert the danger. But the farther I go, the more I advance on this last road, the more the idea imposes itself that there is something else still, another mechanism, that would implicate both of them, and all the others with them, and that wouldn't be unrelated to this radical abandonment. Say there is a desperate population. Abandoned, thrown on its dung-heap, absolutely desperate. Say there is a community that, in the tragedy of its misery, sees added to that misery the misery of being alone, forgotten by everyone, erased from the great global projects, crossed off the maps of the soft-hearted politicians and their compassionate systems. Can't you imagine a kind of backlash, then? A wave of rage and revolt? Can't you picture an immense, mad anger that, like all impotent angers, would seize itself as an object and turn against itself? Individuals commit suicide. Why not countries? Why shouldn't a sick community, stripped of everything, a literally proletarian nation that has nothing more to sell on the market of universal history than the rising extremes of its own collective death that, in a sort of ultimate swindle, it realizes—only too late—interests no one, decide to do the deed? A suicide, yes. A rage of self-destruction carrying everything away with it. The perhaps unique case of an entire population attacking its own country in order to break it apart. You need as much energy to die as you do to live.

Who kills better? A fascist or a Marxist guerilla? The peasants of Quebrada Naïn are still debating about it. A month ago the former arrived in the village, the "paramilitaries" of drug lord Carlos Castaño, and killed twenty people suspected of "collaborating" with the Marxist guerilla movement. Eight days later, people from the guerilla movement turned up, the one called FARC, or the Revolutionary Armed Forces of Colombia, and, on the pretext that the survivors hadn't resisted enough, on the pretext that they might even have fraternized with the enemy, killed ten more of the villagers.

Today, three survivors from this double killing are there, come back to the scene of the crime, to this village at the end of the world, on the outer edges of the state of Cordoba, where they wanted to recover whatever was left of the tools, personal effects, or objects that, in the haste of those two mad nights of flight, they had left behind. There is Juan, the oldest. Manolo, called "the Blond," because he's a little lighter. And then Carlito, the teacher—he's the one who, on the day of my visit to the Tierra Alta camp, administrative center of the municipality, offered to let me accompany them: "A gringo is good for us; it's a protection; that'll prevent them from attacking us again."

We left, early in the morning, in the windowless bus that makes the journey up to the hydro-electric dam of Frasquillo (32).

We drove for an hour, along the Rio Sinu, on a pretty good road, lined with flowering trees, where we didn't encounter any checkpoints (proof that the paramilitaries are at home in Cordoba? That the partition of the country is finished and that, like the FARC, they have real territories where they have taken the army's place?).

In Tucurra, on the river, we passed the dam, along with the permanent camp built by the Swedes and Russians, and we went further on, to Frasquillo, to retrieve a flat-bottomed barge which, two *vueltas* further on, two loops of the river lower down in the direction of Antioquia, set us on the other shore, at the foot of the mountain.

And it's a little after noon, after an hour of walking on a bad path, cleared by machetes, in one of those zones described on maps as *"datos de relieves insuficientes"* (insufficient data) and where all we know is that the FARC, observed from the plain by the paramilitaries, has their most solid bastions, that we arrive in this desolate place that Quebrada Naïn has become.

Peasants are there, come from the neighboring village: How are things in Tierra Alta? Is there work? Money? Is it true that the municipality is giving out land? That it paints houses for free?

There is another group, Indians from another village, further north, on the edge of the Parque Paramillo, in the heart of the FARC territory, who have also come to see what's happened—their feet bare, on mule-back, dressed in scraps of frayed black cloth, some in balaclavas: what is the army doing? Is it true that it no longer protects people and that it is confiscating hunting rifles? Is it possible that it's working hand-in-hand with the paramilitaries? And especially, especially, do we have any information about the assassination, in Tierra Alta, in the middle of the street, of José Angel Domico (35), the leader of the Indians of the Alto Sinu, who had come down to discuss the compensation due in exchange for the 400 hectares of good land flooded by the dam?

But the village itself is deserted. Not destroyed, no. Not even looted. Just empty. Absolutely, terrifyingly empty. Humble houses of wood and straw, scattered beside the torrent, that make one feel, from myriad signs—the doors left open; a rotting sandal; the end of a pipe, on the ground, already rusty; a piece from some overalls almost reduced to dust—that it's as if they'd been blown out by the mad violence of that double assault.

"Why?" Manolo asks, standing stock-still in what had been his house and where humidity, dust, the force of vegetation have already begun to eat away the walls, putrefy the roof, warp, almost overturn, the beaten-earth floor. "Why did they come? Why did they do this? Here, in Quebrada Naïn, we've never known any violence..." (36)

And, from the weary, singsong tone of his voice, one feels that he hasn't stopped asking these questions, day and night, for months; and one feels they've formed the subject, in the same words, and with the same Juans and Carlitos, of dozens of endless conversations.

"Because of the drug people," answers Juan, in the same tone, a rusty pickaxe in one hand, chipped enamel bowl in the other. "I heard they're going to install a *cocina*, a coca factory. So there had to be no one here."

THE HEADACHES OF CARLOS CASTAÑO

"You think so?" Carlito says. "Usually, they want to be far away from town so the 'antinarcotico' helicopters can't come. We were so close to the city..."

"*Pues no se...* I don't know, then..."

Juan makes the sign of the cross. And they recommence, all three, wandering through the empty houses:

"*Ay, sagrado corazon, que calamidad!*"

Colombia at war is also, obviously, Bogota with its killings in the middle of the street, its assassins, those people who are kidnapped "wholesale" and then resold "retail" to the urban units of the FARC. In Soacha, the dingiest neighborhood of the city, a retired police officer with ties to the other side, that is, the paramilitaries, tells how he gathered fifty neighbors in a "social clean-up junta," how he taxed each of them 80,000 pesos, and how he placed thirty contracts on the heads of thirty children who: (1) doped themselves with glue or diesel exhaust fumes; (2) belonged to bands of killers; (3) had the shameful habit of feeding on rats, living in the sewers, and, on top of that, exhibiting their filth under the noses of honest people; (4) hence brought down property values in the neighborhood; and (5) were, twenty of them, eliminated for good.

Colombia at war is the gang—FARC? Paramilitaries? Simple "*bandoleros*"?—who go to find the people living in the city underground, in other words the poor neighborhood tramps, and persuade them, for a down payment of a few thousand pesos, to take out a life-insurance policy that benefits a gang member— "You don't have to do anything," they say to the tramp; "you sign here, on the bottom of the paper; we'll take care of the rest, of the paperwork with the insurance company; and, just for this signature, we'll give you, right away, this nice bundle of pesos"; the tramp, of course, signs; lured by the pesos, he looks no further and signs; except that, once he's signed, the manhunt begins, the pursuit in the sewers or in the slums of Belen and Egipto; and, when they've trapped him and killed him, they grab the insurance premium—a clean Bogota operation!

Colombia is Medellin, where I spent some time trying to find out what new group was hiding behind the strange acronym "MAT," which I saw posted on the walls on the town: *Mouvement, Action, Travail? Mouvement pour l'Ascension des Travailleurs? Mas Amor y Tierra? Mouvement Atypique Terroriste? Mouvement Anarchiste Temporaire? Mouvement pour l'Autonomie du Travail?* No. "*Maten A Los Taxis.*" Literally: "Kill the taxis." Hunt them down, kill them, especially the big yellow taxis, and especially the ones equipped with radios, since the drug cartel has proof that they use these radios to communicate with the police and inform on the cocaine dealers. Since the beginning of the year, twenty-three drivers had already been killed. And thirty in Bogota. Like that. On the basis of a simple rumor. By the bullets of hired killers as invisible as they are unpunished.

Colombia is all that. But the blown-out village of Quebrada Naïn, that humble life petrified by the double savagery of the paramilitaries and the FARC (37), those contented lives broken, that almost silent despair (38), the image of Carlito wandering through what had been his street, hugging the walls, his arm half-raised as if to protect himself from another blow, those innocent people who, faced with these two armies turned mad and whose fighting has become incomprehensible to them, faced, too, with the third army, the regular army of Colombia, which hasn't moved a little finger to protect them, don't know who to turn to or where to place their hope—these men, these shadows of men (39), seem to me the quintessence of this war that, as in Bujumbura, in Luanda, in Sri Lanka, is taking itself out once more, and first of all, on the simple people and the unarmed.

In the past, twenty or thirty years ago—might as well say a century—one went to the end of the world to look for exemplary lives, exceptional people, heroes. In 1969, I went, not exactly to Colombia, but to Mexico, to the villages of Chiapas that were like Quebrada Naïn (40), to meet men and women who, humble as they were, seemed to me carried away, as if lifted from the earth, by the breath of the worldwide insurrection of the oppressed—they interested me only because of that. Juan, Carlito, Manolo, aren't carried away by anything. They are neither heroes nor exceptional individuals nor possessors of unusual fates. They're just small people, minuscule existences (41)—Michel Foucault would have called them "in/famous," without "fama" or "history," whose main aim in life is reduced to trying to survive, and who can't be found listed in any of the annals where the deeds of nations are recorded. There, in the warm night, lying on the beaten earth of the hut where they set up our camp and where the noise from the torrent below and, especially, from the hordes of insects, keep me from sleeping, I can't keep myself from thinking of the road traveled—the other road, the real one, the road of the loops, not of the river, but of the Idea: year zero of humanism; History reduced to its living humanity; by going from the infinitely great of the marble heroes of days gone by and their dazzling biographical details to the infinitely small of those men "made of all men, who are worth all of them and whom anyone at all is worth," going from the salt of the earth to its dregs, we have exchanged infinities—it's like that... (43)

"What happened in Quebrada Naïn? Is it possible that your men have killed in cold blood the survivors of a massacre carried out by members of the opposition, your sworn enemies, the paramilitaries?"

The man to whom I address the question is named Ivan Rios. He is a high-ranking leader of the FARC. And we are in his office in San Vincente del Caguan, the red base, the free zone—the Colombians say "*el despeje*"—which the government, at the end of thirty years of relentless fighting, and in exchange for a commitment to open peace negotiations, ended up conceding to them, in the midst of the Amazonian forest, 600 kilometers as the crow flies south of Bogota. 42,000 square kilometers of good land. The size of Switzerland, or twice as large as El Salvador. And, throughout the entire breadth of the territory, even in the market town of San Vincente as well as on the road that led me to the military camp of Los Pozos, no policemen at all, no soldiers from the regular army, no trace, in short, aside from a vague unarmed "civil guard," of the central Colombian government: just bunkers; trenches; underground prisons where, it seems, the hundreds of illegally confined people kidnapped from the rest of the country are grouped together; fields of coca, vats, drums of sulfuric acid and acetone—in other words, cocaine laboratories that have nothing to fear now, it seems, either from fumigations by the American "Colombia Plan," or from defoliation by anti-drug policemen;

and then, everywhere, at all the crossroads and all the strategic points, men and women in combat fatigues—but relaxed, cheerful, almost casual, so *at home* they seem.

"Anything can happen," Rios tells me, his body small and round, his hair pomaded, trim black beard—he is generally thought of as the brain of the FARC, one of the political advisers of the supreme leader, Manuel Marulanda Velez, alias "Tirofijo," or "Shoot the bull's-eye," about whom the Colombian press like to say that he is "the oldest guerilla fighter in the world."

"Anything can happen. There are blunders in every war. But..."

A woman soldier has just come in. Bringing a message. The arrival, forecast for midday, of Camilo Gomez, High Commissioner for Peace of President Pastrana's republic, who is coming to resume the thread of a dialogue in which everyone in Bogota knows that he is more than ever at an impasse.

"Blunders, yes, they exist. But that's not our line. We're a revolutionary movement. Marxist, Leninist, hence revolutionary. You listen to our opponents too much."

He seems sincere. Nice and sincere. But what does he know about the situation in the field? What does he know, here, in the remote camp of Los Pozos, of all the cases, duly documented by the United Nations, in which it was indeed his "revolutionaries" who burned, raped, tortured, cut people's throats?

"It's not your opponents I listen to," I tell him. "But the victims. The survivors. And all the independent non-NGO's who accuse you of so many crimes: forced recruitment of child-soldiers, massacres, massive kidnappings..."

He cuts me off.

"Collective kidnappings aren't done by us. That's the Guevarists of the Ejercito de Liberacion Nacional, the ELN."

I observe, to myself, but you're the one, right now, with your wall covered with four posters of Che Guevara. But I carry on.

"We'll skip the collective kidnappings. But the others? Three thousand individual kidnappings just for last year alone. Almost half are attributed to you."

"All right, that I do claim responsibility for. We kidnap the rich. That's to say, the ones responsible for this war. They're the ones who wanted war; well, now, let them pay for it!"

I counter with the ordinary people kidnapped for 10 dollars that I learned about from Andres Echavaria, one of the great enlightened industrialists of Bogota, founder of the protest movement against violence, *Ideas Para la Paz*. Rios pretends he didn't hear.

"That's a tax. It's normal for people to pay a tax. Moreover..."

He smiles. He is too shrewd not to be aware of the extravagant bad faith of what he is going to say.

"Moreover, there is a very simple way not to be kidnapped: pay before. Often that's what the people do. Then everybody is happy. Them, because they're not being kidnapped. Us, because we don't have to pay expenses. It's virtual kidnapping. Are we in the age of the Internet, or not?"

Laughing, he shows me a large computer behind him, linked to the Web, which allowed him to find out about me before my arrival and, especially, to find an old article against Castro.

"Because you are pro-Castro?" I say to him. "Cuba is a model, for you?"

"We have no model. That's what saved us when the Berlin Wall fell. But admit that, in Cuba, which is ten times poorer than Colombia, no one dies of hunger."

I evade Cuba. But I jump on the allusion to the wealth of Colombia, a perfect transition to bring up the responsibility of the FARC in drug trafficking.

"That's American propaganda," he growls. "They think only of their cherished young people. Not of our own. Their sole idea is to destabilize Colombia, to destroy its social fabric."

"Of course. But are the FARC, yes or no, at the center of coca trafficking?"

"That's not the problem. The problem is that we are actively involved, in fact, in regions of intense production. So, faced with this concrete situation, the concrete question is: what do we do? Fumigation? Destruction? Do we associate with Americans who fall on the peasants and destroy the country? Look."

He gets up. And goes toward the wall map.

"Those are all the zones that the planes of the Gringos have destroyed, their Turbo Thrushes, their Iroquois combat helicopters. Do you know that, there, in the states of Putumayo and Huila, they are using, at this very instant, defoliant agents of the same kind they poured over Vietnam? No one knows the long-term effects they'll have on the flora, the fauna, our health."

I think of the many billboards on the *zocalo* in San Vincente, then all along the road to Los Pozos: "Don't pollute the water... don't burn the forest... *la fauna y la vida son solo una, cuidemosla...*" Would these people who have to answer for dozens of thousands of deaths, these master extortionists, these kidnappers, these specialists in "dirty war" whose technological imagination is seemingly limitless (they told me, in Medellin, that, in the "pipetas," those cylinders of explosive gas, loaded with nails, chains, sulfuric acid, grenades, which are among their favorite weapons, they have just introduced, in order to infect the wounds, a dose of human excrement...), would these real assassins also turn out to be big-time environmentalists?

"The real question," he continues, "is political."

He sits back down, suddenly sententious, a dialectician.

"It's a question of the rural proletariat that works in the coca fields. Question No. 1: Is it illegal to work, to support your family, to survive? Does that make you a drug trafficker? Answer: No; the farmer who cultivates coca remains what he has always been, a farmer. Question No. 2: Is it normal to see small-scale property owners who, not content to work like donkeys, have their plots of land bought out by large-scale landowners for a mouthful of bread? Answer: No; we won't accept increase in big capital in favor of coca in the Colombian countryside without reacting to it."

"So?"

"So, we tax. We take a tax from the large-scale landowners. And, incidentally, we prevent the enormous flow of wealth generated by the trade of coca paste ending up in the fiscal heavens. And I'll tell you something else..."

He leans over the table, his face very close to mine, as if he were going to tell me a terrible secret.

"Do you know what annoys the Americans the most? It's that coca is a natural resource. It's that it's part of the national heritage. And that, in a world market where all raw materials, which have to contend with the iron law of unequal exchange, inexorably drop in value, it's the only one that keeps a steady course.

They say 'the Colombia Plan.' It's the 'Anti-Colombia Plan' they really mean. But excuse me. It's time. The High Commissioner is waiting for me. Do you want me to introduce you?"

Outside, in the sun, his right arm in a sling, is in fact the High Commissioner for Peace, Camilo Gomez, one of the most threatened men in Colombia, the one whose head is certainly worth the most to Ivan Rios and his people. With him, looking baleful and smiling loutishly, but in deep and hypocritical conversation, there is old Joachim Gomez, a member of the political leadership of the FARC, but actually one of the largest drug traffickers in the country. "Your arm, Mr. High Commissioner?" "Nothing, dear Joachim, nothing, a bad fall." "Good, you reassure me; in case they blame it on us and the press writes tomorrow that you were in a fight with the FARC, ha! ha! ha!"

I return to San Vincente, then to Bogota, in a state of real perplexity. Marxists, definitely. These people must, without a doubt, be Marxists, Leninists. But there is something in this Marxism-Leninism that, despite its irreproachable rhetoric, resembles nothing I have ever heard or seen elsewhere. I used to know Communism as a drift of dreamers attacking heaven and breaking the history of the world in half. I have known, in East Berlin in the 1980's, Stalinist Doctors of the Law for whom ideology was just a knout to train human livestock. But here we have trafficking Communism. Communism with a gangster's face. This is an impeccable Communism; along with Cuba, this is the last Communism in Latin America and, certainly, the most powerful, since it's the only one that has at its disposal a quasi-state, this "liberated zone" of San Vincente del Caguan; and yet it's no more than a mafia (44).

Carlos Castaño, alias "El Rambo," is the other major actor in this war in Colombia. He, too, is at the head of an actual army made up either of disciplined battalions or of death squads, and, in the states of Uraba, Sucre, Magdalena, Antiochia, Cesar, Cordoba, Cauca, and Tolima, he holds immense territories where horrible crimes are attributed to him. He is hard to meet. Until recently, he gave his rare interviews only with his back turned or his face hidden; in Bogota, he was thought of as the country's invisible man. I didn't say I was a journalist. Through various channels—especially a high functionary of the Colombian state whom I discovered, on this occasion, to be in close contact with him—I presented myself as a "French-philosopher-working-on-the-roots-of-violence-in-Colombia." And that's how, at the end of many days of negotiations, I received a telephone call setting up an interview for me for the next day, in Monteria, capital of Cordoba, the same state where the massacre of Quebrada Naïn took place.

Monteria, then. A Toyota. A semi-mute driver. A guy with a hat and a big yellow checkered shirt who, throughout the entire journey, would answer whatever question I asked him with a resounding "Si señor" or "No señor." A third man, in the back, who won't open his mouth. And three hours on a very bad road, in the direction of Tierra Alta, through a landscape of pastures, little lakes, and small villages where soon we meet only cows, riders on horses galloping by, mules dragging loads of bamboo and, sometimes, when we stop, a man on a walkie-talkie who looms up from the thickets and respectfully comes to greet the man in the yellow shirt. Finca Milenio... Finca El Tesoro... The villages, successively, of Canalete, Carabatta, Santa Cantilina... We are in the heart of the zone of the *finqueros*, the big landowners who were, in the 1980's, the originators of the Autodefensas de Cordoba y Uraba that are now called the paramilitaries and that were the embryo for Castaño's army. More importantly, if my deductions are right, we are at the southern border of Cordoba and Uraba, where the front line with the FARC runs.

El Tomate again. The village of El Tomate overwhelmed with heat, with its soccer stadium, its pool halls and its *gallera* for cock-fights. And then, suddenly, a large wooden gate; another; yet another; I count seven of them; the seven gates of Hell? I say. The man with the hat laughs; for the first time since we left, he relaxes and laughs; tents; khaki-colored sheds; tree trunks also painted in camouflage; a garage full of 4X4's and Jeeps; a giant sign: "*la mistica del combate integral*"; a thatched roof beneath which, around a television screen, thirty or so men are gathered, wearing ranger hats; other soldiers who come and go; whites; a few blacks; a busy ferrying of weapons from one tent to another; and, right in the middle of this immense camp, at the entrance to the largest tent, surrounded by armed men in uniform, a small, thin, nervous man, who scrutinizes me: Carlos Castaño.

"Come in, Professor."

No irony in his voice. A respectfulness, rather, for someone he takes to be a university authority come to visit him in his jungle.

"I am a peasant. All of us, here, we are all peasants."

He gestured, modestly and as if excusing himself, toward the squadron leaders who have taken their positions, like us, around the table.

"I might as well tell you right away. What interests me, what I have stood up for, for twenty years, against the FARC, is justice. I am a man of justice."

He speaks quickly. Very quickly. Without leaving me time to ask a question. There is, in his voice, a youthfulness, a fever, which contrast sharply with the uniform, the stripes, the hat proudly placed on top of his head.

"Tell him, Pablo, that I'm a man of justice!"

Pablo, next to me, says it. He puts his straw hat on the table and confirms that Mr. Castaño is, in fact, a man of justice.

"Drugs, for instance..."

He's the one who, right away, tackles the question of drugs.

"I don't want to harm this country. It harms me to harm it. But what can I do if this conflict is tied to drugs and if you can't understand anything about it if you don't keep drugs in mind, all the time?"

The squadron leaders again nod in agreement.

"But watch out! When the question of justice comes up, we don't traffic in drugs; I forbid you to say we're drug dealers; we're just behind the farmers who cultivate; when a piece of land is sterile and when that's the only thing you can grow, what are you going to do? Are you going to forbid the farmers from earning their living?"

I point out to him that he is speaking like Rios, like the FARC.

"No. I also forbid you to say that. The difference is that we, with the profits from drugs, we do Good. Good. Which way did you come? By the Tierra Alta road? But that's us, the Tierra Alta road! It's with the money from drugs that we made that good road!"

Carlos Castaño becomes heated. Almost gets carried away. Beads of sweat are forming on his face. He makes large gestures. Rolls his glaring eyes. He uses a considerable amount of energy to make me understand that he is responsible for this road and that he is a man of justice.

"Am I making myself understood?"

"Yes, of course."

"*Tu crees que entiende?*"

"Yes, Sir, he seems to understand."

The truth is that I find he is becoming stranger and stranger. That breathless nervousness. That vehemence. Those sniffs, with which he punctuates his sentences and which I hadn't at first noticed. Those pains in his ears. In his head. That way of tapping his fist on the table, then of feverishly passing his hand over his face as if to chase away a great weariness, or an unbearable idea.

"It makes me crazy, injustice... Crazy... I'll give you another example. The ELN (National Liberation Army). The talks with the ELN. This idea of giving them, too, a zone. How can Pastrana, President Pastrana, envisage talks with the ELN which is an organization of abductors, torturers, killers?"

I point out to him that his organization seems to me also to practice random attacks on civilians and, especially, this very week, on union activists. He recoils.

"Random attacks, us? Never! There is always a reason. The union activists, for instance. They prevent people from working! That's why we kill them."

How about the leader of the Indians of the Alto Sinu? Who did he prevent from working, this little Indian leader who had come down to Tierra Alta?

"The dam! He was interfering with the operation of the dam!"

The mayor, then, of Tierra Alta? They told me, in Tierra Alta, on the road from Quebrada Naïn, that, just before the elections, the Autodefensas had the mayor assassinated.

"That's another thing, mayors. It's our job to bring the representatives of the people to power. When there's somebody, in Cordoba, who persists in trying to run for office when we don't want him to, we threaten him, that's true—we send him warnings, that's normal."

Yes. But the mayor in question? He wasn't just warned. He was killed...

"He had stolen two million from the city. And then he accused other people of doing it, he made other people bear the responsibility for his thefts. Corruption, then lies! It was too much! We had to be implacable. Plus..."

He takes his time. Catches his breath. Then, in a high voice, almost a woman's voice, and as if he clung to the indisputable proof of the mayor's guilt:

"Plus, it's quite simple: he wore a bulletproof vest!"

The conversation would go on for two hours in this vein. Castaño is speaking so quickly now, in such a rasping voice, that I am more and more obliged to lean toward my neighbor to have him repeat what was said.

President Pastrana whom he respects, but who does not respect him—that drives him to despair... Castro who castrated his own people—and this image makes him laugh with a demonic laughter... All those soldiers, dismissed from the army, who, like Generals Mantilla and Del Rio, rush into the Autodefensas—but watch out! He makes one condition on their joining, since, if he didn't, it would be another reason to go crazy: that they weren't dismissed because of corruption. Injustice again... Always injustice... The litany of injustices, breaches of duty, government malfunctioning: he, Castaño, is there, to take the place of the missing state—he is its ready right arm, its faithful and ill-rewarded servant... And then finally Quebrada Naïn, the crime of Quebrada Naïn and, beyond that, all the crimes attributed to his henchmen, they don't arouse a word of compassion or regret from him: at the very most he admits that his army may have increased a little quickly and that the massacre I mention to him "lacked professionalism": but he won't yield on one thing: if any man, or any woman, has even the vaguest link with the guerilla movement, then they stop being civilians and become guerilla fighters dressed in civilian clothes, and as such deserve to be tortured, have their throats cut, to have a living hen sewed in their wombs in place of a foetus...

Carlos Castaño is becoming increasingly more heated and more feverish. This medicinal smell that pervades the tent. This way of jumping now, when he hears a noise: "What is it?" "Nothing, Jefe, just the generator starting up again." This way he has of shouting, every five minutes: "Un tinto, Pepe, un café!", and a soldier, terrified, brings it to him, and he continues to talk in the same frenetic rhythm. A final quarter-hour to shout a confused jumble of things: that he admires Nixon and Mitterand... that he is in favor of the Colombia Plan... that he's sick of people who say they are Autodefensas but aren't... that he trusts my objectivity... that he is a defender of law and order... that he's sick, too, of being blamed for all the crimes of this dirty war—maybe you think those army assholes are angels?... that he is not, nor will he ever be, Pinochet... he is just a peasant, he told me that in the beginning... all he wants is to make justice and order reign in this world...

And then he falls silent. He gets up, and falls silent. Staggers a little. Leans on the table. Looks at me with such a strangely fixed stare that I wonder if he isn't simply on drugs. Pulls himself together. Offers me a large briefcase in black imitation leather, stuffed with speeches and videos. His lieutenants surround him.

He goes out, unsteadily, into the full noon sun. A psychopath confronting mafiosi. A story full of sound and fury told, either by crooks, or by a murderous clown. A part of me says there have always been people like him, and that the wisest observers have never been taken in by coarse peremptory animals, full of themselves, swelled with importance and power, who reigned over the hell of the "major" history of past times: the grotesque Arturo Ui in Brecht; the pitiful Pierre Laval of Céline's *From Castle to Castle*; Garcia Marquez and his Caudillo; the flaccid nudity of Himmler in Malaparte's *Kaputt*... But another part of me can't get rid of the idea that there is, all the same, a change, an energetic degradation, a fall, and that we had never before seen a war so reduced to this clash of criminals and puppets, clones and clowns. Degree zero of politics. Height of buffoonery and depth of naked, unadorned violence, reduced to the bone of its bloody truth (45). Even monsters are deflated when theological ages draw to a close (46).

There are no roads in the South Sudan. In fact it's one of the few places in the world, along with perhaps Tibet, or the mountains of Nepal, where the idea of a road has the least meaning. So that, in this immense country, in this space that's one and a half times the size of France, there are only three ways to travel. By .foot, when one is a peasant. In a Jeep, but over short distances, and by dirt roads, when one is a soldier. And, if not, by small planes rented in Lokichokio, the humanitarian base on the Kenyan border; as long as they don't travel on the flight corridors reserved for the UN, and as long as, if they're intercepted on the radio, they avoid answering and having to identify themselves, they manage to connect most of the cities of this animist and Christian South which the Islamists of Khartoum have been Arabizing by force, and bombarding, for almost twenty years.

It's by a plane of this kind that I arrived in Alek, in the province of Bahr el-Ghazal, literally the "country of the gazelles"; quite close to the border with the North, it is one of the regions most affected by the war. My journey lasted four hours. I was welcomed, on the grass strip, by a joyous throng of Sudanese soldiers in uniform, civilians in shorts, Kalashnikovs slung over their chests, and naked children, their bodies coated with ashes and urine, in order, they say, to repel insects. I saw, surrounded by his four squadron leaders, Deng Alor, governor of the province and ex-Minister of Foreign Affairs for John Garang, the Sudanese leader, a Christian. And then I arrived in a handsome, completely new camp, made up of a dozen impeccable huts, a thatched fence, a communications center, a large covered space intended for feeding large crowds—but, strange to say, completely empty.

"Where are we?" I asked the young man who showed me my hut. "In a humanitarian camp, belonging to the Norwegian Church Aid." "Where are the Norwegians, then? The humanitarian volunteers?" "On leave, in Nairobi." "All of them?" "All of them!" Asking to visit the rest of the camp, and insisting on seeing, especially, the little adjacent infirmary, I discover that it is closed, and has obviously been so for a long time; then, having gotten it opened, I find a bed, one single bed, which, it seems, has never been used; and finally I see, at the door, a Dinka woman, carrying a malnourished baby, whom no one seems the least bit interested in helping. A phantom camp? No. A false camp. A camp which, more precisely, and upon investigation, was in fact built in the fall of 1998, by Norwegian humanitarians, but was almost immediately offered to the Popular Liberation Army of the Sudan (SPLA) of Deng Alor and Garang—in other words, whether you like it or not, and whatever side you take as to the origins or outcome of this war, offered to one of the warring parties.

The image of those improvised stalls comes to mind, on Kakuma road, in Kenya, where Turkana nomads sold food rations stamped with the UN logo. And vividly I remember my conversation, that very day, with the visa man in Lokichokio, who assured me: first of all, that it's the guerilla fighters of the SPLA who are bringing these packages from the Sudan and who have stolen them, one way or another, from civilians who were the real intended beneficiaries; secondly, that, seeing this, and knowing that it's this diverted aid that allows the SPLA to finance its weapons purchases, Khartoum has concluded that, to stop the aid, the simplest thing is to eliminate the civilians who receive it—either by displacing them, or simply by killing them. Humanitarian hostages. Mobilization of humanitarians in a logic of war that goes beyond them. As if this war, the oldest in the world, which has already produced two million dead (more than Bosnia, Kosovo, and Rwanda combined), four and a half million displaced (three South-Sudanese out of four), had chosen to instrumentalize even our compassion. As if, in Sudan, even Good were brought into the service of Evil (47).

"Do you want to go to Gogrial, on the Wau road?" the squadron leader Paul Malong asks me, leader of the Northern sector. "Yes, of course." And here we are, crammed into a Nissan, four armed men in back, on one of these dirt roads, full of bumps and potholes, which take the place of roads. A landscape of savannahs. Crops burned on both sides. Go right or left, into the brush, whenever you're afraid a section has been mined, or when you have to bypass a broken bridge. Pass men in rags, or with bare torsos, scarcely soldiers, sleeping next to an antiaircraft defense cannon. Pass others, so obviously starving that they have trouble standing up but who, recognizing the squadron leader, or his Nissan, or perhaps not, recognizing nothing and no one, but smelling authority, thus rations, stand to attention. The journey is long. The squadron leader Malong, to pass the time, recounts the capture of the city: "It was a real, big city... it took ten days of relentless fighting to crush it... the artillery support came from Alek... an infantry battalion cut off the road from the Arab reinforcements coming from the north... another, in the west, had the mission of preventing the garrison from fleeing and of taking no prisoners." He also says that Gogrial was, before that, the capital of Kerubino Kuanyin Bol, the ill-named "cherubim," one of the worst warlords of the Sudanese war, betraying Garang for Khartoum, then Khartoum for Garang—"even the dead are still trembling from the tortures he inflicted on them." Finally, despairing of ever arriving and seeing that we're still in a no-man's land of stones and vague ruins, I lose patience and ask, "Gogrial is still far away, isn't it?" and he replies, "You're in it."

I have already seen phantom cities. I've seen Kuito, in Angola. El Quneitra, on the Golan Heights. Vukovar, of course, in Croatia. But this... This desolation... This desert... These little piles of mud which had been houses... These bricks with which they've made bunkers... These fires... These tents... These patches of sorghum, these camp beds, where there used to be streets... These nests of snakes... This filth... This rotting smell of shit and corpses intermingled... These weird dogs, too fat, who are no longer afraid of humans... This immense space... This square... Yes, you can see it had been a square... You can see, from the skeletons of the structures, bordering it, that it was a large square, home to official buildings... But there's nothing, now, on this square, but an immense void, where the dogs and soldiers circle warily... It had been a living, animated square, full of the good life of normal cities, and now it looks like the devastated amphitheater of an ancient city, testimony of a vanished civilization (48)—except you no longer know which, exactly, is the ghost, if it's the people who are no longer there and for whom Gogrial has become a common grave, or the ones who wander about in their place and look scarcely more alive. "Where are the inhabitants?" "Dead, or gone," Marial Cino tells me, the local leader, whom has just been given by his orderly an urgent message, scrawled on a sheet of a school notebook and reporting a movement of enemy troops on the other side of the river... And then, he corrects himself: "Except them..." And he points out a group of children with thin legs, their eyes too large for their small faces, dressed in military rags, doing somersaults over the gun carriage of the T-55 that commands access to the square.

Return to Lokichokio where I am supposed to be told if I do or do not have a chance to see John Garang— and where the meeting will take place. Same plane. Same pilot. The pilot, perhaps because he doesn't know the zone, bears to the east, instead of immediately heading south. At our feet, through the window, the great desert of the Sudanese savannah. And there, first far apart, then closer together, points of light that seem to be brush fires. What are these fires for? Can we see them closer? The pilot descends. Quite low. We discover then, astonished, that it's not the brush that's burning, but huts. We also discover, invisible from the height where we had just been, but very distinct now, a column of poor people, a few dozen, perhaps more, pushing a few cattle, exhausted. And then, a few minutes later, the plane having regained altitude, but barely, this other spectacle:

hangars; trucks; khaki semi trailers that look like military vehicles; a median strip, likely a landing pad for helicopters; a road, new; another one that could be a concrete runway for planes; and an immense space, strangely cross-hatched, which reminds you of a chessboard, or neatly checkered fields, or oyster or rice beds—an oil-bearing field being prospected.

We have actually come upon the oil complex, in principle a no-fly zone, of the Greater Nile Petroleum Operating Company, the consortium that includes the Canadian firm Talisman Energy, Chinese and Malaysian interests, and the Sudanese national company Sudapet. And now we've had confirmed for us what the NGO's, Amnesty International, the Canadian government itself, have suspected for years but which the oil companies and the state fiercely deny: namely that the government is systematically "cleaning" the land, in a perimeter of 30, 50, sometimes 100 kilometers, around oil wells; that the least oil concession means villages harassed, bombed, razed, and columns of poor people chased away from their homes; in short, that wherever oil is gushing, wherever black gold is supposed to bring happiness and prosperity, the desert increases. By chance I have statements in my pocket, which were published in the Kenyan press, by Carl Bildt, former UN emissary in the Balkans, the man who, on the day of the Srebrenica massacre, was still discussing peace, in Belgrade, with Milosevic—this "diplomat" became an administrator of the Swedish oil company Lundin Oil, which operates more to the south, near Adok, and so I have his virtuous protestations with me: "We are building roads, in the Sudan! Schools and roads! Can't you see we're civilizing this country?" Well, yes, roads. I have seen these roads. No doubt I have also seen one of the landing strips where, according to numerous testimonies, the bombers from the neighboring military base of El Obeid come to fill up. And this spectacle is overwhelming.

Is this a forgotten war or a hidden war? Ignored or carefully concealed? And, in this concealment, in this war of shadow and clandestine interests, doesn't the West of the oil companies bear, this time, an enormous responsibility? A suggestion, then: responsibility for responsibility (49). The South Sudan is now nothing but a vast subsoil, where Sudan's oil and Sudan's dead are mingled. If we put pressure on this subsoil, if we act about this oil as we did with Saddam Hussein's, if we show we're just as determined when it sends processions of beggars, without faces and without names, fleeing into the burned savannah, as when it endangers world peace or our own prosperity, then perhaps the other pump, the pump of misery and corpses, will also see its terrible rhythm slowed.

John Garang is late. I've been here, in Boma, near the Ethiopian border, for two hours now, in the heart of a camp of clay and thatch, very similar to the Norwegian camp of the other day. Heat. Gusts of wind. Clouds of sand and dust. Soldiers bustling about, inside. A group of children, outside, behind the wall, who are also waiting for "the leader." A wooden table, under the tree, over which someone has just put a red-checked woolen tablecloth. Chairs. A command car, finally. Is it he? No. Not yet. It's officers who have come as scouts, in olive-green uniforms, who all have the same red scorpion sewn on their chests. Why a scorpion? "It's the symbol of the battalion."

"Yes, but why?" "It's a good animal, the scorpion. Even snakes back away from scorpions." We hear crickets chirping. Roosters. Philip Obang, the "Wise Man" of the village, is here to tell me, to kill the time, about the wild animals that have to be preserved, the mango orchards, the banana trees, lemon trees, guava trees, and about that English colonel in the beginning of the century who buried his wine cellar on the neighboring hill and how everyone since then has been searching for it. And then halleluiah, here he is, preceded by a horde of new soldiers—he's smaller than I had thought, thicker: I had expected (perhaps because of his name, John Garang, which I liked and which evoked some sort of relaxed English elegance) a kind of guerilla dandy; instead of which is this massive, imposing character— same olive green uniform, thoroughly starched, as his officers.

"Did you have a good trip?"

I tell him the pilot didn't learn our actual destination until we were in flight, by radio. I also tell him that we had difficulty, much more than in Alek, in finding the little landing strip, shrouded in the savannah.

"Yes. They exaggerate a little. They take too many precautions. But what can you do? You are in an occupied country. And our strips are systematically bombed..."

Seen up close, when he becomes animated, his face is more interesting. He has a white beard, over a face still young. A disdainful lip. Small, sharp teeth. A cruel gaze, with a cloudiness that, sometimes, whitens his pupil.

"Here—let's start with something to eat."

They've just brought out an enormous plate of roast lamb from which he serves himself heartily.

"What surprised me," I tell him, "is also that, contrary to what I saw yesterday, around the oil fields of Majak, there aren't any destroyed villages here..."

"Ah! You went to Majak..."

His gaze has hardened. I sense that by mentioning Majak, and oil, I've touched a sore spot.

"President El Beshir has made a grave mistake. You can't say to the people: 'Oil is manna fallen from heaven, all the Sudanese will become rich' and, in the end, give them nothing. Especially since..."

He speaks good, refined English. But with a strange way of attacking the sentences—as if each time he had to contain a secret rage. A soldier keeps filling his glass. With water.

"It would only have to happen once. Just imagine the valve being turned off. At the source, maybe... Or at its destination..."

"Do you mean you'd be ready to sabotage the wells? The pipeline?"

"For example, yes. We don't have all the means to do that, today. But one day... Who knows?"

I think of the Jonglei canal, stopped since 1983, when the SPLA took the French engineers of the Grands Travaux de Marseille hostage—and which I also flew over. I know, since I've seen that great, dried-out, dead trench, near Ayod, that Garang is not joking. And it seems to me that the oil companies should also know that this kind of threat, from him, should be taken very seriously. He continues.

"You are right, all the same, to take an interest in oil. That's the key. Do you know, by the way, that it's here, quite close, that TotalFina has its reserves..."

Veiled threat? Or, on the contrary, a way of saying that he has a deal with the French—perhaps against the Nuer tribes of the South Sudan Liberation Movement (SSLM) that hold a part of the zone and are at war with the Dinkas? He smiles.

"Let's speak instead about today," he goes on, serving himself more lamb. "You arrive at an interesting time. The agreement with Hassan El-Turabi, my sworn enemy..."

"Yes, the former Islamist, the mentor of El Beshir. But he's been in prison since he signed this agreement with you. Are you sure he still represents something in Khartoum?"

"Of course!"

He almost roared. As if I had offended him.

"It's like the capture of Kassala," he insists, "last year, near Port Sudan. The most important event of this war, for a long time."

"Because that showed your capacity to strike far up in the north, far from your bases?"

"Yes. And because it expressed clearly that the Sudan, for us, is indivisible. Contrary to what your newspapers say, we are not Southerners, but Sudanese. We are not for the independence of the South, but for a free Sudan, unified and liberated from the domination of the Islamists. Look."

He takes out of his chest pocket, the one where, instead of the scorpion, is sewn "CDR. Dr. John Garang of Mabior," a carefully folded piece of paper where a whole series of circles and ovals are printed—and, from the former to the latter, arrows. His face has softened. Almost ingenuous, suddenly. Moving.

"These are the four possible diagrams of relations between North and South. It's diagram no. 2, the one of the Confederation, that I like."

All the officers present, including me, our eyes open wide, lean toward the graphics... The guerilla leader, this man who, for almost twenty years, has known no other law than that of the armies, in the process of saying that his life, his fate, his combats, are reducible to childlike diagrams...

"And what will make," I ask of him, "El Beshir choose your solution?"

"The people."

The answer came very quickly, in a voice also changed— candid, a little high. And a long explanation follows, about the ferments of revolution that, according to him, are stirring the people of Khartoum: "The regime is only holding on by a thin thread... a giant intifada is being prepared... the regime is in its death throes... twilight of political Islamism..." Does he really believe what he's saying? Does he truly believe that the SPLA, his party, is on the verge of provoking this general insurrection and of winning? As just now, when he seemed hypnotized by his agreement with Turabi, I am struck by his air of credulity: the effect, perhaps, of this strange life, cut off from everything and everyone, in the brush; twenty years of secrecy, guerilla warfare as a job and a destiny—and political judgment which, necessarily, has to lose all its points of reference.

"Don't think I'm dreaming," he says, as if he were reading my thoughts. "Or that I'm cut off from reality. We have agents in Khartoum. And I have precise reports. Very precise."

He's the one, now, who seems lost in his thoughts. Silent. His eyes fixed and white. His Sudan, truly? This great Sudan, unified and non-denominational, the very idea of which is enough to plunge him in this state of dreamy melancholy?

"Ah! The children," he jumps up...

The children have entered the camp—a little choir, come to welcome him, bouquets of flowers in their hands.

"It's normal," he says. "They're happy. This is the first time I've come here in five years."

Then, without transition, the children still there, singing their psalms—and, looking fondly at them, very "grandfatherly"—he tells me:

"No, I'm not dreaming. I am a rational thinker. A strategist. My bedside reading is Clausewitz. Sun Tzu. Mao. Thucydides' *Peloponnesian War*. De Gaulle, because of the French Resistance."

And then, hopping from one subject to another, he confides the following to me:

"Do you know the real difference between El Beshir and me? The Bible. He should read it, don't you think? He should also be as faithful as I am, since we are both sons of the Bible, me a Christian, him a Muslim. Well, maybe not. For if he read Genesis II:8, or the first book of Joshua, he would know that the Cushite civilization has existed since the dawn of time, and that therefore his Sudan born from Islam simply makes no sense."

And there is the old guerilla fighter, like Kurtz in *The Heart of Darkness* who, by dint of "camping alone in his forest," was in desperate "need of a listener"—there is the creature of war and brush who, in front of his officers and his gaping guard, in front of the children still there and still singing, embarks on madly erudite stories all mixed together, stories about the Blue Nile; the White Nile; the four rivers of the Garden of Eden; the story, in the Book of Chronicles, II:14 (he hesitates on the chapter...), of Zerah invading the kingdom of Juda with an army of a million Sudanese; the kingdom of Meroe; the first African kingdoms,

2500 BC; the black Pharaohs of the XXVth dynasty; the Nubian Christianity of the Fourth Century; the kingdoms Darjour and Fung; the Christian kingdom of Soba; all stories, legends, fabulous and grandiose genealogies supposed to plead for this Sudan of mixed identities that seems to be his *idée fixe*.

I think, listening to him, of all those men with an "*idée fixe*" I have met in my life. I think of Massoud (50). Of Izetbegovic and his Bosnia. Of Otelo de Carvalho, in Lisbon, during the "carnation revolution." Of Mujibur Rahman, and of his free Bengal (52). I think of these great unrealistic men whose life seems drawn to a distant chimera. Garang is of course not of their ilk. He is also this coarse, cruel being I sensed at first. And I know the crimes attributed to him—the child-soldiers; famine as a weapon; the city of Nyal, in the Western Upper Nile, in the Nuer zone, razed by the SPLA; I know all this. But at the same time... I can't prevent myself, at the same time, from admiring this stubbornness, this fidelity to a fixed star. A war animal, no doubt. A tactician without soul or scruples, perhaps. But also this resistance fighter, whose long-term obstinacy compels respect.

I knew pretty much nothing about the Nuba before landing in Kawdah. Leni Riefenstahl's photos, of course. The flattering—dubious?—reputation of being counted among the most successful of human specimens, along with the Dogon. A few literary evocations. A stubborn taste for insubordination from which the Anglo-Egyptians had to suffer in the nineteenth century. That their very name, Nuba, came, if one is to believe an old *National Geographic*, from the Egyptian *noub*, which means "gold"—people of gold? Gold of the people? And then the fact, of course, that the Nuba Mountains of today are more inaccessible than ever since to their traditional isolation has been added total war, hence total blockade, decreed by Khartoum eighteen years ago.

So it's with the sole authorization of John Garang that I arrived there.

His staff had alerted, by radio, Abdel Aziz Adam al-Halu, squadron leader of the fifth division of the SPLA and military head, in that capacity, of the Resistance in the Nuba Mountains.

For my part, I had taken, in Lokichokio, a small plane (53): about four hours, up to the emerald green hills—legend has it there are ninety-nine—set, like huge breasts, on the savannah.

And there, in this lunar and confused landscape, for which no precise map exists, I had the great good fortune of being accompanied by the Franco-Polish doctor Zygmunt Ostrowski, longtime friend of the Nuba and head of the humanitarian association ADE (Aide à la Décision Économique), who had just made the same journey a few weeks before, and who remembered the location of the trail.

When pilots land in Kawdah, they know they have no more than twenty minutes to unload, possibly reload, and, especially, refill their tanks with the two drums of 200 liters of fuel carried from Lokichokio—after which the Sudanese Antonovs based in El Obeid, alerted of the mission, take off and come to bomb the runway.

The inhabitants themselves, the hundreds of children and the soldiers who have come, just as in Alek, but this time to the sound of a traditional Nuban round dance, to welcome us, to celebrate our arrival, and, also, to pick up the provisions of sugar and oil offered by ADE, they all know that it's here, in the plain, and, even worse, near a runway, that they are most vulnerable.

Thus the principle is never to linger and, after reaching an agreement with the pilot as to when he'll pick you up, to go very quickly to another village, higher up, in the mountain: two hours on foot, through a landscape of tall grass and acacia, mud huts, burned brush, deep craters meters wide from bombs—and, along the way, impressions, accounts, that only confirm one's most alarmist apprehensions.

The blockade. The semi-total encirclement that Ostrowski had told me about, denounced by the NGO's that, like his own, continue to maintain a symbolic link with the Nuba mountains. I can testify that, where I went, you will find no doctor less than eight hours' walk away. And no medicine. Not a windmill or a pump in sight—the war has destroyed everything. I can testify that you find fewer and fewer real tools there—except the ones pieced together from the molten scrapheap of debris from bombs. And then those entire fields, in the plains, that the peasants themselves burn, fearing that an army besieging them could creep under cover up to the villages. You survive, among the Nuba, by eating roots and bark. There are hamlets where, in the dry season, they're reduced to digging in the sand, with their bare hands, to find water (55).

The bombs. The plane of an Italian NGO was shelled, on April 16, a few days after our stay. The very morning of our arrival, in Kawdah, a tank had just shelled the little village school, point blank. And we hear, throughout the day, albeit intermittently, the sounds of the cannon shelling the neighboring hillside. The account of an inhabitant, the teacher, who will hold his classes, he says—under a tree, in the open air, but he'll hold them: "Twenty bombs, on some days; they fly very low; they know that we only have bad, scrap cannons to return fire; so they fly low, with a very calm, regular flight, like flies circling, and they drop up to twenty bombs a day, and the children are so frightened!"

The deportation, finally (57). The forced displacement of tens of thousands of Nubas toward the so-called "peace camps" set up at the foot of the mountains, especially around Kadugli, or even quite close, in Aggam, in the part of the province already conquered by the army. It's Abdel Aziz, this time, who speaks. It's he, the leader of the Nuba, who, sitting, like Garang, under his tree, his staff set next to him, tells about the ordeal of these people who, tired of being shot at, tired of eating grasshoppers and boiled roots, tired too of seeing their children die of new or, on the contrary, forgotten illnesses that they no longer know how to cure, end up going down into the plains and taking refuge in these camps that are actually nothing but sorting centers for slave merchants. There used to be a million Nubas. Three hundred thousand remain. What's become of the others? Dead? Disappeared? Or prey to the slave traders of Kordofan who have sold them to the Arab families of Khartoum?

Then the question is, of course, Why? Yes: Why such huge misfortunes on the head of such a small people? Abdel Aziz reflects, with good, gentle, intelligent eyes, seeming so unlike a soldier despite the uniform jacket and the revolver at his belt. "Oil. Maybe we're on the oil route." Then, changing his mind: "And, at the same time, no; can one exterminate a people, can one snuff it out like that, quietly, without witnesses, just because it's on an oil route?" And this is the voice of the free Nuba, of the one that, in a few days, upon the death of Yussif Kuwa Makki, will also become their political leader, who, still under his tree, his officers around him, in a tone in which, as with Garang, the precision of strategy alternates with Biblical lyricism, tries out other hypotheses better adjusted to what he calls "the soul of his people."

The Nubas' taste for freedom, he begins. Their tradition of insubordination and revolt. We are a small people, indeed. But a stiff-necked people. Aren't we the ones who rebelled first and set the example? Can you, if you're El Beshir, tolerate such insolence? Can you, when you want to impose shariah law on the entire country, accept that all faiths live together here—animist, Christians, but also Muslims who don't want this Islam of rage and revenge? And then the Nuban "case"... This case that's unique in the world... Do you know that the language we speak in this village is different from the one they speak in the neighboring village? Do you know there are fifty languages among the Nuba, fifty real languages that come from ten different groups, and that it's not rare to see a few hundred men and women keeping alive a language that will stop being spoken a few hundred meters further on? It's strange, yes. But that's Nuban strangeness. That's the greatest singularity of my people. But what's even stranger—and more unbearable for the fanatics of holy war and lost purity—is that far from this multiplicity of languages provoking, in our society, tribal dispersion, the splitting up of minds and bodies, it has the opposite effect and produces a paradoxical community, a strong, proud belonging, a Nuban awareness...

Aziz, while he was speaking, has begun to leaf through, as if it were familiar to him, the copy of Riefenstahl's book that we've brought him. By what miracle, this familiarity? By what mystery of transmission? And is it possible that there exists here, in this country cut off from everything, men who haven't drunk drinkable water in months, haven't seen a doctor in years, haven't read a book or held a newspaper in a much longer time than that, is it possible there are men, or one man in any case, who nonetheless know, with an obscure but indisputable knowledge, that, very far away, in a lost corner of the world that is called Germany or Europe, there lives a paradoxical artist, who was a Nazi, but to whom they owe a little of their immortality?

"Look at what they've done to us," Aziz murmurs, leafing through the book. "Look." It's the photos he's showing, of course. It's the legendary Nubas, in well-composed photos, by the filmmaker. But it's the others he wants me to look at, the real Nubas, his own, with their emaciated faces, their rags, who no doubt seem to him, at this instant, the shadow of these shadows. But his officers have had the same instinct as I and have, as with Garang and his graphics, come very close, very close to the photos, so they can admire them too; the children also come close and slip, very excited, among the squadron leaders; the teacher comes close too, and even the peasant who had climbed up on the wing of the plane to help the pilot recharge his fuel and who chuckles with surprise and joy at the sight of these elder brothers, naked and scarified. I look very carefully at what Aziz wanted me to look at: together, almost superimposed, the shadows and the shadows of the shadows. But I see the opposite in them, it seems to me, of what he was inviting me to see. Not the degeneration of icons. But, miracle of art or of life, I don't know, a stubborn faithfulness to the finest quality the photos had, of which, I am sure, they have only recorded the vibration: a force risen from the depth of the ages; an indomitable courage that, today as well as yesterday, emanates from these ashen faces; miserable, abandoned, pawns for all the governments, the great forgotten ones of this forgotten war, men whose tragic grandeur compels us all the more since their disappearance wouldn't affect the world's economy in the least.

Réflexions

Réflexions

So, these accounts. These travel impressions, these notations, which already seem to me so distant and which, maybe because of that, because I sense they're vanishing, because they had been so alive and suddenly they seem so cold to me now, almost foreign, I wanted to fix in a book. For the text that follows them, for this long "postface," written afterwards, I had a choice. It could be like an instruction manual (once upon a time... how I left... how I wrote some of these texts... how, why, a writer undertakes such an adventure... the logic of my involvement... principles of a journalism of ideas...). Theses (this is what these reports taught me... this is what, thanks to them, I feel I've been freed from... here, in the manner of Walter Benjamin, are some theories on the concepts of History, the End of History, the return of History... here is what they let me say about war and peace...). Thoughts, images contemplated with hindsight, some memories that haunt me, which make me not quite the same after *The Damned* as I was before, and that I might, in this way, try to "give shape" to ("reflection" taken literally... the "Sartrean" connotation played to the hilt...). a newspaper (a chronicle of reporting... a chronicle of post-reporting... the other side of the story... behind the scenes...).

I couldn't come to a decision, in the end (rather quickly a loose, discontinuous form imposed itself, without any principle, at bottom, other than a pure "rule of the game": one text corresponding to another, resulting from the former, proliferating starting from its core or its margin, whose chapters would resemble long footnotes, called such in the narrative and subject to its logic alone—notes, yes, or glosses, or jottings, or marginalia, or commentaries, or palimpsests, or ellipses, I don't know, but I like this idea of an epilogue following the text it prolongs step by step; I like the image of an album of scattered images that nonetheless doesn't lack structure; I like the ordered freedom this convention allows; as Mallarme says, "a book neither begins nor ends; the most we can say is that it pretends"...).

"Huambo... Huambo... he kept repeating this word, Huambo..."

Waterloo... The Chemin des Dames... Dresden... Valmy... Stalingrad... The unique thing about the place-names of wartime geography is that they have a reputation that precedes them and that, like "Parma" or "Balbec," which the Narrator of *Remembrance of Things Past* tells us end up being "more real" than the "places on Earth" that they designate, their names overwhelm the thing; they end up being substituted for it, and one is always a little disappointed when one arrives there by the humbleness of the actual places about which one had, finally, dreamed too much. Here it's the opposite. The names say nothing. They concern, recall, suggest, absolutely nothing. They are, to stay in the Proustian register, like that "obscure Roussainville," or that "boring Méséglise," for which all Gilberte's narrative talents are needed to explain, at the end of the book, that they're other names for the famous "Hill 307" that general staff communiqués spoke of during 1917, and that they could, as such, "become for ever a part of history, with the same claim to glory as Austerlitz or Valmy."[1] So it is with "Huambo." Except for those people who met Dominique de Roux between 1974 and 1976 and heard him revel in both the word and the hellish images with which it was, for him, associated, the name Huambo says nothing, evokes nothing, and, in any case, hints of none of the horror of what happened there—it's only when you get there, when you leave the name and enter the place, that the horror seizes you. Forgotten wars? Wars without names, unnamed. The war damned? Wherever names, even if they exist, say nothing about things: What is one's first objective, then? The traveler's task? To speak these place names. To hear them, to have them spoken aloud. To create, not commonplaces, but, literally, common places. To make it so that whenever you say "Huambo" there immediately arises, absent on all the memorials, the image of the abomination.

There is a literary tradition, in France, of talking about the "beauty" of war. It's Apollinaire's "God, how pretty war is." It's Cocteau and the "faerie" of a war seen like a ballet, a theater. It's Proust again and the dazzling observations he places, in the heart of *Time Regained*, in the mouths of Saint-Loup, of Charlus, but also of the Narrator himself who finds, in the Parisian skies, at night, during the air-raids, a quality of beauty he had forgotten since the stormy days of his childhood in Balbec: the heart-rending summons of the sirens; the airplanes rising, like rockets, to join the stars; this pale stardust, these fragile milky-ways that trail the searchlights, like luminous fountains; the city in the sky; the sky like a glass roof; the pilots; Wagner; Pompeii; Jupien's hovel at risk of being buried beneath some German Vesuvius; the apocalypse at the Ritz and at Ciro's; and, in the spectacle of the socialites thrown, during an alarm, in their nightshirts, out into the street, the reminder of a painting by Greco...

This tradition, I might as well say right away, is not really my own. Or, more precisely, it could have been. I could have been open—my departure for Bangladesh, thirty years ago as a war correspondent; then, again at the end of the 1970's—to this aestheticizing of war seen as an adventure or a spectacle. If that's the case, I'm cured. If the journey to Huambo, Kuito, the place-names of the planet dead from forgotten wars, these cursed capitals of the modern-day Calvary, had only one function in my life, it would to be that of making me mistrust any romanticizing of war and its effects. What "beauty" is there in a destroyed urban landscape? Is it really bewitching, this city that looks as if it's returned to the earth, buried, crushed beneath the weight of an invisible pestle? Where is the faerie in this group of women in rags, shivering from fever despite the heat? And these smells of fever and shit in the hospital in Kuito? And the morgue, its corpses with their clenched, horribly tormented look, so different from the calm corpses of the Sarajevo morgue? And what about Sarajevo? Already in Sarajevo, in the hilltops, that Serbian barracks in Lukavica where, along with Herzog, Douste-Blazy, and Deniau, I was blockaded on the first night of my first trip? The Bosnians, below, were bombing... the Serbian soldiers, as well as the UN Blue Berets, had gone down to take shelter in caves... and since we were neither Serbian nor UN people, they planted us there, locked up in our car, in the middle of the main road, with the continuous thundering of bombs above our heads, the machine-gun fire, the sirens, the searchlights that seemed to be activated by a virtuoso stagehand, flares from spraying rockets that exploded high in the sky and crossed each other... a Proustian night, if ever there was one! Apollinairian images and night! But, frankly, I've never been so frightened in my life!

I've reached that point. I've reached that fear, that horror. And, with regard to literature, I feel more moved today by another tradition, less fashionable, less poetic, but closer, it seems to me, to what the reality of wars is: Henri Barbusse's

Under Fire; Roger Vercel and his *Capitaine Conan*; the war chapters of Roger Martin du Gard's *Les Thibaults*; Céline, of course; the later Malraux; the one who, in *The Walnut Trees of Altenburg*, reverses the "virile" mythology of the lovers of war by making fun of those "intellectuals" who "are like women" since "soldiers make them dream"; the great Malraux who, against the esthetes of war, against those who love war without participating in it, risks the other theorem, which was, a few years earlier, the theorem experienced by the anti-fascist fighters, and who, on the contrary, recommends waging war without loving it; Claude Simon's *The Flanders Road*; Norman Mailer's *The Naked and the Dead*; Kurt Vonnegut's *Slaughterhouse 5*: Gide's exasperation when, on August 14th, he sees appear before him, dressed like a soldier, very agitated, skillfully mimicking the terrible slaughter of Mulhouse, a Cocteau who had been given a strangely "healthy" complexion[2] by the "fillip of the present events"; all those who, faced with the horde of mutilated and downtrodden who make up the armies, understood, in a word, that war is not beautiful, but hideous, and that the aestheticizing of war is always dangerous.

"...whose most beautiful buildings are reduced, like the Kuito
Hotel, or the Bishop's Palace, or the five floors of the
Gabiconta building, to their concrete skeletons..."

Faced with a devastated Kuito, faced with the catastrophe that is a
city reduced to almost nothing, once again there are two points of
view, two theories of ruin, between which the history of philosophy, hence political history, has oscillated for two centuries.

Hegel, of course—the Hegel of the *Philosophy of Right*, the
one who explains there's a "moral element to war" and that, far
from being the "absolute evil" we think it is, it has the purpose of
maintaining "the moral health of the people": History is a field
of ruins, he says; in this terrible field of ruins "resound" the
"nameless lamentations of individuals"; but if the weeping individual's first instinct is to give in to this "profound, inconsolable
pain," if his natural inclination is that of a grief "that nothing
can appease," the task of the historian, of the philosopher, of the
rational individual, of the dialectician, is to go beyond this "first
negative balance sheet," to "rise" above these "sentimental" and
"pathetic reflections," then it will be obvious that this spectacle
of misery was just a trick, an illusion, a method in the service of
the "true result of universal History," that is to say of the "realization" of a "World Spirit" that passes over bodies and carries
them away—"patience! patience! all this desolation, all this suffering, will end up, one day, becoming clear!"[3]

And then there's the other theory, belonging to those other thinkers—in my *Sartre: The Philosopher of the Twentieth Century*, since they refused the idea that Hegel was a secular Messiah announcing the End of History, I enjoyed christening them "Hegel's Jews"; their prototype was indeed early Sartre, or Kierkegaard, or even Walter Benjamin of the 1940 *Concept of History* (his last, and most passionate, work, written just before his suicide). The question asked by "Hegel's Jews," and, in particular, by Benjamin, is this: What if ruin were "the natural state of modern things"? And what if modernity were that particular state of the world where "all production" is destined to be "immediately destroyed"? And what if, faced with the scenes of ruin in modern life, we had to return to an "attitude like that of the seventeenth century confronting Antiquity," which was never perceived as anything but the definitive accumulation of ruins? And what if ruin, in other words, were the first, but also the last, word of the world we're entering: ruin as such; a ruin that neither promises nor hides anything; a cold ruin, without recourse, where the sun shines only as a dead star (Benjamin says, using a phrase of Nietzsche's: a star that, suddenly, shines "without atmosphere"...)? A ruin without theodicy? without a tomorrow? an absolute ruin, an absolute disaster?

I map it onto Kuito. Ruin onto ruin. Metaphysics against metaphysics. The indecent optimism of people who, to men and women who survive in muddy craters, in this tiny life that war has deigned to spare them where they go on bleeding, will always find a way of saying: "Stop complaining; dry your tears; you just have to change your point of view, to raise yourself above your sheet-metal and tar roofs, all you have to do is project yourself forward in your mind into the future, and you will understand that all this, all these ruins, this desolation your city has become, this end-of-the-world landscape, these corpses all around you, these living beings almost as dead as the dead, this life of hunted animals or insects at bay, this unhappiness, is an obligatory stage of History, an annoying but temporary phase of globalization—almost a stage set."

Opposing that is the pessimism—seemingly desperate, but actually more stimulating—of those who, clinging to ruin and taking it for what it is, refusing to see in the ruins more than ruins and sensing in this putrid life, this universe of disarray and remnants, the whiff of some new kind of genesis, at least have the merit of not adding insult to injury, not adding the denial of unhappiness to unhappiness itself. Yes, there are the pessimists, who spared the damned the final outrage of having to hear that the greatest suffering permits the finest redemption, and that it's when you crush him that a man shows his worth. In the pure scandal of these ruins, their insurmountable horror, there does not exist, anywhere, a point of view that allows one to see in this cesspit the Annunciation of some kind of new world order, world market, etc., secretly beginning its metamorphosis and its course.

Benjamin against Hegel. Dry, indignant anger against the consolation of dialectics. One is always right to leave ruins, but also to hold onto them.

"It's too late," the hotel manager tells me, an old white-haired
Portuguese, with the hoarse voice of cancer and with a
musketeer's goatee..."

This idea that war isn't what it used to be... The good old days
of "real war," to which modernity has put an end... There
again, there are two ways of understanding this. Two distinct
"laments," about which I realize I've perhaps done nothing,
here and elsewhere, from war to war, for thirty years, nothing
other than try to dissociate one from the other.

The aestheticizing lament. Complacency. Once upon a time
we had wars of real men. Schools of courage and virile virtue.
Once upon a time there were real heroic wars, based on physical
contact, for which technology has sounded the death knell, and
that's such a shame...

That's what Henry de Montherlant says, in *La Relève du
matin* and, especially, *The Dream*, that hymn to the "holy male
order" of true military virtues—that's what Alban de Bricoule,
his hero, says, in the famous episode [4] where, drunk with sensu-
ous pleasure, he gathers in a final carnal "embrace" the young
and handsome German boy he's just killed, face-to-face, in
hand-to-hand combat, in an abandoned trench.

It's what Ernst Jünger never stopped saying, from *The Storm
of Steel* up to his later interviews with Frédéric de Towarnicki[5]:
"Our time is a time of battles of equipment"; alas, we are in the
era of "technology," and war, having become hyper-technical, has

become an "abstract operation." Oh the indignity of those battles where, as in Les Eparges, I fought for months "without seeing a single one of my adversaries"! Ah, the wonderful "shiver" the warrior experiences, his "wild, delirious joy," when, "from his hiding-place," he sees "the enemy" appear at "closer range," "in the open"![6] Beware of that moment! Beware of the "temptation of throwing down your weapons and leaping towards him like a fatal mirage that the senses have been deprived of for too long"! That's the "instant of supreme danger"—the moment of pure ecstasy "where you forget your cover and where you get yourself killed as if you were completely intoxicated"![7]

It's Drieu La Rochelle's obsession, in *The Comedy of Charleroi*, later in *Socialisme fasciste*: shame on bad war, which has "conquered men"; shame on "modern war," this war "of iron and not of muscle, of science, not of art"; of "industry," "commerce," "offices," "newspapers," this war "of generals and not of leaders, of ministers, union leaders, emperors, socialists, democrats, royalists, industrialists, bankers, old men, women, little boys"; shame on this war "of iron and gas," fought "by everyone, except by the ones who created it"; shame on this war "of advanced civilization"; shame on its "knowing and perverse scrapheap"; shame on these new wars where to fight is to be "flattened, sprawled, prostrate." Once upon a time war "was men standing up." Shame on this cursed era that, by replacing men with machines, has sullied everything, defiled everything, dishonored everything, even the holiness of war. Long live the wars of long ago, wars like those "Joinville or Monluc" described—long live the big, beautiful, homosexual wars where, as with Montherlant, it was a question less of fighting than of "intertwining" and "embracing."[8]

Finally, it's a theme you find, even today, in what remains of wartime literature; it's the core of what was said especially during those two "smart" and "ultra-technologized" wars, which were the Kuwait war and then the war of Kosovo: long-distance wars, the armchair strategists lamented... wars without contact, added the Saddamists or Milosevicists... wars where, for the first time, the warriors did not use their *thymos**, their courage, their manly battles, the traditional warlike virtues... Shame on these wars without risk where sophisticated machinery, as in Iraq, allowed them to reckon a thousand-fold fewer deaths of their own than of their opponents, or, as in Kosovo, to drop their bombs from high enough up to be out of reach of the enemy defense systems and not to take any risks at all... And glory, with the same people, the ones still nostalgic for hand-to-hand combat and its real embraces, countering those who, as soon as night fell, in Belgrade, organized their open-air rock concerts: "Strike! strike! We've drawn a target over our heart! We're waiting!" sang the Brave Ones, and those present applauded, without realizing what a powerful tribute they were paying to the restraint of the allied air forces...

I don't know what's "worth" more, in the absolute—long-distance or close-range wars. I can't settle the question of what is "morally" preferable, wars where the enemies touch, or those where they evade each other. Coming from wars where they kill with knives as well as with cannons, having had the opportunity to observe the damage done by warfare that keeps oscillating between extreme distance and extreme proximity, I'm not even able to say which ones kill more (all in all, if I absolutely had to choose, it seems to me that a good provisional motto would be Keats's "I don't hate my enemy, and I don't love the one's I'm defending"—in other words, distance is preferable,

*Greek, "spiritedness" – Trans.

the reduction of enthusiasm and passion; but who knows?). It's a story of ideas I'm speaking of here. It's the circulation of images, the recycling of fantasies and imagined worlds, that I'm interested in now. And the only thing I'm saying is that the essential argument of the "pacifist" camp, during Kuwait and Kosovo, was tuned to the viewpoint of Drieu, of Montherlant, and of their great homosexual and phallic carousel.

And then there's the other way.

There's the other nostalgia, which is that of the old Angolan musketeer of Porto Amboim, and which expresses regret, not for virility, but for meaning.

There's the memory of that time when wars, as hideous, detestable, and bloody as they were, still had stakes.

It's: "Once upon a time there was a Revolutionary war, with its procession of heroes and martyrs" or; "Once upon a time there were political wars, simply political, like the first war in Angola" or; "Once upon a time there were just anti-fascist wars; once there were wars of resistance that, by means of war, resisted the worse-than-war."

Literature for literature, it's these other writers who, in the middle of the 1930's, and then in the grim times of the anti-Nazi protests, together envisaged, calmly, the absolute hideousness of war and the obligation, nonetheless, to wage it: there is Aragon of 1942; the Bataille and Breton of *Contre-Attaque*; the interventionists in Spain; Orwell and his *Homage to Catalonia*; Malraux again; there's this whole other way of thinking about war, not as virile, exalting, or a source of greatness or self-accomplishment, but quite simply as a necessity, since the alternative to this war would be, not peace, but hell...

That there are, in this second way of thinking about war, other fine distinctions to be made; that it's not the same thing to extol the virtues of war against Nazism and war against imperialism; that one must regard as highly suspicious a concept— "political war"—that would force one to put in the same category both the act of the democrat aspiring only to conquer totalitarianism (Nazi, Stalinist, Islamist-fundamentalist) and the act of the nihilist dooming the dry earth of old Europe to the purifying fire of revolutionary war (the young Aragon, all the Leftists), I am the first to be convinced. And it's clear, also, that the dichotomy is, in any case, never quite clear-cut, and that a full analysis remains to be made of the secret relationships, the undisclosed points of contact, the links, between the two types of nostalgia and, hence, the two "families": Hemingway's case, straddling the two temptations; the case of *Farewell to Arms*, the quintessential book of the genre, about which we forget that the preface to the first French edition was written by Drieu, at the time a specialist in military affairs for the NRF (Nouvelle Revue Française), and about which no one has been able to say for sure if his farewell was to "arms (weapons)" or to "arms (arms)," to the possibility of "embrace" and "grip," hence to Montherlant's sense of war (similarly, the hero of *Across the River and into the Trees*, the sad old officer, in love with his "contessa," who, as if by chance, is named "Cantwell," the one who "can't... well"); or again the case of Malraux, the evolution of André Malraux himself, not to speak of his ambivalence—there is a Malraux, the one of the fragment from *The Walnut Trees of Altenburg* quoted earlier, but also the one who, in *Man's Hope*, has it told to Scali that one has to distinguish the "combatants" (whom he likes) from the "warriors" (whom he mistrusts); to Shade that war is a horror and that one should hate it as one hates his own disfigured face; to Garcia that, if "there are just wars," for instance the anti-Franco war, there has never been a "just army," incarnation of the Fine, the True, and the Good—in short, there is a Malraux who keeps showing the abject side of this war that can be legitimately waged only on condition one is sure of hating it with all one's soul. But there is another Malraux, the one of *The Conquerors*, of *The Royal Way*, and also of some other pages from *The Walnut Trees*, sometimes the same ones, who believes, like Montherlant, like Drieu, like Jünger, that war is the best arena for the accomplishment of a man's fate.

But finally, having made these reservations, I see nothing absurd or reprehensible in this second version of nostalgia. I am not at all afraid of saying that I, too, like the hotel manager in Porto Amboim, have had nostalgia for this nostalgia. Maybe not in Angola. Or in Burundi, Colombia, the South Sudan, or Sri Lanka. But eight years ago, in Bosnia, where it's this lack of nostalgia, this incapacity to regret, thus to imagine, the old notion of anti-fascist war—in short, the failure to make a claim for even the idea of a just war—that was responsible for the non-intervention of the West and, thus, for the prolongation of the siege of Sarajevo, and for its rows of murdered civilians. Have things changed with the era of "suicide attacks"? And did the West have to be struck in its heart to regain consciousness, as well as its ability to defend its own values? We shall see. The only thing we can say, for now, is that the disappearance of meaning is not an idea, but a fact; and that, for this fact, for this actively experienced nihilism, we are already paying the price.

But that too is an idea. The disappearance of meaning is a fact but it is, still, an idea. And I'm not even sure if this idea, this envisioning of a war capable, without the least sense or reason, without anything at stake, of producing an infinite amount of devastation, is very easy to conceive of. Anti-Hegelian? Yes, of course, anti-Hegelian. Anti- everything that Hegelianism has taught us about the economy of Evil in this world. But it would be too simple if this idea were only anti-Hegelian. It is also *anti-Kantian* (insofar as *Idea for a Universal History from a Cosmopolitan Point of View* forms, in 1784, well before Hegel, the hypothesis, if not of a "scheme," at least of a secret "design" that would act on men without their knowing it, would give "distressing contingency"—the seemingly "absurd" and "aberrant" course of their actions—a rational significance, and would prevent their "actions and gestures" from being that "web of madness, of puerile vanity, and also often of puerile malice and thirst for destruction" that they seem to be at first glance. "There is no science of the individual," Kant insists, following Aristotle; no science of the singular; in view of which he appeals to a "new Kepler" able to "explain the universal laws of the historical evolution of humanity," in other words to give a meaning to what, at first sight, had none).[9] It is *anti-Leibniz* (insofar as all the stress of *The Monadology* lies in positing: 1.The impossibility of a phenomenon, however little, local, unique and seemingly erratic it may be, not finding its justification in universal harmony. 2.The non-existence in this world of any element, any event, or any conflict that, provided one takes it as a part of a whole, and then one takes the point of view of this whole, does not prove, not just the rationality of life, but its supreme goodness. 3.The short-sightedness, on the other hand, of those who, pleading the case for the radical nature of Evil, or noting the sheer gaping abyss of human suffering, are like those naïve people who, seeing a city "from different sides," think they see "different universes" where there are "only various perspectives of a single one"[10] and prove thereby merely their inability to be fully free, to taste the pleasures of universal language and to adopt its point of view).

Finally it is *anti-Christian* (wasn't it Christianity's great feat to resolve this business of Radical Evil? Doesn't the heart of the Christian Revolution lie in the idea that there is no unhappiness, misery, suffering, war, that, if only you look carefully, doesn't turn out to be *ad majorem Dei gloriam*? Isn't it the very function of Providence to say to the humble, to the small, to martyred, desolate humanity: "Divine goodness is watching over you, it speaks to men through History, you just have to know how to wait, yes, to keep waiting, and to hope"? Wasn't hope given to men so they could have, in the words of Saint Irenaeus, the strength to wait for that moment of "divine pedagogy" where what one has known forever, which doesn't need, as in Hegel, to be revealed via work, labor, or dialectics, will be expressed: that we never suffer in vain, since "God treats us like his son"?).

It's an idea that goes counter to the essential part of the philosophical, theological, and political tradition of the West. It's a perspective that attacks from the rear the whole sedimentation of beliefs, convictions, self-evident facts, and instincts that, necessarily, make up "common sense." And that's why it is at the very limit of the thinkable—that's why we find it so difficult to imagine this idea of a war *for nothing*.

"Is that why I came all the way here? For this spectacle of
looming death?"

Political activism, all right. Humanism of the other man. To
draw the world's attention to these wars, these sufferings, that
are never spoken of. All the virtuous reasons intellectuals give
themselves for doing what they do and that, in my case as well as
in that of my elders, have, obviously, their share of truth. But the
others? The rest of the real reasons? The ones you prefer to keep
to yourself and that you sometimes hesitate to confess, even
to yourself? Adventure. I would have to say, if I intend to say
everything, the taste for adventure. A testing of self. A taste, as
Foucault said, for changing yourself, for thinking differently
from the way you usually think, for living differently from the
way you thought you should live. A love for diverse identities. To
be one person and then another person. Above all, not to be the
person whose identity is ascribed to you, here or there. Not
romanticism. I don't think this is a return to romanticism, aes-
theticism, etc. But Michaux says: One wants too much to be
someone. Or: One wants too much to be faithful to oneself,
one's wretched "to be myself"—how can you break that? How
can you betray yourself? How, every now and then, even if you
know quite well that it's almost always an illusion, how to twist
the neck of His Majesty the Self. Freedom, then. That kind of

freedom: to be many, everything and nothing, many and no one—the sacred duty of infidelity. But this other form too, the ancient dream, that I've only found here, in these wartime situations, these reports, and that the game of truth, played to the end, will force me to say: to live in my own way, according to my rhythm, my rules; their morality, my own; their principles, my own. New emotions. New feelings. Another regimen, suddenly, for the mental (which is also, often, the physiological) engine. These "borderline situations" which Sartre says, extracting the subject from himself, reveal to him his share of contingency. Bataille calls them "paroxysmal situations"; because they "go beyond" the subject, because they detach him from himself and from his inertia, they initiate him into a new algebra of sensations. All right, Bataille says: ludic, erotic, revolutionary, mystical situations. But why not war situations, as long as you're there? Why not war instead of games, mysticism, revolution? And why not a situation that, instead of linking man to a lost organicity, as with Bataille, would lead him back to the extreme point of himself, to his—radical singularity, released from all continuum, ab-solute? That's it. Sartre within Bataille. The Sartre-effect within Bataille-situations. The Sartrean absolute subject instead of the orgiastic fusion of the author of *The Blue of Noon*. And sensations, then. New perceptions. There are writers who use the novel to explore the unknown possibilities of existence. I write reportage. Perhaps because I, like Sartre again, regard journalism as the literary genre par excellence. Perhaps because today's novels are all, in any case, in the process of becoming reportage. The fact, however it may be, is there. It's in reality, not in fiction, that I have looked for a long time now for unfound perceptions.

There are "great" perceptions, of course. Major perceptions. There is the journey through hell. Experiencing the Devil and Nothingness. I've always told myself that a writer should, at least once, have had the experience, in himself, of the diabolical, of nothingness. I always told myself that the famous "History is a nightmare from which I am trying to awake" surely had a precise, concrete meaning, and that it would be good to know what that is. Well there it is. I've done it. A season on the other side, the hell, of contemporary History. A few months spent in testing *the* great forbidden hypothesis: a world created, not by God, but by the Devil—God reduced, as in Isaac Luria's Kabbalah, to a few sparks of holiness. But there are also little, very little, perceptions. I am someone who, for instance, doesn't "see" into everyday life. I ask those near me to tell me what the weather is like outside. It's they who, quite often, tell me the color of a landscape that I like or about a sound that moved me. Then, since reporting demands it, I see. I hear. It's as if my body were on alert. My radar switched on. It's as if all my capacities of perception were, suddenly, operational. Colors. Sounds. The sickly smell of blood that the wind brings among the coffee trees of Tenga. They always say "the sickly smell of blood." But I didn't know that a sickliness could be so strong, so harsh, so violent. All the nuances of the night. All the possible colors of a morning. There are no two mornings, or two evenings, that resemble each other—and that's what I have realized in Africa, in Sri Lanka, in Bosnia, in the long watches of my journalism for thirty years. Gleams of dawn in full darkness. The moon rising between two clouds and flooding the camp, on the summits of Donji Vakuf, where the Bosnian forces were secretly preparing their attack.

Days slow to start, almost black, as in Maglaj, a few weeks earlier—and there, on the contrary, it's a godsend, I surprise myself in blessing, as the soldiers do, this extra darkness that aids movement. Unknown murmurings. Mysterious shouts. I didn't think there could be so many different ways to shout, so many distinct tonalities of cries —short or prolonged; drawn out, like a silent reproach; hooting; screeching; bellowing; whinnying like the cry of a wounded horse; rising up to the sky; plunging into the depths; shouting to make people afraid; shouting because you're afraid; shouting, then moaning, as at the Last Judgment; the alphabet of emotions, the gamut of feelings, legible in the color of a shout. Moments of grace, too. The smallest pleasure—not the pleasure of war, of course!—the tiniest pleasures, rather, that war has not stolen away! The slight pleasures of living won from and against war! A ray of sunshine… a corner of shadow… a breath of air in a heatwave… the smell of freshly-cut pine trees in a Bosnian bunker… the pause after a long march… a mouthful of warm water… a shower… real sheets in a real bed when I go back to Luanda… a telephone that works and that allows you to hear the voices of those dear to you… —the tiniest pleasure, I say, that takes on the aspect of a miracle. Laughter. Fear. Abysses of sadness. The extreme surprise, when the bombs fall very close and terror is at its height, of hearing only the sound of the blood that throbs in your temples. The calm, on the other hand, an almost heavenly calm, the gift of saints, when the bombing stops—"magnificent and terrible peace, the real taste of the passing of time" (Debord). Your head exploding again, your lungs burning, drops of frozen sweat that in the full sun burn your eyes, when, the firing having started again, you have, in Grondj, to rush back into the trench, then run down very fast, along the line of the ridge, with the Serbian mortar-shells following in your tracks. Is it very hot or very cold in hell? The Gospels say, Very hot. Isaiah says, Gehenna of fire. Milton, Blake, Fénelon of *The Adventures of Telemachus*, speak of rivers of fire, volcanic lakes, boiling cesspits, boilers whose covers the angels lift to observe the contortions of the damned. But Pythagoras, according to Ovid, claims that the Styx is frozen. There are a number of theologians from the Middle Ages who, troubled by this fire that burns without destroying and preserves the flesh of the victims as salt preserves brine, people the realm of the dead with fountains of frozen tears, whirlwinds of snow, deserts of ice, frost-covered lakes. Dante himself says, Cold, very cold—the core of the air, in hell, is terrifyingly cold. And as to Baudelaire... It's in the Bosnian trenches that I realized, for the first time, that I knew some Baudelaire poems by heart. And it's here, in Angola, that, twelve years after my *Derniers Jours de Charles Baudelaire*, some of their "diabolical" lines came back to me. Another way memory works. Buried memories that surface. Recent memories that emotion submerges, erases almost immediately. An unexpected sound, the noise of a tambourine in a district south of Bujumbura, the crackle of an old rusted drum I stepped on by accident, the oily sound of my feet in the mud of the Bubanza trench, and it's a whole host of memories, absolutely incongruous, that begin to vibrate. Fear, also. The effect of fear on memory. I am afraid, yes, I am so intensely afraid, in Tenga, Burundi, during the gunfire, then on the road back, with the wounded soldier who is dying next to me, that, under the effect of this fear, in the whiff of horrible life it breathes into me, it's other fragments of memory, with no connection to the situation, obscene, intrusive, that rush into my mind: a caress, a sigh, a Mexican sunset, A.'s hair in the light of a Mediterranean landscape, a word from her, a gesture that's familiar about which I understand, for the first time, that it was hers alone, a snow-covered landscape, a cup of tea, a sunset on the Positano bay, a childhood treasure-hunt, a film shot that I didn't realize had impressed me so much. The panic of time. Its landmarks brought to a boiling point. Sometimes it's those slack, leaden days, when nothing happens and when the minutes count double—"the hideous universe" and its "too-heavy instants." Sometimes it's the opposite: a time that goes very quickly; minutes divided in half; loose, uncontrollable ideas, that buzz about like insane insects. Books, of course. To continue reading, but in a different way. To remember forever the passage from *The Death of Virgil* that I was reading, the first night, until lights-out, in Massoud's guest house, in the Panjshir. To know immediately—with a strange, somewhat magical, but definite knowledge—that the smallest details of the edition of Malaparte's *Kaputt* begun again for the umpteenth time, in Huambo, in the little hotel in the former General Norton-de-Matos Square, across from the government palace, where I found a room, were in the process of inscribing themselves, with an indelible ink: the meaning, of course; the words; the attack in Chapter 3 ("that morning, I had gone with Svartström to see the horses freed from their prison of ice; a greenish sun, in the pale blue sky, was shining," etc.); but even the typography of the book; the arrangement of its chapters; a telephone number scrawled on top of the page that I'll always remember; a stain of red ink, on top of another, that had run onto the "huge crowds of Jews fleeing through the streets." To learn again how to be quiet. To laugh quietly, in discreet staccato gasps. To wait. To run. To breathe. To run again. The body, pinned to the ground, in danger, tries to be in control the soul. Which wants very much to trick the body. And asks only to face up to things. But the body resists. The body holds on for dear life with the single wish to survive and, sometimes, calculates wrongly, makes a wrong connection. Hence, in Maglaj, where we had to run in the open through an orchard, to go from one trench to another: the soul is determined to dash forward; it knows you have to move fast and reach the second trench without lingering; it is aware that everything depends on a few seconds and that, across the way, an artilleryman's eyes might be beginning to take aim; but the knees won't follow through, they live their own autonomous life and, thinking they're doing well, stop me halfway, in the orchard, on all fours. For there is another feeling of existing. Another experience of self. Not the soul, really. Nor strictly speaking the body. But the animal. My untamed but intimate animal. This animal that resides in me, more inseparable than my shadow, which, that morning, had the upper hand. Another game between life and death. A life that, suddenly, is no longer completely given to me. A part of me that I discover and about which I tell myself that I could, without too much difficulty, rid myself of. This experience, again. Which, they say, only the dying have. But it seems to me I have come close to it, myself, twice. Once in Jessore, in Bangladesh, the day the city was captured, when a Pakistani soldier, with a belt of grenades, put me against the wall. Another time, twenty years later, on the heights of Sarajevo, the first night, in that famous Serbian barracks in Lukavica, bombarded by the Bosnians, where I also thought my last hour had come. This experience, then, of seeing in fast motion, or of encompassing it within a single glance, the film of one's whole life. A feeling of rebellion, each time. A terror, and a rebellion, at the idea of possible nothingness. But not that. Not nothingness. That's not enough, nothingness. I wouldn't have felt, if it had been only nothingness, either this terror, or this rebellion. The real secrets being unveiled. The truths one was hiding from oneself and that, suddenly, come to the surface. Death, always. Death in the heart of life. Death, not as the truth, or the limit, of life, but as its hard kernel. A taste for playing with this death. A taste for outwitting it. A taste, said Perken, the hero of *The Royal Way*, for playing not with, but *against*, one's own death, and maybe, too, for averting it. Portrait of the adventurer as gambler. A gambler of outwitting death. Of the art of cheating one's death, of entering its game and triumphing over it. I see myself a little, then, like those big cargo-planes that carried out the airlifts in Sarajevo and that, when the radar told them they had Serbian antiaircraft defense pointed at them, produced a decoy, a fictive image of themselves, that they sent to float further away, in the clouds, as a way of tricking the gunners and diverting their attention. The syndrome of the deep-sea diver. The famous Sartrean theme of lead shoes that bring you down from your philosophical empyrean and bring you into the nakedness of the human condition and of life. I've done my share of pointing out this attraction to lead in others—that is, a bad conscience; I've talked enough about the dimension of expiation and penitence with which intellectuals have almost always been involved. I've made enough fun of this way of thinking of engagement only as a "shot" of reality in a soul that, rightly or wrongly, thinks it's weaned of it (Nizan and the temptation of Aden, Aragon's "real world," all those intellectuals with too-clean hands coming, during the 1930's, and then the 50's, to join the school of life to expiate their original sin...), I've spoken too much of this nostalgia for the concrete in others, in ancient times, not to suspect it in me, today, at a time (internet, cloning, unbridled potentiality) when the real, not content with hiding itself, is in the process of exploding, of eclipsing itself. A taste for chaos. The extreme curiosity of the advanced Westerner faced with these images of confusion and disaster. Destruction was my Beatrice. Not to camp, but to write, on the ruins. To save bodies of course. But also—how can I deny it?—to observe how a suffering, dying body, at the extreme boundaries of life, functions—obscenity of great reportage, shame of the grand journey, wild entomology, passionate vivisection. Nostalgia for asceticism. I have friends who go, in wars, to feed their taste for the epic, for lyricism. Not me. Not the epic. Not lyricism. First of all because I have always thought, rightly or wrongly, surely wrongly, but I have thought it, that I had, without that, without dispatches, my dose of private lyricism (inner life, etc.). Then, especially, because I definitely do not believe that war is a place for the lyric or the epic. But asceticism, on the other hand, yes. A taste for a life stripped of what usually furnishes and, perhaps, encumbers it: habits, conventions, urbanity, money, that whole part of life that makes life secure—and that, suddenly, shatters into bits—all that's left is a fragile body, three shirts, the old copy of *Kaputt*, some dreams. Of all that, of that other heap of secrets, of that strange pleasure I feel when I act the ascetic, of the shadows that, at this instant, haunt me and of which I surely want to make myself worthy, I don't want to say any more—maybe because I can't, for now, see any more clearly. That's it.

Watch out for Drieu. When you start talking about "playing with one's own death and in that way maybe averting it," watch out for being too friendly with the fascist writer Drieu La Rochelle. Perken? Yes, all right, Perken. But also, before Perken, Drieu's book *The Comedy of Charleroi* where it says, "What's the use of living if you don't use your life to clash it against death, like a saber"; then: "If death isn't at the heart of life like a hard kernel, what a soft, and soon overripe, fruit life is." And, when I say "before" Perken, I mean it literally—anteriority, authority, direct influence: Drieu will answer Malraux in his other book *Gilles*; the end of *Gilles*, the final journey to Spain, the plane crashing on the beach, the very character of Walter, or of Manuel, the Falangist who joins Walter, all will be a reply to *Man's Hope*; why shouldn't *The Royal Way* be an answer to *The Comedy of Charleroi*? Don't we know that influence is exercised in both directions between these two works? And how can we be sure, when we think we're admiring Malraux, that we're not having a dose of *Charleroi* palmed off to us, on the sly, like a bad drug?

God knows I don't like Drieu. I don't like his fascism. I don't like his literature. And, as to his views on war, it's like Montherlant at his worst: from among a thousand examples, still in *The Comedy of Charleroi*, a few pages before "what's the use of living if you don't use your life" etc., the "flash of inspiration" of the proto-fascist leader "rising up from among the dead" and from "among the larvae," discovering "the boiling of his blood, yellow and hot" and feeling the welling up in him of a man, a real man, that's to say "a man who gives and takes in the same ejaculation."[11] All that I find displeasing. Even a little disgusting. And, honestly, I don't think I feel any kind of fascination for the author of *The Man on Horseback* and *Rêveuse Bourgeoisie*— nothing comparable, for instance, to Régis Debray's turmoil when he evokes, in *Les Masques*, that "empty suitcase" side, that "hatred of self," that "taste for isolation," that "remorse for missed communions," that "curiosity about death," that "inability to experience happiness," which are the "nocturnal aspect" of Drieu and which make him the most "fraternal" of the "sacred monsters" of the interwar period.[12] But at the same time...

At the same time, if I'm honest with myself, if I choose to say everything, to the end, how can I avoid remembering those summer days, thirty years ago, a few months after I had played the role of Paul Denis in Michel Favart's and Françoise Verny's film of *Aurélien*?* A pink villa on the coast of Naples. Cascade of rocks going down to the beach. The sea, at my feet, that had the time, in two days and one night, to pass through the whole arc of its colors—light blue, dark blue, rose-colored, almost black. And, being the total Aragonian I was then, the dazzled feeling I had when I read that strange draft of *Aurélien* that Drieu's 1939 *Gilles* was then—a reply to *Man's Hope*, indeed, but also, with the same self-evidence, a first draft of Aragon's *Aurélien*...

"Dazzled" isn't the word. One is never dazzled by Drieu. One is moved. Curious. Seduced by a sad charm. Surprised.

---

* The title character of Aragon's *Aurélien* is supposed to be based on Drieu—Trans.

Often overwhelmed. Sometimes touched, or moved to pity, or strangely melancholic. And I think I felt all that when I read *Gilles*. That whole gamut of emotions. Plus—and this is the main point—that astonishment I felt at the powerful connection with the other book, the masterpiece, the one I thought of, at the time, and not just because I had performed in it, or because it had been the occasion for me to meet Aragon himself, as one of the chief books of my life: two bodies for one single soul; two signatures for one single novel; the rough draft and the finished work, Albert Cohen's *Solal* and *Belle du seigneur*, Proust's *Jean Santeuil* and *Remembrance*, but here borne, not by one author, but by two distinct writers. For the second one, for Drieu, for this first-draft writer of genius, for this inventor of an imaginary world to which Aragon would give its finished shape, I feel a real, if somewhat troubled, liking, about which I'm ready to bet that it was of the same nature as that other liking, so enigmatic and into which I would, quite a bit later, in *Les Aventures de la liberté*, try to enquire, that the Nizan's, the Malraux's, the d'Astier de La Vigerie's, felt, often up to the end, when Drieu had ended up dishonoring himself, towards this friendly enemy, soon to be execrated, but who had, in their eyes, the unsettling strangeness of mirrors.

In short. A return of memory, I suppose. An obscure progression through earlier scenes. And, at the finish, which is to say today, this reflection on my taste for "a life stripped bare of all that usually furnishes it," this page in the old copy of *Kaputt* tirelessly read, re-read, and annotated, where I am indeed forced to hear the echo of this other page and, through that page, of all that I do not want, in principle, to hear any more: "there is within me a terrible taste for depriving myself of everything, for leaving everything; that's what I like about war; I've never been so happy—while being atrociously unhappy—as in those winters when all I had in the world was a fifty-cent book by Pascal, a knife, my watch, and two or three handkerchiefs, and when I didn't get any letters."[13]

There was a time when people fought for God (crusades, traditional wars of religion, the great clashes of Ideas prophesied by Hobbes...). Then there was a time of idolatrous wars, where people fought for ersatz Gods (wars between nations, races, classes, rival memories, madnesses—all of them just vehicles for a divine principle recycled in secular forms). Here, in Angola, or in Burundi, at a time when the ersatz itself seems dead—here the last stage of the interminable Death of God has arrived, which Nietzsche, in a fragment from *The Gay Science* called, aptly, "The Madman," called the moment of the "decomposition" of the gods, a twilight of the idols, the vanishing of the last traces of the divine, the completion of nihilism, new humanity "straying as through an infinite nothing," new historic time or, perhaps, post-historic, where reign the "cold," "night," the "breath of empty space" on our face, and where wars appear where no one believes any longer in the great pagan signifiers of long ago (which I call "senseless" wars and which a faithful Nietzschean would call "atheist" wars).

After that? After this "last" stage? Perhaps a final last stage. Perhaps the war to end all wars, but a real one, combining in a new synthesis the characteristics unique to the three kinds and endowing them, by the very fact of the combination, with a new, unheard-of energy. Serbian wars, for instance: they were wars of the first kind when some sort of bully was baptized "the son of Jesus Christ," in the beginning of Bosnia, by extremist Orthodox bishops; of the second kind when they fought, in Kosovo, for a territory, an acre's worth of memory, a few old monasteries, a heap of stones supposed to embody the reliquary of true faith; of the third kind, in the irrational, insane brutality of massacres and ethnic purification. Or else wars in the name of Islam: they're of the first kind when they invoke, although by distorting them, the imperatives of the law of jihad; of the second kind in their pagan, idolatrous fascination with martyrdom; and, again, they are wars of the third kind, pushing to their most extreme consequences the laws of nihilism, when they take the shape of suicide-attacks—irrationality, pure vertigo, the taste of death for death's sake, endless fall, the world backwards, no meaning in sight.

Still, are things so simple?

Am I so certain, for instance, that the wars of the past had so much more "meaning" than those of today? What do Barbusse and Dorgelès say about it? What does Céline say? Isn't his *Journey to the End of the Night* precisely one of the books of the twentieth century that best describes war as a delirium, a madness, a chaos of passions thrown against each other, an "absurdity" (Bardamu: "War was everything you didn't understand...")? And what about Dada? And the Surrealists? And Vaché? Cravan? Breton? And the early Aragon, howling against a war whose main characteristic is that it already made no sense? And what, even, of the heroic wars à la Malraux? What is it about these political and revolutionary wars which are of course thought to be invested with great and noble values but which, if they were told not from the point of view of Tchen, but of the coolie, would seem as stripped of meaning, as absurd, as the wars of Angola and Burundi?

Is it absolutely certain, on the other hand, that the wars of today have as little sense as I say? Can't I envisage the hypothesis that they obey, secretly, a manner of rationality, of order? Shouldn't I, at least provisionally, for an instant, *in order to see,* try to take seriously what some of these "madmen" tell us about their wars? The Hindu fanatic who devotes his life to beating up Buddhists... The South Sudanese Dinka bent on his war against the Nuer... The Tutsi civilian who's convinced he's resisting a genocidal operation planned long ago by the Hutus... The Hutu who has the opposite feeling of struggling against discrimination and oppression long wished by the Tutsis... Is it so completely certain that these viewpoints have no meaning? Isn't it actually conceivable that they touch, here or there, on the truth of these wars? And should we, under the pretext that it tells us nothing, or that it is expressed in a language that is not familiar to us, deny that this meaning exists?

For, what does "no meaning" mean, really? Should it be understood from our point of view or from the viewpoint of the interested parties? Don't we call "absence of sense" a sense that just makes no sense to us? Aren't these wars that have "no more meaning" wars whose meaning is either unintelligible to us or doesn't concern us? Aren't I in the process of qualifying as meaningless those wars whose meaning has only the fault of not being inscribed in the great game of world history? What if this is the last ruse of Hegelianism? The last trick of Western-centrism? What if it were enough, this time, to change your point of view, to take the point of view of the Angolan leader, of Savimbi, of the Tutsi fighter, of the leader of the Tigers I met in Batticaloa, in short, of Tchen or of the local follower of Tchen, to see this disorder of actions, this upheaval of shadows and aberrant forces, suddenly settle into place, like the pieces of a puzzle?

Who, moreover, decides on "world history"? Who is the judge of what is inscribed there or not? What if the witnesses don't know any more about the question than the people involved?

And if the people involved know no more than the witnesses? And if the future witnesses knew no more than the contemporary ones? And what if one were never sure of seeing, in the first place, what matters to world history and what doesn't matter to it? One could cite wars that were charged with meaning in the eyes of those who waged them and that now have no more meaning in the annals of the world. One could say, on the other hand, that Priam's soldiers didn't know they were writing the *Iliad*; nor did those in the Peloponnesian War know they were marking the borders of the Athenian empire and the Greek world; nor did the Germans of 1914 know, plunged into unprecedented killings, so horribly useless, about which propaganda had tried to make them think they were advancing the cause of France, Europe, and the Right—they never for a moment suspected that they were the destroyers of a civilization as well as the midwives of the new century. So, who knows if, about these forgotten wars of Angola, Sri Lanka, Burundi, they won't one day come to say that they, too, without their knowing it or our knowing it, for better or for worse, conspired at burying one world and making another emerge from it?

And then, what is a meaning that doesn't have a world-historical meaning? When I say, "A meaning that is unintelligible to us but wouldn't be in the eyes of the interested parties," or, "A meaning that has no sense for us, but does for the local Tchen," who, exactly, are the interested parties? Who is the local Tchen? In the eyes of whom, precisely, will this sense make sense? And aren't there grounds, there too, for distinguishing between them? This Angolan war, for instance. I want there to exist, for the leaders of the two rival armies, for the leaders of the MPLA as well as for Savimbi's comrades, a meaning about which the West doesn't give a damn and yet which illumines their war. But the fighter himself? The rank-and-file guerilla? The miners? The diamond slaves? The ones I call "the damned," who are the only ones, after all, whose fate matters? Do they not give a damn, either, about this meaning? Aren't they, at least as much as I, convinced they're part of a war whose significance has been lost and whose outcome, whatever it might be, will change nothing of their fate? And aren't I justified, in my name but also in their own, in saying that this war is insane?

Another question. Where are the greatest number of dead? In wars "with meaning" or "without meaning"? In the ones where they know why they're killing or in those where they don't? And what should we fear the most, the knowledgeable or the ignorant barbarian, the one armed with ideology or the one who doesn't believe in anything? When I wrote *Barbarism with a Human Face*, I said, like Camus: Ideology is a multiplier of massacres; one kills all the more easily, and in greater numbers, when one kills in good conscience, hastening, by doing so, the arrival of the Good—Communism, fascism, the exterminating angelisms of all kinds, the logical drunkenness of assassins. Now, back from this series of travels, I don't know anymore, I hesitate, and, under the shock of what I've just seen, I almost have a tendency to say: No; it's the opposite; the worst are the indiscriminate massacres; the things most to be feared are the exterminations that nothing sets off, but that nothing, as a result, is able to stop; watch out for those for whom the act of killing a man has no more meaning or importance than slicing a head of cabbage. Watch out for the demon, not of the Absolute, but of Nothingness. And then changing hats, again, after the shock of the terrorist attacks on Manhattan: the fighters for Islam; a massacre, no longer indiscriminate, but lit by the terrible light of a death-bearing faith; and, at the finish, victims of what must be called an ideology, a belief, a religious fanaticism, a vision of History and of its meaning, thousands of dead in a few seconds, a furious, bloody energy that hasn't seen its like in a long time, the world record for civilian massacres per hour in a large city, a threat of apocalypse—how, after that, can you continue to be certain that the most devastating wars are the ones whose protagonists have, at bottom, nothing in their heads?

And another question: Should we miss the times of wars "with meaning"? Do we want the wars of today to "rediscover" their lost meaning? Would the world be better, worse, or unchanged, if wars had, as before, the meaning that used to justify them? Part of me, the part that feels nostalgia for the wars of resistance and the anti-fascist wars, tends to say, Yes, of course; nothing is more distressing than indiscriminate, insane war. Civilization is when men, waging war, know pretty much why they're fighting; all the more so since, in a war that has meaning, when people know pretty well what their aim is in war and what the aim of their opponent is, the time for reason, for negotiation, for transaction always ends up following that of violence; and all the more so (another argument) since meaningful wars are also the ones that, in principle, are the most accessible to mediation, to intervention—they are the only ones over which third parties, arbitrators, involved observers, can hope to have any influence... Another part of me hesitates. The part that suspects that wars with meaning are the bloodiest, the one that regards the "meaning machine" as a machine of slavery, and regards the act of giving meaning to what has none, that's to say to the suffering of men, as one of the most underhanded tricks by which the Diabolical takes hold of us, the one that knows, in a word, that the best way to send poor people to the front is by telling them they're participating in a great adventure or working to save themselves—this part, then, replies: "No, the worst war is the one with meaning"; the worst is, as Blanchot said, "that the disaster take on meaning instead of body";[14] the worst, the most terrible, thing is to clothe with meaning the pure insanity of war; no question of missing the "cursed time of meaning."

I should be more specific.

And I should, above all, distinguish between situations.

I see five different kinds of situations, in fact—five cases each with a distinct face, as many "insane" wars as journeys: and perhaps this unspoken taxonomy was not irrelevant, either, to the choice of the place for these articles.

There are the wars that had meaning once, a real political meaning, but about which everything now indicates that they have lost their meaning, that everyone has forgotten why, exactly, they were fighting—there are wars that, in fact, have loyally kept their role in the great spectacle of cold war; now that the cold war is over, now that the great global participants have packed up and abandoned the territory, these wars have had their political responsibility switched off like a candle blown out: that's the war in Angola, as the old musketeer in Porto Amboim mourns it.

There are wars that had meaning once, a real political meaning, and that, like the war in Angola, and for the same reasons, seem to have lost it. But, in their case, it's a trick. A maneuver. It's a dialectical conjuring trick intended to take the new meaning that has risen up and hide it inside the ruins of the old meaning. This seeming non-meaning, working as a lure, has the chance to veil the truth. That's the case of the South Sudan, abandoned, it's true, by the protagonists of the old East-West confrontation—but all the better to leave room for the other war, secret, hidden, but so charged with meaning, and even with self-interest, that is the war for the appropriation of oil resources.

There are wars that reveal a contrary meaning, that even produce tons of meaning in the display-case of reason and its advantages, and where the two camps rival each other in their enthusiasm to put to sleep the words of the great cause intended to oppose them. Except that this meaning has lost all meaning. These words make no more sense. It's just an easy way to hide the enormous hold that non-meaning has on the world and on the war. It's become a way to make people forget that this war has no other purpose than the struggle for power, the appropriation of goods and wealth, the triumph of a mafia, traffickers. That is the case of the war in Colombia. That is the case of this war that is seemingly ultra-political, where the "Marxists" pretend to oppose the "anti-Marxists," the "revolutionaries" oppose the "counter-revolutionaries," the heirs to "Che" oppose the right-wing "paramilitaries." But that's all a joke. A masterly and bloody illusion. It's the other ruse of the Devil. His other way of proving his acceptability and making us believe he doesn't exist. No longer is it, as in the Sudan: "See how all this has no meaning, fix your gaze on this spectacle of chaos—that's the best way not to see the new reality of the implacable oil business." But it's an extremely symmetrical lie: "See this profusion of meaning, admire this farandole of viewpoints where it's a question exactly of waging war to change the world, or to fight the ones who want to change it, or to defend noble ideas"—and the truth is that nothing of all that has any meaning any more, that all these meanings have lost their meaning, that, in Bogota, they're living during a time of "zero sense," or of the "zero degree of sense," and that any appearance of meaning is there just to make a self-righteous smoke-screen to cover the sordid reality of mafia squabbles.

Fourthly, there are wars that once had a meaning; that, unlike the war in Angola, still have one; that, unlike the one in Sudan, do nothing to hide this meaning, make it a secret meaning, an arch-meaning; there are wars whose avowed meaning is truly a meaning and not, as in Colombia, an illusion of meaning, a meaning that has lost its meaning, a chimera; except that this true meaning is a meaning for some but not for others; it's a meaning, especially, that has nothing to do with what makes sense in the West; and it's this meaning, this abuse of meaning in a way, since the meaning that animates them is a purely local meaning and since any outcome, if there is one, will have no more effect on the world's affairs than the waging of war had—that these wars, this fourth type of war, are the insane wars. That's the case in Sri Lanka. It's this clash between Buddhists and Hindus about which I said, at the time, that it seems stripped of meaning only in the eyes of the Judeo-Christian Westerner for whom otherness stops at the border with Islam.

And then there should be, in principle, a final case. For the roster to be complete, there should be wars that truly had, this time, not a jot of sense—either local or global, either from this viewpoint or that, either understood from Tchen's point of view or from that of the coolie: wars about which no one, really, knows why they go on; wars that have utterly bidden farewell to every kind of meaning, whether it be secret, coded, avowed, or misleading; wars where it's the very idea of meaning, almost its memory, whose sense has ended up disappearing and hence that fully deserve the qualification "insane." That's the case of the war in Burundi. The most insane of the insane wars. The most forgotten of the forgotten wars. The damned among the damned.

"...armies of lost soldiers, whose real objective is less to win than to survive and kill..."

I'm sick, every time it's a question of war, of hearing talk of courage, heroism, surpassing of self through military action, fraternity of fighters, strength of soul, honor. Sick of this boy-scout vocabulary, with no relationship to the reality of these wars where the protagonists confront each other by means of interposed populations, where it's the civilians, that's to say the women, the children, the sick and unarmed men, who pay the price for the battles. Here, then, is my vocabulary. My words. The style and appearance of these wars, the passions they put into play, the real actions they mobilize, seen, lived, spoken, through this other grammar book.

Waiting. You always imagine fighters attacking, in battle, or, at least, performing maneuvers. And it's always the first thing a war reporter asks when, reaching the site of a military theater, he comes into contact with an officer: that he be brought "into the operations." But the first law of war is waiting. The normal, almost natural state of combatants is inaction. Most of their time they spend buried in trenches, huddled up in mud shelters or bunkers, crammed in, numbed, dulled by immobility or cold, on the lookout for orders for movement which never come. Law of the least effort. Tacit, unwritten rule, but equally respected by both camps, of maximum avoidance. To search each other out, yes. To spy on each other. To skirt round the opponent's position almost imperceptibly while reinforcing one's own again and again. That is the look of most of the wars I've seen. Those are the most common occupations of the combatants. I never understood how wars could produce so many dead when head-on clashes are really so rare. I never admired a war story more than George Orwell's *Homage to Catalonia*, since he tells, rightly, about this law of waiting and the patience that is the first law of the combatants. What a difference there is from a Hemingway and his mythology of head-on engagement, the charge, the fighting! How I prefer Orwell to this Hemingway so stupidly fascinated, for instance, by the "go-get-'em" side of Patton. (The military imagination of the man who had written *A Farewell to Arms* is structured around these two great antagonistic figures of the overheated Patton on one hand and the wise, prudent, thrifty Montgomery on the other, who waited till there were ten against one before giving the sign of attack—"a Monty, one," whispered the author of *A Farewell to Arms*, on his bad days, to his favorite waiter at the Ritz or at Harry's Bar, and that meant: "a whisky heavily diluted with water or soda; ten to one; insipid. . . .")

Submission. How dare war novels talk about surpassing the self? About accomplishment? About "the wonderful atmosphere of friendship and youth" (Montherlant, on Philippe Barrès's *La Guerre à vingt ans*)? About brotherly communion, joy? How dare they tell us—Drieu again, and even Malraux, and Tolstoy in *War and Peace*—that there is "nobility" in war? that man discovers his true nature in it? that there you are educated in holiness, in the epic ("We demand a great breath from the epic poem," exclaims a ridiculous character in Céline...)? How can they have the effrontery to celebrate war situations as opportunities for emancipation and freedom? War is discipline. Maximum subjection. Slavery. It's one of the situations in which man is most subject to man, and has the fewest ways to escape. He is seized. Requisitioned. Buffeted back and forth by mechanical orders. The object of a sadism that suffers no argument. Exposed to humiliation or being shot. Numbered. Crushed. Forced to perform menial tasks. Caught in very slow, very obscure, absolutely indecipherable collective movements, which, even to the most naturally rebellious, leave no other choice than to bend to their will. War is the circumstance above all others in which this power of letting people live and making them die is, according to the best philosophers, the characteristic of absolute power. The man of war is the least of men, that's to say, he is an absolute slave.

Fear. The universe of war is not boldness, valor, courage, etc., but fear. Silent, spineless panic. The human animal rearing up. The rebellious flesh, which stiffens. Bent shoulders. Head lowered. Bad alcohol you have to swallow to be able to dare, in Burundi, but also in Bosnia, to go under fire. The combatant wants above all to be forgotten. He would like to melt into the mud of a sunken lane or trench. He has just one idea: to save his skin, to go scot-free, to defer as long as possible the moment of attack, maybe even to flee, to desert like the regiments of the Lunda Norte. He has just one dream: a wound, an honest-to-goodness wound, an accident of God that would leave him with one eye, or maimed for life, but that, like the self-inflicted mutilations of the fighters from the Vendée in 1792 who objected to "Republican" conscription, would at least have the merit of getting him out of this hell. If this chance to be wounded passes him by, he has just one serious activity: counting the hours, the days, then not even counting them anymore, since time passes so slowly; the important thing is that the order not come, the essential thing is this heavy, viscous time, spent above all in not doing battle, not having to die—let someone else die in his place! It doesn't matter who! It doesn't matter what kind of cowardice, yes, even resourcefulness or baseness, are needed—anything so that he himself can keep from fighting and dying! Subjected, and rearing back. Prostrated, but dodging. The egoism of the survivor, the final ruse of the slave, the infinitesimal freedom that remains to him.

Suicide. The suicides of soldiers are never spoken of. Or else they're spoken of, but in veiled terms, as of a shameful secret. A military secret, General Pavalic had told me in Sarajevo. Confidential military information, an Angolan leader told me when I was questioning him on a case of mass suicide, in Moxico, that the leader of a humanitarian agency had reported to me. Where would we be if we knew that there are, in the Angolan army as well, no doubt, as in all the armies in the world, people who prefer the certainty of dying right away to the risk of dying on some future day? The last freedom. A black freedom, certainly. A negative, desperate freedom, etc. But there it is. It's still a freedom. The last, only resource of freedom. Like the character in Jünger. Yes, Jünger. In a little novel from his youth, *Sturm*, published serially in the *Hannoverscher Kurier*, and which survives only in the *Complete Works*. He can't bear any more, this character. He dies from not dying. And, considering he's lost everything, already, he ends up killing himself in the toilets in his barracks. That's the only character in Ernst Jünger who has ever managed to move me deeply.

Absurd. The natural state of the herd is waiting, patience, vegetative stupidity. But all the same it sometimes has to move. Sometimes it has to wage war in the sense we usually understand it. And then it's just idiotic and misunderstood orders, disordered movements, confused shuffling in place, colossal or, on the contrary, minute commotion: it's the night where you can't tell friend from enemy, dead from living; the days darker than the nights where the units coming up to the front advance blindly, look for the leaders of the units already under fire, can't find them, take a wrong turn; it's attacks that aren't attacks; it's firing at random, it doesn't matter how or where—to kill or to cause fear? To aim at the enemy or to reassure yourself? Those terrible blind men, groping in the dark with their rifles! That Bosnian battalion, above the Donji Vakuf, which, on the last night, couldn't manage to figure out if it should advance, withdraw, shoot, or cease fire, and which, at the moment of taking action, realized that orders had been given to the soldiers, the night before, to get rid of their ammunition, in order to advance more quickly—so finally they mounted their attack holding their rifles by the barrel, like clubs. These are parodies of men; puppets; the living confused with the dead; men with heavy gestures who drag themselves along the front lines.

Animality. The animal becoming of the humanoid. Dirtiness. Dust. Water up to your belly. Your head in hardened mud, when the bombs fall. Putrid bodies that stagnate. Getting the runs when the first shooting begins. Toilets, for everyone, out in the open. Vermin. Words reduced to grunts. Torpor, most of the time. Days spent sleeping, as in the trenches in the south of Burundi, mouths open, in a heap. Hunger. Excitement when it's time for mess. How many dead today, in the battalion? So much the better, more rations for the survivors. At least, tonight, they won't have to venture beyond the front lines to rummage through the dead men's knapsacks. The mingled exhalations of night. The smells. The ugliness. "The lofty sky, not clear yet still immeasurably lofty, with gray clouds gliding slowly across it" above Prince Andrei, when he loses consciousness: come on! The low sky, you mean! A sky that's low even when it's lofty! When Prince Andrei gets his wound, the sky, as it does for all the dead, falls on his head—the rest is a joke. This halo of mystery, this impression of the supernatural, that those who return from the front and who have brushed with death emit, according to Proust—I myself have never felt, near the front lines, anything but evidence of ugliness, pestilential smells, herds fixed in place; I have seen black Saint-Loups, their eyes staring off into space, their breath become one long word—wild animals, pariahs, or paralytics.

That, then, is the true face of war. That is what we should be able to present to all those who feed the romanticism of war. "The worst thing of all," said Geoffrey Firmin, the Consul in Malcolm Lowry's *Under the Volcano*, "is to feel your soul die." Well, war is, every day, the soul's day of death.

"...I see again the Portuguese captains of April, those reds..."

And, at the same time, it's not just that. And I realize that I have sometimes, at least during my years in Bosnia, been witness to scenes that don't exactly play that way. Waiting, certainly. Fear. General reduction to a kind of bestiality. The life of the trenches, like all the lives of trenches, sucking out the last drop of human dignity. But there are also, when I think about it, cases of unexpected fraternity. Heroes. Sarajevo hoodlums who in one night became, like Captain Conan de Vercel, admirable defenders of the city. Celo. The hoodlum Celo. I often speak of him, this Celo-Conan. I like to tell about the day I met him, with his bleached-blond rocker look, his guns, his sinister-looking bodyguards, his pockets stuffed with hashish and black-market Deutsche Marks, wandering, like a soul in pain, through the ruins of the burned library where he was collecting, in the midst of the ashes, the few drifting pages that hadn't burned. And I am well aware of the questionable quality this fascination with the vigorous but large-hearted crook can have, revealed under fire: that other character in Jünger, in *Das Wäldchen 125* (Copse 125),[15] whose "adventurous tendencies" as well as his "past" as a smuggler, a criminal, and a professional fighter, have made him "a bad soldier" but a very "good warrior"; or also, in a soppier version, *The Return of Dr. O'Grady* by André Maurois: "Members of the police force will arrest more than one bandit whom, two or three years earlier, their general had embraced." But is it my fault, though, if Celo had his moment of grace? if this war had the virtue, for the space of an instant, of hoisting men like him up above their villainy? if it succeeded in making a thief into one of those spontaneous resistance fighters thanks to whom the city did not fall, on the first day, into the hands of the Serbs? General Morillon shutting himself away in Srebrenica. The Serbian general Jovan Divjak, choosing, out of love for Bosnia and the values it embodied, to remain in the besieged city. Samir Landzo, my undying friend from that day on, Samir Landzo, in the Grondj raid above Sarajevo, taking the risk of dying in order to cover me. That old reservist, professor of physics and chemistry at the Zenica high school, whom I saw, in Maglaj, confronting the Serbian bullets in order to walk between the lines, looking for a dead friend. That other one, a sort of priest, who claimed, out of bravado, to be a collector of last words and also went to look for them, under hails of bullets. That civilian who, in Sarajevo itself, in front of the Holiday Inn, rushed to help the UN blue-beret who had just been shot by a sniper, with a bullet in his throat, just between his helmet and flak-jacket: the killer was still there, surely; he could shoot again and have a second target; but there it was; the UN man was dying; his head half off, swimming in a pool of blood already black, he was untransportable; and so the Bosnian didn't move, he held his head like a mother and waited for help. And the unit that had received orders to withdraw but that didn't want to move, as long as its officer wasn't dead. And Izetbegovic. Yes, the case of Izetbegovic, this literate man, this man of texts and laws, whom I can still hear telling me, during the shooting of *Bosna!*, facing the camera: "I was not made for the role; nothing and no one prepared me for it; it just happened to me, this role of a Bosnian De Gaulle that you're giving me, like a bad fate to which I had to conform." The man Izetbegovic whom I saw again later, well after the war, when Sarajevo had resumed its pace of a small capital of a tiny Balkan state: he was tired; a little somber; he, too, had become again a modest little man, without grace, or, more precisely, whom grace had deserted, leaving him nothing but the melancholy shadow of the war leader that, against all expectations, he had succeeded in becoming; the war had transformed him; it had hauled him above himself; now that the war was over, like the Chouan leader in Balzac leading his cow to the market, he had rediscovered his true size and knew it.

So? Bestiality or greatness? Horror or dignity of war? And how can I separate myself from this contradiction, this antinomy, or as Sartre would say, this "turnstile"? Two qualities of man, above all, two modalities of being in the world; this aptitude that some have, more than others, for living two lives in one. Two levels of truth, two forms of self-evidence; both theses are verified according to how you envisage war—from the point of view of the rule or the exception, judged by the ordinary or by certain instants of grace. But, above all, two kinds of war. The same two kinds, again. Except this time I see them a little more clearly. Not atrocious wars and the wars that are less so: they all are atrocious—look at Céline, look at Barbusse, look at my experience of the nameless abomination of the siege of Sarajevo. Not wars that have a meaning and wars that don't: the distinction is blurred; it is neither as solid nor as clear as I thought; look at Céline again; look at the aporias named above; look at the ambiguity of those wars that, depending on whether you envisage them from the point of view of those who wage them or from those who witness them, from the point of view of the leaders or the infantrymen, from the civilians or the soldiers, take on a meaning or lose it. Not political as such: for by what right could I decide, as I have said, that the war in the Sudan is less political than the war in Bosnia? And the war in Sri Lanka, taken from the point of view of the little leader in Batticaloa, isn't it as charged with stakes as our great Western wars? No, the real division, the only one that counts, is the one simply of wars that make possible or do not the Conans, the heroic thieves, the heroes, the Izetbegovic's— I wonder if the real dividing line doesn't pass between wars that make a place for greatness (roughly, the "just" wars, the "antifascist" wars) and those that don't...

I know it sounds strange, this word "greatness." I know that the Nazis, the Fascists, the Soviets of the old era, the Cambodians, the Cubans, also spoke of greatness. And I know that this idea of thinking great for man, this dream of a humanity knowing how to raise itself above itself and above its baseness of principle, this illusion that man is something who can and must be surmounted, I know that all this was at the heart of all totalitarian projects. But have the totalitarians made off with the word? with the idea? Can we imagine they have monopolized a share of the nobility that, sometimes, rises up from the depths of horror? I call "forgotten wars" those wars where not the least move toward greatness is brought about anywhere. And I have a nostalgia for those other wars—Spain, the Resistance, and even Bosnia—where, despite the horror, the mud, the waiting, the bestiality that are also their lot, men do in fact sometimes touch on something that surpasses them. May my country, Europe, remember this something, and this nostalgia, if, by chance, a new adversity comes to threaten it.

"The problem is the head..."

I said: Those days are over, when there were wars where you knew, when you died, why you had been fighting.

I also said: Now the time of absurd, insane wars has arrived, when, unlike Guy Môquet walking to his execution with the certainty of sacrificing himself for a certain idea of liberty piercing his soul, now the combatant has the feeling of dying, and even of living, for nothing.

Well, that's not quite true.

Because this is the caricature of Guy Môquet.

This is the horrible caricature of those figures whom I, along with everyone else, so admired, whose example shaped me and who, long ago, in the time of the wars with meaning and panache, died in the name of an ideal, for an ideal.

Here—in the persons of the Sri Lankan kamikazes—are people about whom I could, at first sight, say pretty much the same thing as what I had said about those heroes: they, too, know why they are going to die; they, too, are sacrificing themselves for a cause that surpasses them; they, too, have the feeling, while they walk to their execution, of defending a certain idea of humanity, of the world, and even of the divine.

What is a kamikaze? The grimace of a hero. His monstrous other side. The ridiculous and hideous forgery of the Hegelian "heroic character," the man who is "fully man," ready to go beyond his "purely animal instincts," desiring what other men desire, involving himself in a struggle to the death for recognition and prestige, willing to take the risk of dying in order the better to reach his "elevated aims."

What is a kamikaze? The shadow of a martyr. His parody. The caricature, obviously abject, but still a caricature, of the magnificent figures who have peopled my anti-fascist pantheon since childhood. Take the death of Kyo, in *Man's Fate*. Take the last profile of the revolutionary mingling with the "sleeping crowd," joining this "assembly of the conquered," who are going to die with him, "even in its murmuring of complaints" and its "fraternal quavering." Take the man who has the feeling, even till his last breath, of having "fought for what, in his day, was charged with the strongest meaning and the greatest hope." Listen to him who, at the instant of dying, goes into raptures over the feeling that he is inhabited, for the last time, by the invincible dream that gave sense to life. What does death matter? Malraux insists. What would "a life for which he would not have been willing to die" be worth? And when he replies: "It is easy to die when you don't die alone," and then: It is good and beautiful when you know that you are becoming a "martyr" and that, from your "bloody legend," others will make a "golden legend," you can't keep from thinking that you aren't very far from the words that the Sri Lankan kamikaze must have in his head when he puts on his suicide vest.

They say history always strikes twice: the first times as tragedy, the second time as farce.

On the subject of humanity ready to die for an idea, Sri Lanka has taught me that it, too, has two faces: that of Kyo (and of the hero), and that of the kamikaze (and of the swine).

"... she wants nothing more of life than a visa for London or
Paris."

I find this remark by Hannah Arendt, in her *Men in Dark
Times*[16], explaining that the best thing, "in the Hegelian system
of historical revelation of the world spirit," that can happen to
any individual is "to have the good fortune to be born among
the right people at the right historical moment": Greek, not
barbarian, in the times of Solon and Pericles; Roman, not
Greek, in the time of Augustus and the beginning of the Pax
Romana; Christian, not Jewish, when Europe was becoming
Christianized and when the pogroms were beginning; a theorem
that, transposed to today, in the beginning of the twenty-first
century, at this time when the "Universal Spirit" continues
more than ever, in the words of Hegel as read and commented
on by Arendt, to be embodied in the "particular principles" of
people who, giving it its "specific form," are the "privileged
agents of History"; at this time when, moreover, the "special"
people of the moment, in other words Westerners, lay claim to
the additional privilege of being the last of their kind, the final
stage of the history of the mind, the only ones about whom it
is certain that no other candidate will come, as they did themselves, to dethrone them from the great theater of world
history—a theorem, then, that becomes roughly: The best that
can happen to a subject is to be born a Westerner; the worst, the

irremediable catastrophe, the very figure of misfortune, of the tragic, of damnation, is to be born Burundian, Angolan, South-Sudanese, Colombian, or, like little Srilaya, Sri Lankan.

I also remember that day, in a restaurant in Sarajevo, when one of my friends realized, a few hours before the departure of the big UN plane that carried out airlifts to the Croatian coast and which he was, in principle, supposed to board, that he had mislaid his passport. It wasn't such a big thing, when you were French, and a journalist, to mislay your passport in Sarajevo. But it made life complicated. The bureaucracy of the United Nations being what it was, it prevented him from taking the plane he had planned to take, and even—who knows?—the ones in the next few days. The journalist was tired, too. He was just returning from a difficult assignment, outside of Sarajevo, and for days now had been hoping, without saying so, just to leave the hell of this war. And there we were, with our Bosnian friends, starting, calmly at first, and then with a certain nervousness, to look for this wretched lost passport: under the restaurant tables? in the cloakroom? forgotten in another café? at K.'s? at the hotel? stolen? Wasn't there, in besieged Sarajevo, a trafficking of stolen passports, and wasn't it possible that a valorous foreign correspondent, a friend of Bosnia if ever there was one, was its latest victim? That's the time, I remember, when our Bosnian friends didn't have any passports at all. Or more precisely they did, but they were useless passports, passports for nothing, almost false—they were passports that forbade them to take any plane they liked and, in fact, sealed them away in their own besieged city. So that there was something at once distressing, pathetic, and a little obscene in the spectacle of this shared searching fever: like looking for a rope in the house of a hanged man... or papers

in the house of a man without any... those without papers
themselves who, out of a mixture of kindness and unawareness,
as if they forgot for an instant their fate as definitive paperless
citizens, or that they found in this—who knows?—an occasion
to play at being normal Europeans who had known in another
life (and who suddenly remember) 1.what "papers" means; 2.the
trouble it is, for a normal European, to lose the papers in
question; 3.the slight panic that seizes him when, as he is
supposed to board a plane, he discovers he is temporarily—oh
very temporarily!—without papers—the real paperless ones,
then, getting involved in the fever of the search for the lost
papers... As absurd as that seems, I have the impression, looking
back on it, of having rarely felt as close to my Bosnian friends as
during those few hours of confusion and hesitation when the
inconvenience of a passport lost by a compatriot who could have
been me made me put my finger on what they actually mean
when they spoke of Sarajevo as of a giant prison to which the
UN held the keys. And above all I think I rarely experienced the
shame I felt than when, at the end of those two hours, when, all
together, the real prisoners and the false ones, the ones locked up
for a day and those locked up forever, we had turned the restaurant upside-down, Kemal Muftic, with the enigmatic half-smile
of one who had understood everything and who was surely not
the last one to size up the indecency of the situation, announced
they had found the precious document, and that a friend was on
his way to bring it back just in time for the departure of the
flight of "Maybe Airlines": the comedy was over, and so was the
brief illusion of this sharing of fate—the French journalist recov-
ered his right to leave, and his inestimable privilege, and he
abandoned the Bosnians to their solitude for good.

These two notes—Arendt, the passport—what do they say? That, as time passes, as experiences accumulate, I've acquired the conviction that the major inequality between humans, the one that separates them the most irredeemably, the one for which progress, History, the good will of some, can do, for now, almost nothing, is neither good luck, nor knowledge, nor power, nor know-how, nor any of the other graces that nature or the world dispenses, but this other division that, in situations of extreme distress, distinguishes those who have the chance to be able to leave from those who know they are going to stay. The allies of the damned on one side; the friends of the modern Job; the companions of a day or a few days; the infiltrated ones; the mercenaries of Good; all those fortunate ones who, whatever part they take in the suffering of others, whatever ardor they have in being an activist, a sympathizer, of becoming the spokes-people for the voiceless, of going on-location, trekking all day, following them into their trenches, under their bombs, all of them do what they do knowing that there is this little difference that changes everything: they can leave whenever they like... And, on the other side, the Bosnians locked up, the Burundians riveted to their night, the Angolans for whom the entire horizon seems to have to be, till the end of time, the liquid mire of those mines where they work like forced slaves, or else my young Sri Lankan kamikaze who knows she is hunted down, pursued, con-demned to death by the sect she has deserted and who, when she confesses to me that she hopes for nothing else from existence but this visa for London or Paris, means that the most invaluable of all rights is the one to move, to leave—this inalienable right to leave about which Baudelaire said it should be inscribed, along with the right to contradict yourself, in a declaration of the rights of man worthy of this name—but she knows, herself, that it will certainly be the last right granted her.

These two notes—the grave inconvenience of being born Sri Lankan, Burundian, Angolan; the way Sarajevo was, for four years, transformed into a shooting range, a laboratory for the inhuman, an open-air prison where a few of us went, sometimes, to visit—like a humble codicil, really, to this *Portrait de l'aventurier* by Roger Stéphane that was one of my childhood books and about which I rambled on so in the final pages of my *Sartre: The Philosopher of the Twentieth Century*. Two types of adventurer. There are two methods of sharing suffering and fate on which, it should be said, neither Sartre nor Stéphane dwells. Those who, like the heroes of the detective novels I always carry with me and that I devour, like Sartre in fact, when covering a story, hear themselves saying, during their infiltration into the country, behind the front lines, or in the heart of an enemy network: "If it turns out badly, you'll manage; you'll exfiltrate through your own means; the CIA won't recognize you"—the "Mission Impossible" syndrome, the "River of No Return" schema, absolute heroism, supreme merit, but who, today, can aspire to that? And the one who, on the other hand, like most war reporters, like humanitarians, like the Blue-Berets, like me, knows, the instant he leaves, and whatever risk he may be inclined to take, when and how he will return: by parachute, yes, but with exit guaranteed—that's the limit of his fraternity.

I'll return to this idea of dying, or not dying, "for an idea."

Often, they say: A cause for which men are capable of dying is a holy, invincible cause.

Or, conversely: A cause for which I would not be ready to sacrifice my life—a revolution, or a hope, for which I would not be willing to take the risk of death—would have no chance of triumphing and, moreover, wouldn't deserve to triumph.

Or again—the argument of Régis Debray in a page of *Loués soient nos seigneurs,* as well as the argument already advanced by Alexandre Kojève in the famous interview with Gilles Lapouge for *La Quinzaine littéraire* which was, unless I'm mistaken, his final discourse and in which, reasserting that the end of History "was not Napoleon, but Stalin," he declared he had been living, for fifty years, as the true "conscience of Stalin." Debray: If the events of May '68 don't deserve respect, if it was nothing but a weak and inconsequential psychodrama, that's because they cared about "unfettered enjoyment," whereas the true activist is one who is ready to "die for the cause." Kojève: If the rebels of '68 were people who weren't serious, if they were false rebels who forgot about the idea of revolution at the very moment they thought they were restoring it to its prestige and its symbols, that's because they had neither the sense nor the taste for the "Tragic," and the idea of taking the risk of dying, to make it prevail, was foreign to them.

This proof through martyrdom, this idea that it's in the blood that the truth of a world or a combat lies, is also the theorem of the kamikaze.

This myth of blood, this blood as myth, this prejudice according to which blood is nobility itself, the vehicle of the highest virtues, the absolute marker of truth, which would, when it is put into play, mark the courage or greatness of a man—this is an idea that's both racist (Boulainvilliers and the birth of modern racism) and dangerously topical (the kamikazes, all the kamikazes, whether they are Tamil, Palestinian, or Afghan).

Or: this drunkenness of bloodshed, this passion of sacrificing yourself so that the promised kingdom, whatever its form, can come, this haematology, this haematomania, was, beyond the kamikazes of yesterday and today, one of the motivating forces of the various kinds of fascism in the twentieth century, and it was even, if you listen to people of the time, the real reason for their influence over the overcautious, cunning democrats, ready to do anything except die to defend their ideas. It was, moreover, one of the obsessions of the "Collège de Sociologie" that urged the swift creation, to face up to the "Nazi religion," of a counter-religion, even, for some, a "super-fascism," which would have the merit of returning the sense of the Tragic and of blood to those who had lost it.

But let's make no mistakes!

It was also, precisely, the principle that in the end guided the best of those contemporaries in question.

It was the heart of the anti-Munich discourse of 1938, then of all the anti-fascists who, in the following months and years, ended up by waking up and realizing that there was something worse than war, worse than death, and that this worst thing of all was Hitlerism.

It was the conviction of the fighters in the Warsaw ghetto, then of the insurgents of Sobibor as Claude Lanzmann tells about them in his film, when, in the second-to-last stage of their martyrdom, having the feeling of reaching the end of what is humanly possible to endure, they placed their lives at risk and preferred the danger of dying to the certainty of being treated, till the end, like dogs.

It had been, long before that, and would be long after, the driving force of all the rebelling populations in the world, the instant they decide to say "no" to something intolerable that, until then, had imposed itself on them under the guise of a so-called necessity. There is no revolt, no insurrection against tyrants and barbarians, no serious venture for liberty or equality, without this leap into the unknown of a dreamed-of salvation. And for this leap to be possible the risk of nothingness must be taken knowingly.

Even better, and more unexpected, is, if you believe Emmanuel Levinas, the correlation of the theme of "the chosen," that is to say this "moral sovereignty" that makes a nation, any nation, and not just, of course, the "Jewish nation," conduct itself as if "it had to answer for all nations": being chosen is nothing other, he says in a very curious passage in *Difficult Freedom*, than taking this risk of ontological responsibility; being chosen is nothing other, consequently, in his words, than "the ability to die for an idea."

In short, the worst and the best.

The worst bastards and, also, the honor of mankind.

This idea that the proof of an idea is that to defend it one is ready to go to the end of one's own life is the classic example of those twofold ideas that, in the long war that brings them into conflict, the friends of freedom—the democrats—and the enemies of freedom in turn seize hold of.

What is the difference, then? What distinguishes the taste for blood of some from that of others? What separates the "dying for one's ideas" of the perpetrator of a suicide attack in Jerusalem from that of the wonderful writer of *Difficult Freedom*? In a word, what makes the division between the sacrificial exaltation of the kamikaze who is persuaded that, thanks to his deed, he will go straight to heaven, to the right hand of the Lord—and the reasoned disturbance of all the instincts of survival in one who, suddenly, decides to be no longer content with simply surviving?

I see again Srilaya, in our hotel restaurant.

I think back to her hardness, of course. Her clinical coldness when evoking those former comrades with whom she shared a part of her adventure. Her very concentrated manner, eyebrows furrowed, like a man, when she lit a cigarette. And then, suddenly, with no warning, and as if she had changed genders according to currents in the conversation, a nuance of gentleness, then tenderness, and even, I'd swear it, of flirtatiousness in her expression or gesture. Her pink eyelids. The childlike trembling of her lips, over magnificent teeth, when she tried not to smile. Her finger on her lips, mutinous, when, still smiling, she insisted on not answering. Flashes of mischievousness in her gaze. This streak of gaiety, of good humor, that her season in hell obviously had not exhausted completely. I intuit that she is joyous. In love. I try to guess, under her mask of gravity, and under her light dress, the exquisite lover she could have been, or that she will one day be, but whom this war has thwarted. And then the fixity of her pale eyes, again, when a customer entered the room—she knew that her killers were hot on her trail, that they were looking for her and would surely end up, if she remained in Colombo, finding her whereabouts.

I do not know what has become of Srilaya. Maybe she ended up getting her visa for London or Paris. Maybe not. All I know is that she wanted to live. Just to live, and not to die. She knew, of course, that by leaving her sect of assassins, and by bearing witness against it, she was placing herself in the position of being killed at any moment. But risk is not certainty. All witnesses are not martyrs. There was hope in Srilaya. There was joy. Whereas there was, with the Tigers, only hatred for others, hatred of self, despair, sad passions: not just to put your life at risk to defend your ideas and take the risk of dying, but to die, really die, without the shadow of a hesitation, or of a doubt, or of a regret, or of a choice.

Some risk death, but through love of life; others don't risk it, they run to it, because in reality they love nothing but death.

Some (as in the story of the Warsaw ghetto and, as Lanzmann says, of the Jews' reappropriation of violence) don't have a choice: you either risk death or you die; you prefer a possible death not just to humiliation, to being reduced to the level of an animal, but to certain death. Others (this is the root of the kamikaze mentality and, as Foucault said about the Iranian revolution, the state of mind of these "crowds ready to advance towards death in the drunkenness of sacrifice")[17] have a choice: they could not die;

no final solution threatens them; they have the possibility, for instance, of negotiating with the Sri Lankan authorities; and so it's freely, with sovereign power, in full and absolute awareness, that they make the choice of *viva la muerte.*

An anti-fascist is someone who, in other words, resolves to shed blood (his own, or that of others) only in desperation and in the hope, by doing so, of loosening the vice that condemns him to death—this mixture of despair and hope, of the blackest pessimism and of methodical optimism, about which I have always thought that it formed the heart of the culture of resistance. A fanatic, a kamikaze, has the cult of death for death's sake, pain for pain's sake, and yet they walk toward martyrdom, and wish for their own execution, full of hope, with joy in their hearts, in a state of jubilation matched only by the desolation of their victims—the same mixture, but the other way round; the same combination of darkness and light but in symmetrical doses; a fascist, a fundamentalist, an extremist, is neither, as everybody usually thinks, "a pessimist"; nor, as I have sometimes said, "an optimist"; he is a failed crossbreeding of the two—the only way, in this case, to escape moralism.

I'm not saying, however, that the two kinds are completely distinct.

I don't think they are like two distinct, incompatible substances.

The case of Che Guevara, for instance, and the very strange cult devoted to him from one end of the planet to the other. Secular or Christian warrior? Did he die in combat or commit suicide? Did he love revolution at the risk of dying for it, or was revolution a pretext for his love of death?

Or else the case of that Iranian revolution as Foucault experienced it, then told about it in a series of famous but little-known texts. The authenticity of the uprising on one hand; the risk, lost but that matters little, taken for a greater liberty; the good exchange, in a word, of an almost unlivable life for a life that is less so and that involves, in this hope, the very principle of survival (Foucault was right—whatever they say, and whatever the horror of what was to come—to admire these men and women who preferred, he said, and each word counts, "the risk of death to the certainty of having to obey"; he was right to be moved by this very brief moment when "in front of the gallows and the machine-guns, men rise up" and when, the "powers" now "powerless to do anything more," life, suddenly, "can no longer have value"). And then fanaticism on the other side; hatred; total war, not against the Shah, but already against the West; and, faced with this contemptible West, the drunkenness, not of hope, or of possible victory, or of a moral superiority for which confrontation would provide a proof, but sacrificial dementia, self-abnegation, expiatory masochism, death given and welcomed (and that's, obviously, the dark side of the event—that's what very quickly established Khomeneism in the lineage of great barbarities).

But finally the distinction, even if it is not perfect, functions.

It isn't a bad marker, in any case in my opinion, of those revolts about which I no longer think, as before, that they were "always right" to carry out.

And above all it allows us to see what kind of actual relationship there is between both of them—it allows us to understand better why it can't be said that, in his struggle against the democrat, the kamikaze always, necessarily, has the advantage.

Do not be afraid of the kamikaze.

What interests him in risking death is not the risk, but death.

What he loves in war is not "to conquer or die" but to die and above all not to conquer.

His main concern is not, as Clausewitz says, to adjust his efforts to the force of the enemy's resistance, to bring him down, to crush him. His main concern is to die.

"I had come there to meet Sirimavo Bandaranaike, back from
Bangladesh and its war..."

I was a little over twenty years old. I was one of those who, at the
age of twenty, would never have said it was "the best years of my
life." I said the flesh was sad. I claimed I had read all the books. *
And, in the manner of Rimbaud, I added that nothing was left to
the "valorous" but to "flee, to flee away," to escape the boredom of
this Switzerland of the Spirit that France had become. And into
this principle of departure, into this plan to "flee, flee away" to go
look elsewhere, in the heart of deepest Asia, for the breath of great
History, which was stifled and exhausted where we were, there
slipped a mass of reasons, not all very acceptable, some of which
even seem to me, in hindsight, outright laughable or regrettable.

An old story, in fact. The eternally old story of belated adolescence, leaving for the ends of the earth to look for a remedy
for your malaise. Bangladesh, in this case, was not my first concern. It was a pretext. A theater. It was the occasion for an egotis-
tical production in which I couldn't say which mattered
most—romanticism, nostalgia for action, fascination with the
East or even with the very warrior aesthetic that, today, fills me
with horror. If I went there, if I stayed there much longer
(September 1971 - May 1972) than was necessary for the series
of articles I was supposed to write about it and that I had, of

---

* Alluding to "Brise marine (Sea Breeze)," the sonnet of Mallarmé—Trans.

course, not written, if I forced myself, first in the jungle, and then in liberated Dhaka, to share, as much as was possible, the life of the Bengalis themselves, it was less, I'm afraid, to help them than to help myself, to save myself, to redeem myself and expiate some sort of shortcoming—scholarly, middle-class, or French—it's not entirely as a journalist, or of course as a fighter, or even in the manner of the "engaged" intellectual that, afterwards, I wanted to take as example, but rather as that more light-hearted, more uncertain, and, at bottom, more irresponsible adventurer who surprised Sartre, in his preface to Roger Stéphane's *Portrait de l'aventurier*, by "asking men who didn't choose their fight to legitimize a death that he, himself, had utterly chosen." I had not, of course, reached that point. But neither was I more reasonable or more lucid. And there was, in this Sartrean portrayal of the adventurer, a lot of characteristics that fitted the person I was then.

I didn't read—my generation didn't read—much Sartre back then. But I had read Byron. I loved the idea of D'Annunzio, flying over enslaved Trieste and scattering his liberating poems below. I had read T. E. Lawrence's *The Seven Pillars of Wisdom* and Victor Serge's *Memoirs of a Revolutionary*. I extolled Malraux—the Malraux of *Man's Fate*, of Indochina, of *Man's Hope*, of the war in Spain, of the "España" squadron. In short, I was living in the shadow—not to say under the tutelage—of those mercenary writers who, from Missolonghi* to the International Brigades in the Spanish Civil War, passing by the Winter Palace or the deserts of Arabia, had in common the fact of having fought in countries, under flags, or for causes, which they had, in all logic, no reason to call their own. And it's clear that

---

* Missolonghi, Greece, where Lord Byron died—Trans.

it's these models, these lessons of lyric and epic illusion, as well as, let's be frank, the example of another of my fellow-students, older than me by a few years, Régis Debray, whom I first held in mind when, after having heard Malraux—pathetic, convulsed, and, at the same time, magnificent—launch on television his appeal for the formation of an "international brigade for Bengal," I took, one October morning, the path of my "Red India."*

Officially, I was a serious activist, a died-in-the-wool materialist, steeped in Marxist culture, who was leaving for the vanguard of a "just struggle for liberation" with the firm intention of creating a theory for it. And that is, moreover, what I finally attempted to do in the book that, as I look back on it now, is a strange mixture, absurdly scholarly, filled with notes and references, and, to my eyes today, almost unreadable, that I brought back from the adventure and that, on Louis Althusser's recommendation, François Maspero published: three hundred pages of dense analysis on the functioning of the post-colonial states, the role of the single party as "arbiter of the dominant classes," or the necessity, in Bengal and elsewhere, of "dislodging the feudal elements checking the development of capitalism"; a somewhat insane erudition on the "proletarian internationalism" of Abdul Huq and Charu Mazumdar; terribly weighty developments around the concepts of "internal colonialization" and the "nationalization of imperialism" that I thought of, in my first text on the Chiapas, as my personal contribution, my stone added, to the theoretical edifice of triumphant Althusserism; no first-person accounts, in other words; no portrayals, or self-portraits, or anecdotes, or personal thoughts; I was indeed, from this point of view, the child of my time, of its frenetic theoreticism,

---

* *Les Indes rouges* is the title of Lévy's book on Bangladesh, first published in 1973 —Trans.

of its religion of "structures," of "epistemological building-blocks" and other "procedures without a subject"; I would have felt I was dishonored—and with a dishonor that had the name (oh how ignominious!) of "idealism"—by the very idea of wasting my time with subjective impressions of Asia; I insisted on saying very loudly that the only acceptable thing, in political literature as I conceived of it, was the great abstract rhetoric of the most rigorous Marxism-Leninism.

In reality it was, obviously, more complicated. I was, in my inmost depths, and despite the censorship, the punishments, that I inflicted on myself, more a Malraux than an Althusser; more an adventurer than a dialectician; in love with action, with panache, with physical and political prowess, at least as much as with thought; and, even if I needed ten long years to admit it, even if I didn't agree to write it until the preface to the 1985 reprint of the book, I am well aware, in hindsight, that these interminable thoughts on the Chinese concept of "social-imperialism," on the necessity of "Vietnamizing the Ganges delta," or on the political and economical misdeeds of "communalist ideology," were an alibi, a cover, or in any case a mental exercise—I know that, relatively speaking (but did I know, at the time, how to "speak relatively"?), what I expected from this journey was what my other teachers, my teachers in turmoil, expected from fraternity, from the great light rising in the East, or from the flight to Aden: an increase in lucidity, an extra quantum of existence, a transformation into awareness of the greatest possible accumulation of experience, an expansion of my self to the dimensions of an unknown theater, a way of feeling important, a form of Salvation—all things that had nothing to do, I repeat, either with the rights of man or with the misery of the world. Oh the childish disappointment and, almost simultaneously, the obscure pride when, having arrived in Calcutta, and presenting myself at the French Consulate, I discovered that I was seemingly the only person to have heard Malraux's summons, and that there wasn't a trace, at the scene, of his Brigades being formed!

Do I have to make it clear that all this happened in 1971, just a little more than three years after that other commotion, the "May uprising," in which, according to rumor, I was supposed to have taken part from my room, between a transistor radio and an ordnance map?

It's too beautiful to be true, this legend. And the truth is that I am one of those people who, on the contrary, immediately felt the importance of the event as well as of this event-within-an-event that was the birth, in Paris, of an intellectual current, Maoism, whose radicality, wish for purity, desire to "break History in half," to make a "tabula rasa" of the past and to reshape man "into the most profound part of himself," made an overwhelming impression on me, and seemed to me to be the harbinger of a new age—as the last words of the foreword to my *Barbarism with a Human Face* (and other passages) testify, where I characterized this Maoism, a bit bombastically, as a "major page in the history of France," in accord with Louis Althusser, or the series of enthusiastic articles that I had, a few days before my departure for Bengal, written for Philippe Tesson's *Combat* and devoted to the hundred flowers of the "Leftist" press of the time (Hallier's *L'Idiot international*; the Proletarian Left's *La Cause du peuple*; *Tout*, the mouthpiece for the small anarchist-Maoist group "Vive la Révolution").

But it's not completely false either, this legend. Its share of truth is that I was not a major actor in the movement. Although I took the small revolutionary groups that were the guiding light of those days for their true worth, although linked both in thought and in friendship with a number of figures of this Maoist movement, although understanding rather quickly, it seems to me, what was really at stake in this affair (roughly: it was the only "language" that the men and women of my generation had available to take leave of Stalinism; a supporting foundation that was used, making it bear the weight of the lever, to dismantle the entire system of "revisionist" ideologies; a wedge in the tenon; a Trojan horse, a vanguard of enemy forces that, from within, was working to destroy it; a way, a detour, a trick of History, the eye of a needle, where the threat of this leftist anti-Communism was beginning to inch its way in, the elaboration of which, I maintain today, was the honor of my generation), I was not an activist in the strict sense of the word. The truth is that I was too individualistic, too skeptical, too resistant to all forms of indoctrination, too neurotically rebellious towards any kind of belonging about which I could not have the feeling, even if illusory, that it began, ended, and found its reasoning in me alone and with me, to be a true revolutionary. I don't take pride in that. I don't draw from that any more glory than I do any particular shame. That's just how it is. There was—there is—an association of former "thisses." There was—there is—a brotherhood of former "thats". The fact is I wasn't one. The fact is that I am still not one. And the fact that I am not one is perhaps not unconnected, incidentally, to the necessity I suddenly find myself feeling to produce, to fabricate from whole cloth, starting from nothing in a way, my own adopted family, my own belonging—my opponents would say: my "network"...

So, is this linked to that? Did I go to Bangladesh because I was angry at myself for not having done enough in May '68? And, since I've said the word, did some share of expiation, of penitence, enter into this way of adding to the requirement, of overplaying militant activism, of raising a little higher, in short, the bar of radicality in order to forgive myself for an involvement that I deemed too half-hearted—a bit like, *mutatis mutandis*, the Sartre syndrome that, although behaving beyond reproach during the Occupation, though founding "Sous la botte" and then "Socialisme et Liberté," though, after his return from captivity, steadily maintaining his link with people like Cavaillès, Kahn, Leiris, and, more generally, the team of Les Lettres françaises, he still felt remorse for not having done more, despite everything, and for not giving enough of his life as an intellectual in order, afterwards, to feel forgiven for it? Maybe. Maybe this entire adventure, the book I drew from it—as well as everything in my life up to now, including this book, which came out of that original scene—can be read from the point of view of my half-missed encounter with the events of '68 and, beyond the events, with that post-May of all the radical movements where the most active, the most turbulent, often too the most brilliant, elements of my generation were launched.

If I needed only one proof of what I am suggesting, one single sign, then it would be, in the book itself, *Les Indes rouges*, where I hardly recognize myself, the excessive importance I assigned to the great schism that was, at the same time, tearing apart the international Communist religion and of which the Indian sub-continent seemed to me to be the epicenter, with its Russian and Chinese influences, its two parties officially at war, who settled their arguments with revolvers in the streets of Calcutta, its "Naxalites"—the local Maoists—whom they shot at like rabbits on the roofs of their prisons. That the question of the schism as such interested me passionately—that, in effect, is one thing. It is conceivable that this duel of legitimacy between Soviet and Chinese communisms seemed to me to give matter for reflection, that I could spend months and months collecting, all throughout Bengal, the "pamphlets," both moronic and insane, that the Naxalites produced and then in having them translated as if they were invaluable documents. Moreover it's from that point, from that thinking on Communism in general, and Sovietism in particular, that the few pages of the book came that seem to me still relevant today. But was so much dialectical acrobatics necessary to defend the indefensible Chinese foreign policy? so much rhetorical energy to develop the theme, which was a commonplace in the Maoist literature of the time, of the heroic "war of the people" mutely stifled by "Socialist-imperialism"? And as to the Naxalites themselves, as to those Maoist fighters no doubt killed in the prisons of Calcutta, but who all the same had distinguished themselves, previously, by a political line advocating terrorism, the physical elimination of territorial ownership, generalized popular war or, in the style of Cambodia before the fact, the "surrounding of cities by countrysides," would they have inspired in me such a confused indulgence if I had not, through them, paid off all my other debts? Ah! this somber logic of raising the ante whose consequences I know only too well and that has, throughout my entire life, made me do so many stupid things! It's obviously at that point that everything takes shape. There where the very first act is played out. As if I couldn't manage to absolve myself for my activist half-heartedness except by going to extremes in some way and by adding defiance to radicalism.

To be brief. Nizan left the Ecole Normale because he saw in it "a comical and often odious object, presided over by a small, patriotic, hypocritical, and powerful old man who respected the military." Half a century later, the set had changed. The comical object had become the den of Althusser. The old school, lair of the "watchdogs"* of the author of *Aden Arabie*, had become the place where, for years, the immense Jacques Lacan officiated. And under guise of "the military" one often met there frightening young people whom I saw, with the military writings of Mao in one hand and the epistemology of Georges Canguilhem in the other, mount an attack, without me, on a heaven that seemed to me, nonetheless, eminently desirable. So that, if I left, if I took the path of my Indian Aden, if I put into effect this initial distancing, which would be followed by many others, and which made me, for almost a year, desert, for a time, all the student and activist scenes, it was less out of disgust than out of pique; less to leave the scene than because I was desperately looking for a way to enlist in a different way, and for good; less to turn my back on a time whose spirit I had, in my soul and conscience, disavowed, than to find this spirit elsewhere, on a terrain that was my own and where I was quite certain, this time, of not being too disturbed by my contemporaries. Pride. Drunkenness and love of self. I'm not sure I have so much sympathy for this character that I was and who seems to me, seen from here, so uselessly complicated.

But that's not all. I fully realize, while I write these lines and while the images from that time come back to me as pale

---

* Allusion to a title of Paul Nizan's—Trans.

reflections, that I cannot reduce this story to that alone. And, whatever precautions I might take to avoid the traps of complacency, whatever concern I have not to let myself off easily with a pleasant role, I can't content myself with saying that, during the six months of this Bengali adventure, I lived only with the bad conscience of May '68 and its sequel.

For I also remember another May, and another Ecole Normale. I remember those absurd evenings when we rambled on, as if the fate of the proletarians of the whole world depended, not to speak of our own, about some detail or other of Engels' *Peasant War in Germany* or Lin Biao's *Long Live the Victory of the People's War*. I remember those parodies of knightly vigils, in the Cavaillès auditorium, where we listened in a pious silence to a young leader of the "Core Vietnam Committee" from the Rue d'Ulm explaining to us, on the blackboard, the thousand and one "philosophical" subtleties of the strategy of Pham Van Dong. I remember those coarser, almost violent debates where we confronted each other over what meaning should be given to the concepts of "the gap," "rupture," "reversal," "turnaround," "revolution," without it being made clear that these dichotomies were only "epistemological" and these ruptures "theoretical." I remember subversions that were never so stern, so pure, so grimly led and proclaimed, as when they concerned the peasants of the High Middle Ages, the distant soldiers of North Vietnam, or the "practice" of a scholar opening, closing, exploring, or re-exploring a continent of science. And finally I remember those early winter mornings when Louis Althusser, via a short and deliberately enigmatic telephone call, summoned me to the Rue d'Ulm; where, with the air of a conspirator preparing, far from prying eyes, his big philosophical night, he led me, scarcely arrived, into the inner courtyard of the school, just behind the office-apartment he occupied until his wife Hélène's death and where, in the rare moments of peace that his illness, repeated hospitalizations, and trephinations granted him, he received his students; Hélène, sometimes, looked in through the half-open leather door; they exchanged a funny knowing look that for a long time seemed to me the very sign of love between equals; and we stayed for hours working there, in the gravel path, then around the "basin of Ernests"*—I, listening, and he, with a pensive brow, his fine thickened by a slightly puffy mouth (overuse of medication?), his hands in the pockets of his wool plaid bathrobe, his glance charged with hints that I had to figure out for myself as he explained to me, without saying too much, the place he was reserving for me in his strategy for conquest, for control, for subversion of intellectual power in France!

There weren't many people left, you'll say, who would respond then to this bizarre summons. And the actual "Maos" had long ago stopped following Althusser. True. But in fact they had followed him. They had received his imprint. They had all, to a greater or lesser degree, kept his warlike, almost military conception of political debate and of the world. And the phenomenon was even in the process of taking on extremely unsettling proportions with the strategy called the "Nouvelle Résistance Populaire," which I have always thought was a distant effect of this hallucinatory Althusserism, and in which France was becoming nothing less than a new Nazi country; its middle class, a new occupying army; its communists, collaborators; its factories, concentration camps; its workshops on strike, the "Maquis," "free zones," "bases of support," "partisan regions"; and they, the "Maos," a people of

---

* The fountain in the courtyard of the Ecole Normale; the "Ernests" are fish—Trans.

"Resistance members," "veterans," "conscripts," in the process of fomenting, in the shadows, the conditions of the great anti-fascist insurrection of tomorrow.

I am making none of this up. I am not even exaggerating. For that's literally what was being formulated. That is how, every week, in *La Cause du Peuple*, in *Tout*, or in *Les Cahiers du Mai*, these intrepid revolutionaries expressed themselves. And the more time passed, the more the madness increased—and the more I had the feeling of living in a strange world where, by dint of covering the sky with dreams and chimeras, the best of us (the most brilliant, the most learned, but also, it should be said, the ones who pushed the demands of morality furthest) ended up inventing for themselves false wars waged with false weapons against phantom enemies.

Well, in a sense, of course, so much the better. Yes, so much the better that these wars were false. So much the better that the weapons were loaded with blanks. And so much the better, as they've said a hundred times, and it's true, that these "new resistants" remained at the stage of imaginary terrorism. But, at the time, it troubled me. This insistence on feigning war, this comedy of violence and challenge, these crucifixions for fun and these schoolboy pranks transformed into great resistance operations, ended up seeming obscene to me. And whatever seriousness there was in me, as well as, probably, whatever authentic anti-fascist tradition I possessed, reared up every day a little more confronting what seemed to me an unbearable imposture, mixed with sacrilege.

Pierre Goldman, at the same time, was nursing similar feelings about the "psychodrama" of '68. And Régis Debray, as I was to learn a little later, after his return from Camiri, during our first meeting at the Socialist Party Congress in Grenoble, wasn't very far from this standpoint either. I knew the texts by Georges Bataille, thirty years earlier, denouncing, in the "surrealist attitude," the same "style of exaggerated provocation," without repercussions in reality. It's while thinking about that, as well as about Sartre and Nizan, that one October morning, tired of hearing talk about invisible enemies, unfindable revolutions, and civil wars that everyone knew existed only in people's heads, I decided to react—by going, without delay, in search of actual History.

Oh! of course, this wasn't the Spanish Civil War. This wasn't the great anti-fascist war that I too dreamed of. I didn't even have, it seems to me, the feeling of certainty that I would have twenty years later, in Bosnia, when I chose the Bosnian side. And truth forces me to say that I was somewhat disappointed, right away, by these obscure, indecipherable battles, where, not content with spending my time, like Stendhal's Fabrice at Waterloo, looking for and not finding the battles that hid themselves (I have learned, since then, that such is the usual lot of all wars), I had the greatest difficulties in the world, between the Soviet tanks supporting the Bengalis and the Pakistani army rabble whose crimes were enumerated for me, in maintaining my bias.

But in the end it was a war. A real war. With tanks. Strategies that were deployed. Men who really did go underground, who grew moldy in their trenches, who busied themselves with trifling chores in a state of vegetative stupidity quite similar to what I observed in the countries of my "damned"—but who, because they believed, unlike the Burundians, the Angolans, or the South-Sudanese, in the sacred cause of their country's independence, still fought a little. It was a war of positions in Jessore, where the Pakistani army withdrew without encountering any opposition—it was a war of attack a little lower down, in a village whose name escapes me and where units of elite Indians mounted an attack using knives. It was a clean war in one place, where you saw enemy officers negotiating cease-fire around a cup of tea, in the shadow of a palm tree—it was a dirty war in some other place, where they said the mutilated bodies were found of those who weren't able to flee in time, half devoured by dogs. In short, it was a complete war. It was a perfect war. It was a war for real, the one I had come to find.

I had my dose, if you like. My shot of reality. And if, in hindsight, I had to calculate what this first expedition to the damned brought me, in the short and the long term, I would say, in no particular order: to be able to put a finger, for the first time, on the substrate of crime and cruelty that is the real secret of the human species; to understand what a mass grave is, what kind of smell it gives off, and how decomposing human meat is the inescapable horizon of today's wars; the cities; to sense how, in the cities, on moonless nights, when the evil rumor of an attack or bombardment arrives, humanity enters into turmoil, everyone for himself, sacred egoism, the wailing of children that are trampled underfoot you'll find, in the early morning, crushed into the dust; what Bangladesh taught me is a little bit of the underside of things, a little of their hidden face, a little of this basis of carnage, of primal butchery, on which the illusion of even successful communities is built; it's not impossible that these few months were the experienced origin, the first intuition, of that series of books that, from *Barbarism with a Human Face* to *Sartre*, finally did nothing but try to isolate this obscure home of Evil that is at the heart of the social bond and that war causes to flower.

Does that mean I liked it? That I could take pleasure in these abominable scenes? And was he even a little bit right, the young commander of the Mukti Fouj who, one night, when he was recalling the memory of one of his best supporters, dead a few days before, and that, for another, Muslim, supporter, they had just finished digging a little grave, a little further on, suddenly declared: "You journalists, that's why you're here... admit it, you're still goddamned filthy voyeurs." This commander's name was Akim Mukherjee. I remember his words. I remember his attitude. I can see again, as if I were there, in the gleam of the storm lantern placed on the table between us, his teeth made red by betel nut, his fierce gaze and smile, when he said: "damned voyeurs." And I think, above all, of the appearance I must have presented, of the panic that seized me and of my sudden inability to give any kind of reply to a remark that was certainly common-place, but that troubled me beyond reason.

For on one hand, of course, there was horror. On one hand, yes, there was the share of savagery that this war freed in every-one, and that terrified me. There were empty villages, where there remained, when we arrived, nothing but beggars or madmen. There were those dead bodies, mutilated or burned in their Jeeps, that were rotting by the roadsides. There was that fragile, happy student, the day he joined Akim's company, to whom they passed his cartridge belt and rifle—I learned later on, a long time after the war, that he had chosen to commit suicide rather than partic-ipate in a particularly dangerous attack. There were, also later on, when the war was already over, those two "Biharis" (collaborators with the Pakistanis) chained up, on the main square in Dhaka, their hands painfully joined in a gesture of supplication, their gaze mad, where all that could be read was the meager request for a gentle death: as the excitement mounted, as the crowd shouted its wish for revenge and blood, they were stabbed first, then killed with bayonets, in front of a handful of representatives of the international press, especially photographers, and especially the young correspondent from *Combat*, who expected nothing else. There were, there are, abominable images that I find it hard, even today, to look in the face, even though I feel they are engraved in the depths of my memory. There were, there are, all those scenes that suffice to explain my horror of war today and that make it so that I cannot, even retrospectively, accept Commander Mukherjee's phrase without protesting.

But, on the other hand, how could I deny it? There was, in the very young man I then was, a kind of delight. An exultation in hell and Evil. There was a real complacency for anything that could give me the feeling of existing more, or more keenly— whether it was the spectacle of the death of others or the risk I took of my own. There were times of intense, almost beatific, happiness in the moments of respite between bombings, forced marches, or maneuvering over destroyed bridges; a cup of boiling tea taken one morning, at dawn, in one of the last remaining huts of a carbonized village... the most exquisite siesta in my life, one late afternoon, on the impeccable English lawn of a golf course at an abandoned garrison... the mad laughter of the children with Akim one night when his Chevrolet, launched at high speed, almost overturned into a crater... the delicious, almost unbelievable, feeling of being still in this world, after a night of bombing that seemed, at each impact, to shake the very walls and foundations of the hotel... the image, another time, of that Soviet plane, hit in flight, that seemed to stop, hesitate, and then fall slowly, like a paper bird... or that impression of lightness, that I haven't found anywhere else since, that affected the least of my gestures—as if my body, my head, my very voice or my ideas were struck with a sweet, aerial, vaporous precariousness... Of these kinds of emotions, some of them still speak to me, say something about the person I have become, and they are not, moreover, the opposite of what my tribulations in the lands of the "damned" inspired in me. Others though seem hateful to me, unbearable in their complacency, bad Drieu, bad Jünger— and that's how I measure the path I traveled in thirty years. Everything is there.

"...a kind of cauldron..."

Imagine Germany in the 1920's. Picture it, this Germany, like a giant cauldron. Imagine a chemical or primeval soup boiling in this cauldron. Imagine that in this soup simmers the good old ideological stew of all ages—nationalism, socialism, communism, etc. And suppose, in the cauldron, in this soup, there is a whirling movement that, stirring up the old pieces, jarring the traditional political molecules against each other with an unprecedented force, splitting them, separating them, making them crack as in catalysis or a big bang, forms, working with their liberated atoms, completely different molecules, previously impossible, unthinkable, unforeseeable. Thus is born, from the contact of nationalism with bolshevism, the "national-Bolshevik" trend of the Strasser brothers. Thus are born the "revolutionary-conservatives," close to Rauschning, von Salomon, Jünger, who also make use of ambiguity—no one can tell, for the time being, if they belong to the left or to the right. Thus are born the sinister "beefsteak sects," brown on the outside, red inside, formed by Communists who have infiltrated the Société Anonyme to struggle against the main social-democrat enemy. Thus is born, in a chaos that is only the expression of the ignorance of observers and of our own, the terrible Nazi synthesis. Thus is born, in the tumult of a chemistry gone mad, a word, just a word, not even a word, a hyphen, but one that suffices to give history its new course and momentum: "National-Socialism"...

Now imagine Russia in the 1980's. Or, better, Milosevic's Serbia. There too, nothing has changed. There too, at least to all outward appearances, it's still the same old Communism, the same very old Nationalism—except that there is a new element, only one, that is both minute and immense, almost invisible at first and, nonetheless, of a stunning impact in Europe: another hyphen; just a hyphen between these two signifiers, "National" and "Communism," which, taken singly, are nothing but rehashes of the past; to most observers they both seem condemned by History, a bizarre coming together, perhaps a hybridization. Everyone talks, at the time, of the very official "hyphen battle" that, in Czechoslovakia, has to do with the question of determining if the name of the country should be written with or without a hyphen—if it should, in other words, remain unified or be split into two states; nothing less than the political talent of the great European Vaclav Havel is needed to resolve the argument without blood being shed. Well, there is another argument, at the same time. There is another "hyphen battle," this one never openly declared, never named, waged by that sinister European, that anti-Vaclav Havel, who is Slobodan Milosevic. This other argument goes well beyond the question of the hyphen. The hyphen is a way to represent a telescoping of signifiers—national...communism—that are as explosive as they are improbable; one says "hyphen" and one thinks, or should think, of a mixture, in the Serbian "cauldron," of the seemingly antagonistic discourses of nationalism and communism; this is going to have far more radical consequences and will, in fact, re-launch an entire political debate in Europe.

Is it the same thing in Sri Lanka? This soup where scraps of Maoism, tatters of Pol-Potism, a twist of fascist populism, a dash of fascination for the Japanese kamikazes of the Second World War all marinate together, in a stock of militant Hinduism—is that comparable to the soup whence the Nazi big bang burst forth? And then the Serbian big bang?

Is it the same thing with the Muslim fundamentalists? This other soup, where scraps of distorted Islam, the stench of fascist hatred of the West, a twist of technological modernity, bits of badly digested Marxism-Leninism, a real fascination for all kamikazes, Japanese or not, apostles of supreme sacrifice, all bubble together, in a stock of the cult of death and martyrdom—is that comparable, too, to the Nazi soup? the Serb soup? the Sri Lankan soup? Isn't it another sign of this History that is setting itself brutally in motion—new actors, new discourses, new risks?

That the conscription of children into these armies of lost soldiers is one of the great scandals of these wars, that there is, in this use of their recklessness to expose them on the front lines and wage battle through them, a revolting cynicism, that here, with this sacrifice of children, we are dealing with the transgression of one of the major prohibitions fundamental to civilizations (or in any case to the civilizations that were born from the deferred sacrifice of Isaac)—all of that is unquestionable and should be steadily denounced. Yet at the same time, you have to have seen these children. You have to have heard some of their stories. You have to have listened, as I have done, for long hours, to young Dayaparan telling me how these children are quite often the hardest, most brutal, wildest, most enthusiastic, craziest of all the fighters. When he recalls the way his regiment finished off with their knives the other children of the villages of the Wanni abandoned by the adults, you have to have seen pass over his little angelic face this look of joyful ferocity that you usually see only in the most hardened killers. When you have seen these things, you perceive that it's jumping the gun to turn these child-soldiers into pure victims of adult perversity. There is also a perversity of children. There is, as with the Chinese red guards, the child informers of Cambodia, the battalions of Hitler or Mussolini Youth, a meanness, a cruelty, an impetuosity in evil, that is specific to divine childhood. Despite the twaddle of new Western adults, despite the attitudes of this new religion—the only one, at bottom, that everyone agrees on and believes in—according to which childhood, as such, is pure, holy, a source of truth, beauty, and morality, still one can be a child and a monster. I'm all for the cause of tortured children. I'm all for launching actions, at the UN and elsewhere, with the aim of rescuing the greatest number of children from this hell that wars are. But I'm not for feeding, through these actions, the old prejudice of innocent and holy childhood. Faced with Dayaparan and his like, faced with these hordes of devouring and terrible gremlins, it's impossible not to think of Freud and his sense of a perverse, polymorphic, disillusioned childhood; impossible not to recall Baudelaire and his theory of possessed children, sometimes demoniacal, since they're close to baptism and, thus, to original sin—the Freud-Baudelaire line against the piety of sinless childhood.

"…sometimes, in the villages, there are five times more women than men…"

Accidents of the calendar. Passing through France, between Sri Lanka and Burundi, I am for a few days in Grignan, in the south of France, where Raoul Ruiz is filming his version of Giono's *Les Ames fortes* (*Strong Souls*). I reread the book. Am plunged, beyond the book, into other books by Giono that I only knew by hearsay. Discovery of *Le Grand Troupeau** (translated into English by Norman Glass as *To the Slaughterhouse*), his great pacifist novel, the existence of which I was, at the time, barely aware. Order or disorder, he asks. Does war produce order or *disorder* of societies? Order, of course, if you think of the rigor of the rules, of military discipline, etc. But disorder on the other hand, an immense and terrible disorder, when you see the deserted fields, the animals left to fend for themselves, the earth lying fallow and widowed of its men, the women especially, all those women deprived of men, widows also, or simply abandoned—to my great amazement and humiliation, I discover that, for him, for Giono, as for me, in Sri Lanka, the procession of women, the village abandoned by its men where one sees nothing more than abandoned wives and widows, is the very image of the desolation of war. Is this some new trick of political discourse (Giono, a sort of trap)? New literary danger (beware of

---

* Translated into English by Norman Glass as *To the Slaughterhouse* —Trans.

Giono, as, before, beware of Drieu)? Or is it the necessity, simply, of knowing once again how to distinguish between the two (to speak like Giono and yet not to say the same thing as Giono)? That's it, yes, of course. The necessity to work through, to take up, one by one, the words of Giono. The necessity to reread them, especially in view of their true context—those other texts for instance, that I didn't know well either, and that make up the *Ecrits pacifistes*. The trap is there. It's the way that Giono comes close to fascism. Not, I see clearly, his image of the village of women as such. But his idea, completely different, of an organic community, of a natural order, let's say that of the village, that the war comes to destroy. Giono's naturalism. His organicism. His nostalgia for a harmony, or for a good community, or for a lost purity. His hatred, not of war itself, but of the modernity from which war emerges and of which it is the completed form. I do not believe, myself, that war is the completed form of modernity. So I do not believe that its greatest crime is distorting an archaic cosmic order. And that is why I can use the same words—and say the opposite of Giono.

"...Yashoda's story..."

This man whose voice floats next to his body. It's his voice, without any doubt. I look around us, we are alone, it is indeed his voice. Except that it floats. It seems to be borrowed from someone else, or to emanate from a strange region, very low, that is no longer entirely his body. Sometimes it changes in the course of a sentence: a flying voice, a voice on loan. Sometimes it dwindles: minuscule trickle, pure trace of a voice, that will soon disappear. Sometimes it strangles itself, or gargles, as if it were no longer capable of an entire word. A strange voice.

This woman, Yashoda, who, while she tells her story, keeps passing her hand over her face. Her nose. The wrinkles, under her eyes. Her mouth. Her chin. Her cheeks. The faint down on her cheekbones. First, I think it's to wipe away a tear. But no. There are no tears. Her face is dry. Completely dry. And then her hand will touch her hair, the nape of her neck, her neck, her ears. It seems a kind of fear, in fact. It's as if she wanted to reassure herself that everything is still there. All her features, one by one, very gently, as if she feared they might take advantage of a moment of inattention to disappear. It's all that's left to her, this face. She doesn't have a house anymore. Or a life. Very thin, almost crippled, she scarcely has legs left to walk or flee if the

Tigers, or the Navy, decide to return. Imagine then this little face also defaulting... Imagine it playing her the mean trick of disappearing in its turn... This effacement of faces that would become the obsession of the century, its secret horizon, and that would so enigmatically pervade its painting, its literature, its philosophy—did I come here to see this program carried out?

That other woman, all those others, in Sri Lanka as well as in Angola and, soon enough, in Burundi, who seem not to have a gaze anymore. It's so beautiful, a gaze. It's the sign of the soul. It's the area of the body, above all others, where light filters through (from the mind... from beyond the mind...). It's the infinite within reach of faces. Their divine portion. Their grandeur. That's another thing that strikes me—another characteristic of these "damned": faces without gazes; gazes without light; that look of broken birds, faces so shattered they seem to have lost that obscure radiance, that superhuman dignity a gaze usually offers. They see people, of course. They have eyes to see. They are useful eyes. They are eyes to live, to survive. Real eyes, usually, aren't content with seeing; they look, they love, they dislike, they think, they question, they dream. These eyes seem to serve just to see: eyes without gaze.

Laughter. In those camps of misery and in the death caravans of Angola, in Batticaloa as in Huambo, Kuito and then Quebrada Naïn or Gogrial, I didn't see anyone laugh. Or smile. Never. Or else weird sorts of laughter and smiles, turned inwards, forced, nervous, almost ashamed. People, usually, laugh outward. They project themselves, through laughter, to the outside. It's as if, by laughing, they were showing themselves to others and to the world. Here it's the opposite. People who gather their laughter in.

Fearful beings, withdrawn, who shrink into themselves to laugh and through laughter. There is something infinitely painful, inhuman, in this way of treating one's laughter. Laughter, an uncertain habit? A threatened practice? A perishable trait, less "unique to man" than one thought? The first thing that leaves when subjectivity departs? Perhaps. . .

I'm not sure what to do with these questions and observations. Say them. Write them. Notice this disappearance of laughter, of smiles, of gazes, all these traits that function, in principle, to individualize a subject. And, faced with this disappearance, faced with this radical and general desubjectification, in this night of non-subjects, this hell where all subjects are grey, in this indifferentiation that offers a pretty good image, after all, of this triumph of the impersonal "one," or "Das Man," of "existence without an existent," prophesied by the philosophers, and about which I had never, till now, really understood what their look or smell could be, in this empire of the mass and the identical, of the anonymous and the intensely close, in this midnight of souls that seems, for eternity, the time of the damned, to force yourself all the same, somehow, in charcoal, exaggerating the features, to spell out the names, distinguish fates, to locate faces and describe them.

Names, to counter barbarism? Faces, to counter the damnation of these wars? Are there, here again, two kinds of humanity: a humanity that is spontaneously named, the one for which having a name and a face is not just a right, but a fact, something self-evident—and then the other, with the subjectivity and, thus, the humanity, of the impossible face crossed out? And, faced with the scandal of this distribution of names and faces, faced with the unequal development, according to the individual cases and the regions of the world, of this culture, of this care, of this labor of self on self, that make a being a subject and that are expressed in a face, faced with the fact that one is a subject neither in the same way nor with the same intensity according to whether one is master or slave, dominating or dominated, people of little or almost no means, European or Sri Lankan—faced with the reality, in a word, of these destitute people, these fallen people, these excess men, to whom it is forbidden to give shape and style to their lives, should the chronicler become a sort of Christ on the Mount of Olives, or a kind of Elohim on the day of the creation of the world, or a new Adam invested with magic power granted by the language of Paradise: "And I will give them an undying name"? That's the risk. And I can clearly see the absurdity, the ridiculousness, the odious quality of the situation. But at the same time... The fact, at the same time, is there... There are, in this world, fewer faces than you think. There are lives that are worth something only through a gesture, a word, a moment of grace, an episode, what I used to call, referring to Conan or to the Bosnian thief Celo, a possible pass to greatness—and there are lives that don't even have this pass. There is, today, only one serious political problem: the tragedy of the disappearance of the other.

Marx[18]: "the oppressed" wait for the recollection of the wrong done to them as well as for reparation and justice.

Horkheimer[19]: "It is bitter to be misunderstood and to die in obscurity; to shed light on this obscurity, that is the honor of historical research."

Brecht: "The additional insult inflicted on the wounded lives of the poor by the fact that their sufferings remain in obscurity and aren't even retained in the memory of humanity."

Well, it is not enough to speak of *the* lives. Or of *the* poor. Or of *the* oppressed, in general. It is not enough to say "a man made of all men, who is worth all of them and who anyone at all is worth." You have to say who. You have to give each person, precisely, back his identity, his name. There must be a recollection that, to have a meaning, truly to struggle against oblivion, to return or try to return to this damned humanity the features it has lost, it must be concrete, embodied in bodies and represented in faces. And finally you have to realize that, in these matters, no one takes the place of anyone else: to quote Srilaya doesn't obviate quoting Yashoda; and to quote Srilaya and Yashoda, to have observed them and questioned them, to have reverently gathered the story of their lives from each of them, should not have exempted me from quoting some other woman, seen from the last bridge, at the entrance to Batticaloa, standing in the lagoon, water up to her stomach, plunging her hands into the sand, like a person digging for gold, except that she was looking not for gold, but for shrimp—or some other woman, so wretched, accompanied by a very old man, her father perhaps, or her husband, he is in rags, but he has a fine net that he casts very far into the lagoon—the last fisherman to use a casting net, they tell me, since it's getting late and fishing is forbidden at night.

Did I do enough, then? Did I quote enough, name enough, of Srilaya, Yashoda, etc.? That is the only question. That is, above all, my remorse. This "etc.," again. This horrible "Srilaya, Yashoda, etc." that betrays me. If history is the vengeance of nations, journalism is the revenge of faces. And I have not, I see it now, told enough faces.

"... long lines of men and women walking aimlessly, their gaze empty..."

That phrase of Sartre's that, as a doxa, summarizes his philosophy and to which I myself attached so much importance, that certainty, repeated in so many different ways, that a man is not what he is but what he does, that he does not have a "nature" but an "existence," that laborious and, in the true sense, poetic definition of a humanity snatched—and so much the better!—from the fatality of being and of *étance**, in other words, whether you like it or not, from their roots and their race, this idea taken up again, recently by a prime minister thundering that a man is not what he hides but, still and always, what he does—what are all these ideas worth confronted by these men, these women, who do nothing and whose final wealth consists, precisely, in their "miserable pile of secrets"? Expressed differently: If one is what one does, if to be oneself is to produce and perform, if the nature of one's singularity is not to exist but to achieve, if each of us can be defined by the way he exists in the world and by his active enrollment in this world, if, contrary to what the eternalists believe, or want to believe, we have no substance that precedes what, by our actions, we become, what of those who have no actions?

What, then of those who can not act, can not work, scarcely move? The living-dead of the South Sudan, those bodies that

---

* physical existence

drag themselves along, those men with the limp gestures, those shadows that, sometimes, seem already to be no longer alive except in a few details—their limbs numb, their lips blue, their eyes or smiles extinguished—must we conclude that, being not good for anything, they are worth nothing? Must we, in the name of a neat philosophical idea, condemn this half, what am I saying, this three-quarters of humanity to nothingness? In short, don't we have a choice, in dealing with the damned, to choose between the old system that locates subjects in their essential nature but that still runs the risk of turning into racism—and the other system, the good one, the one that refuses to cement the subject to the glue of his fate yet which can condemn him, suddenly, to be nothing more at all and to be thrown in the trash? Trash...: the word the checkpoint leader used, in Rutana, when he was telling me of the fate his unit reserved for potential Hutu prisoners. Trash...: the best way, in the Third World, on a background of absolute misery and confusion, to create generations of desperate people.

"...this unspeaking, worn-out despair..."

The question asked by the survivors of camps, the great and terrible question they found it so difficult not to ask when, after the war, in life or in mind, they happened to meet one of their former persecutors: What is the relationship between him and me? Between the torturer he was and the victimized flesh to which he reduced me, what connection is there? Is there a relationship of species, can we still speak of the "human species," when torturer and tortured face each other?

Almost more terrible, this other question that assails me from being in contact with these war damned, that is to say these thwarted, gagged, broken subjects, about whom I observed, in my notes to the Sri Lankan account, that so many characteristics are erased from their faces that, in fortunate peoples, make up a person: between them and me, what relation is there? Between their suffering and the suffering of someone well-off, between their experience of the world and that of a Frenchman, between our idea, for instance, of dying and that of a malaria victim from Kamengué who breathes his last in the same way one spits up a blood clot, what is the connection between our mindframes, our busy activities, and a life whose entire meager meaning stems, as for Faustin, from a hunt for decapitated, dismembered, enucleated, castrated Tutsi corpses, what "unity" is there?

Or again: what kind of memory do these men have? what thoughts? what dreams? Does one experience pleasure in the same way when one has, in one's mind's eye, the image of one's father disemboweled? Do they have the same type of imagination when the major business of the day is to make it through the coming night and reach the next day? How do they sleep? How do they make love? Does Oedipus work in you in the same way? More? Much less? Do they have the strength, still, to lie to those close to them? To be jealous? To be bored? To get carried away? You need strength to get bored. You need an extraordinary kind of power, and vitality, and faith in life to be jealous, to deceive, to get carried away. Whereas here... This exhausted humanity. This terrifying de-humanization. Is this de-humanization a business of bodies alone? Doesn't it also affect souls? In these extremities, doesn't this distress operate like punctures in one's inner life and soul?

I will put aside these questions, of course. They fill me with fear and horror. As earlier the idea of the chronicler distributing names and faces filled me with fear. But it is there. It doesn't leave me alone.

"...bursts from automatic weapons now coming from both sides..."

"The only courage there is, is physical," said Michel Foucault. What if the opposite were true? If true courage, the most difficult, admirable kind, were intellectual, moral courage? What if the only courage that lasts, the one from which all others come, were the courage to reflect for oneself, to think against the grain, to live or conduct oneself differently, to look evil in the face, to stare into the eyes of your enemy and tell him the truth? What if this courage, the kind Foucault talks about that is usually called physical courage, the courage to go and meet an ambush, or to cross Burundi under fire and sword, or, in Sarajevo, to brave the Serbian riflemen by walking down "Sniper Alley" and lingering at dangerous crossroads, were, at best, only the epilogue to the other kind, its crowning—and at worst, which is to say the most common case, the sign, either of an obscure fascination with martyrdom and death, or of a lack of imagination about the possibility of one's own death? Thus Colonel de Bardamu, in *Journey to the End of Night*, a brave man among the brave, so courageous, in fact, that he ends up dying of it: "a monster," writes Céline, "worse than a dog, he didn't imagine his demise." Thus the child-soldiers of Sri Lanka or Burundi: sent to the front line because, drugged or not, they are unaware of the danger, stripped bare of an instinct of self-preservation, impermeable to fear—will people say of them that they are "courageous"? Hence this secret confided to Malraux by Saint-Exupéry, reported in Malraux's *La Corde et les souris*, not without a hint of coquettishness: My courage? what courage? I didn't believe in death in any aerial combat; I didn't believe, in Gramat, that the firing squad was going to shoot at me and, if it had gotten the order to do so, I would have, until the volley, believed they wouldn't fire; I never thought, even when the bombs were falling right next to me, that the next one would hit me; when I was ill, whenever they anesthetized me, I was never afraid of not waking up; I have never been able, in short, to picture my dying body. And thus the chronicler risking the front lines and the forbidden zone of the coffee trees of Tenga: he was unaware, too; superstitious, but the other way round—convinced, no doubt wrongly (but the calculation, once more, was correct), of the lucky star protecting him; never believing in his own death. He usually says, not without boastfulness, "an atheist of the unconscious"—well, he adds here, but no doubt it's the same thing, not believing in his own death; not exactly invulnerable; or beyond reach; but completely incapable of conceiving (still the same problem, the same lack of imagination, of awareness—plus, in the circumstances, a good dose of vanity) of a world going on without him; what's the use of being "courageous"?

"...the old theme, which I have so mistrusted, of the famous 'End of History'..."

I understand that the End of History is, for those who believe in it, a somewhat felicitous perspective.

I know it designates, if not in Hegel (who scarcely speaks of it and who, if we are to believe Eric Weil, in the last pages of his *Hegel and the State*, refused, when it came down to it, to conclude the prosopopoeia of universal history with the constitutional state), at least in Kojève (who sees in it the hidden heart of *The Phenomenology of Spirit*, the esoteric and magical thesis that the master didn't dare to articulate but that he, his faithful and learned disciple, has managed to read between the lines and to expose), the resolution of "contradictions," the reconciliation of "subjective will" and "rational will," the realization of "liberty" on earth, the substitution of "mutual and equal recognition" for the old master-slave relationship—an entire series of events about which the least one can say is that they don't have much to do with the scene of desolation offered by Burundi, Angola, Sri Lanka, the South Sudan, or Colombia: or shall we say, once and for all, to keep it simple, the black holes of the planet.

Putting an end to the work of dialectics and thus of negation, the End of History also has finished with deprivation, evil, and, consequently, the evil genius of division, the contradictions internal to societies, the conflicts, the controversies; hence the fatality of wars and their procession of senseless acts of violence—see, from among a thousand different choices, that page in Hegel devoted to "paintings of Dutch interiors created by a population that, after the great wars of history, wanted to celebrate its emergence from them by savoring anew the spectacle of its own pacified and aseptic condition": Hegel does indeed say "after" the great wars; he insists on the "pacification" unique to the new human "condition," emerged from the time of these great wars; he speaks of this time of "post-History" as of an interminable "Sunday of life" that "equalizes" all things, "distances any idea of evil," and allows us to have done (as he says) with the fatality of war. Does he hesitate over this the perspective? Does it occur to him, in his Philosophy of Right, to think that there will be more wars in the time of the End of History, other types of wars indeed, but wars all the same? Kojève rectifies the position. He suggests that it's the desire for recognition, the mimetic rivalry of pride and love of self, and thus the very need for battle and the source, since the dawn of time, of war, that disappear when History disappears. What of Burundi, in this scheme of things? What of the black holes, in this scene? Isn't the very fact of being at war the best proof that History is not over?

And then I am well aware, finally, that there is one final reason, if the others aren't enough, that should dissuade one from uttering the End-of-History phrase about this isolated, asphyxiated Burundi, a country which the cancellation (the week I was traveling through) of the last Sabena flight after the attack on the airport had just plunged a little more into darkness. There is no real End of History, without a process of planetary unification.

When Hegel and Kojève say "the End of History," they are speaking of a universal becoming of the world, or of a world-becoming of the universal, or, even more precisely, of a world-and-universal-becoming of this very particular category of Being that philosophical tradition, from Kant to Husserl, calls "Europe" and that is also, in Hegel, the homeland of the "type of man" that is the most "universal," the "freest," the one most liberated from "natural principles," in short, a matchless principle, in himself alone, of universality and liberty. In the "End of History," in other words, each word counts. History as End. And it is indeed a History that is in question, one single and unique History, where all the peoples of the earth, all the provinces, even the distant ones, of the new homogeneous empire, are supposed to enter in turn, solemnly, in great pomp, linked more and more to the capitals of the world empire. Hegelianism for Hegelianism's sake, and on the whole, wouldn't it be more accurate, then, and in any case more conforming to the concrete reality of this Burundi cut off from everything and, above all, from Europe, to mobilize another text: the "African" chapter from *Reason in History*, which has nothing to do with these hypotheses about the End of History and that even supports the opposite point of view, because it is a question, a few pages before the considerations on the "type of man" offered by European universality, of an Africa that, "as far back as history goes," has remained "closed, without a link to the rest of the world"—an "ahistorical" Africa, an Africa that "is not part of the historical world," an Africa that does not have to emerge from history since it has never entered it?

Still. I have, despite these reservations, three good reasons at least for having this idea of the End of History in mind while I work my way, this morning, towards the penultimate episode of my reportage, from Rutana to Bujumbara—I have three reasons, even today, to think that the Hegelian texts have something to tell us about these long processions of women, their piles of sheet metal on their heads, who are walking towards Tanzania, abandoning their homes to the "accomplices of the attackers."

The *negative*, first of all. The notion of the end of the negative and what it signifies in the Hegelian text. The end of division? Maybe. The end of controversy, of war? All right. But also, before that, upstream from these particular ends, the end of this work of self on self, and of self on nature, which is the definition of History at work.

Hegel expresses it very clearly in some beautiful pages in *The Phenomenology*: what characterizes human time, what distinguishes it from the fixed, ossified, spatialized time of things, is what he calls the "serious," the "pain," the "patience," the "labor" of the negative. He expresses it, even more distinctly, and a contrario, in the "African" fragment already quoted in *Reason in History*: if Africa is outside of history, if "a series of accidents" have occurred there but no real "events," that is because man remains fixed in his "immediacy," that is to say in his "passions," and because, if he already "distinguishes" himself from nature, he has not yet learned how to "rebel against" it. In other words, what characterizes man in History, man as he is History and as he produces it, is this "anxiety," this taste for "transforming" nature through *techne*, this "surpassing" of existence as given by moving towards conceptual thinking and reasoning, which are the true work of dialectics. Let this movement stop, Hegel suggests, let men stop being these spirits that always deny, let the given appear to them as the definitively given and not as the point of departure for some technological development, or of a work—let them break with the principle by which every given is supposed to be transformed, and with the principle that what is unique to human action, what makes him fully human, is to mount an attack against nature and against the world—and then that will indeed be the end of History, real History, historicizing, not historified, history, to use Spinoza's words.

But I observe the Burundians. I observe their silent immobility. I observe these little groups of men and women who seem to have no other care, throughout the entire day, than to move very slightly, on their sidewalk, to follow the trajectory of shadow that the roofs of the houses make. I see the abandoned houses. The idle soldiers. The depopulated landscapes with their ill-defined front lines, their poisoned land bristling with steel brambles, their fields lying fallow. I consider this prostrate humanity, with nothing to do, out of breath. And I don't think I need to appeal to any facts or any authorities when I say a pretty good image can be found here of this pathetic positivity, of this non-relationship to nature and to the world, of their renunciation of the very idea of confronting the given in order to work it over and transform it; all this signals, according to the Hegelians, that the time limits have expired and that we are beginning to enter into the time of non-History.

Time. Whoever says "the End of History" says "the end of time." Whoever says "End of History" says end of this double property that time had, and end of the time that included

History—in other words, the property that time has had since Augustine of leaning back on memory and pointing towards the future. When Hegel says End of History, when Kojève takes up and develops the "encrypted" prophecy of Chapter 6 of *The Phenomenology*, when Fukuyama, the third apostle (and, contrary to what is said everywhere, not necessarily the least pertinent—I have not stopped insisting, for my part, from the early days on, even if I found myself in disagreement with him, that the debate reopened by the author of *The End of History* was one of the most serious, the most fruitful, debates of our present period), when the Hegelianism of the third generation actualizes the proposal by presenting "democracy" as "the final shape of every human government" and "the liberal State" as "the most perfected" form of "the homogeneous universal State," what is at stake, each time, is the end of the process of "temporalization" that has lasted for two thousand years, that gives meaning to the human adventure, and whose characteristic was to be attracted both by the upstream and the downstream, by the past and the future—what is at stake is the appearance of a lax time, fixed in an eternal present, immobile: the "surpassing of time," Kojève says very precisely, in its double profundity of before and after; a new way of "being in time," says Heidegger commenting on Hegel (and reproaching him, in passing, for having stayed with this image of a time reduced to discrete succession, the old Aristotelian problematic of physical, natural time—a time by being, as much time as there are creatures and as there are nows...). For Fukuyama, his universal and homogeneous State has as its element the "no future" of the moderns and the "no memory" of the post-moderns, an alignment of juxtaposed,

When Hegel states that singularity is never anything but a moment of conceptualization or self-awareness of the absolute, when he characterizes the "individual" as a "subjectivity that realizes the substantial," a "living form of the substantial action of the spirit of the world," isn't he implying that with the occurrence of substance, it is he, the individual as such, who disappears? Doesn't Kojève say that if, "at the End of History," man remains as a "given being," or an "animal in harmony with Nature," what, on the other hand, must disappear is "man properly speaking," "action negating the given," the "Subject opposing the object"?[20] Won't Fukuyama go even further when, like Nietzsche, like Leo Strauss (and one can never insist enough on the imprint of Nietzsche, not just on Fukuyama, but on Kojève himself and on all the theoreticians, basically, of the End of History), he announces the advent of the "last man," that is to say the man who is completely satisfied by nothing more than universal and equal recognition"[21]—a man whom a taste for "comfortable self-preservation," as well as a "calculation of long-term self-interest," have persuaded to sacrifice the "mechanism of his desire" and, along with this mechanism, an entire collection of ancient virtues (courage, imagination, art, philosophy, idealism) henceforth eradicated or useless; a "bestialized" man who, in accordance still with the Nietzschian prophecy, will now need nothing more than a little poison now and then: that maketh pleasant dreams. And much poison at last for a pleasant death"?[22]

Animalization, precisely... This becoming-animal of humans on which all three authors, in various ways, insist... Doesn't Kojève, in a canonical note to the second edition of *Introduction to the Reading of Hegel*, ask us to "take it for granted" that the

heterogeneous instants, shining in the uniform and somber brilliance of its devitalized history, which define the world of these new children about whom Nietzsche prophesied that they would one day be born "with grey hair."

It's pretty close, here too, to what I said in the forward to Part One of this book, when I spoke of wars without memory (hence without past), without outcome (hence without future), fixed in the instant (hence in an eternal present). And it's exactly this experience of time to which, when questioned, the survivors of all these wars and particularly of the war in Burundi testify.

The protagonists of wars usually capitalize on their victories and even on their defeats. From this capitalization, whether it be glorious or painful, they draw a part of the energy they need to continue fighting. And this double process (capitalization, then re-mobilization, energetic recycling, re-injection of memory into the cycle of History that is being produced...) supposes a work of inscription into time, of indexation on a common *durée*, of commemoration, monumentalization, documentatio—it supposes nothing less than the writing of a History and the formation of a tradition (thus the Serbs and the exploitation of the national catastrophe that was, in Kosovo, their defeat by the Turks; thus, in all of central and eastern Europe, this drunkenness of History that becomes the true fuel for irredentisms, national aspirations, political and metapolitical battles; and here I am speaking, of course, only of pathological cases, purposely setting aside the living relationship of democracies to their past and their memory). Here, though, nothing like that. No archives. No memorials. No historical plaques. Scarcely a press. And, in conversations, in the oral testimonies that I have gathered, an incredible indifference to all that could allow one to date the battles, the turning-points of the war, the atrocities, the crimes, or even, on the other hand, the deeds of resistance of the civilian society.

"One day," say people who have escaped some massacre that was perpetrated a few months, or just a few weeks, before my arrival... "That happened one day"... A little later, they would say: "*in illo tempore*... at that time... very, very long ago..." And much effort is needed, much insistence and many questions, to make them emerge from that dead time, from that nowhere-time, that uchronia,* from that abstract and semi-legendary temporality that is, obviously, the time of war as they experience it, where nothing resembles yesterday's crime more than the next day's crime—where a final crime indefinably like all those that preceded it, and, gradually, like the first one, keeps occurring.

It tells me something, of course, this un-situated time; it inevitably says something to a philosophical ear, since it is not the opposite, is it, of the time of Jewish metaphysics and its fixed calendar? Except that if the Jewish time is also an immobile time, if it is, in many respects, an ahistorical time (Rosenzweig said a "meta-history"; Levinas, an "anti-History"), this anti-History is (unlike that of the damned) sacred, ritualized, punctuated by celebrations, hence determinate, even over-determinate.

One also thinks of Joshua stopping the movement of the sun to gain the time necessary for his victory; one thinks of the revolutionaries of July about whom Walter Benjamin recalls that they shot at the clocks so they could be assured of suspending, then of reversing, the course of the time of the masters and nobles; but, there too, it's another matter—this Burundian time

is a time that is not suspended but empty, truly e content, mechanical, automatic, repetitive, homog is, truly, the time of *malheur*, the 'evil hour,' misfo

One thinks again of the time called "archaic"; that time without dates or reference-points that e the 1960's attributed to so-called primitive societ had not yet entered History, where events suppos only in the manner of shots fired with blanks, with points, hence without echo. But Burundi did ent was, in Bujumbura, a time when time had the smell of plans; there was, as all history testifies, not just but great pre-colonial African monarchies, events i understand from the philosophy of Western histor is; there are no more; it's like an exhaustion of tim dates; it's a humanity so profoundly worn-out th seems to have exhausted its resources and its momen time, yes; a sempiternity; a time without dates, wit to hold onto, where horrors indefinably identical keep piling up—a true time of the End of History.

The *individual*, finally. The end of the individ and perhaps, more generally, of what the West has "Man," about whom we have long known that, depe accomplishment upon the future of democratic and on its illusions, he has little opportunity decline. For all the theoreticians of the End of H another of its characteristics. In the time of the homogeneous State, this is another sign, the third, observer that humanity has entered the last stage of

* A fictive time, literally "no-time," on the analogy of *utopia*, "no place"—Trans.

return to animality is the main sign indicating that humanity has entered post-history? Doesn't Fukuyama insist on the idea that to live in post-history is to live like a dog, really like a dog, happy to be "fed," "content to sleep in the sun all day," never worried "that other dogs are doing better" than he or that "his career as a dog has stagnated"?[23] It's difficult, here again, not to think of the fact of dehumanization that I have steadily witnessed in the course of my travels. Difficult, for a philosopher, not to hear the echo of these texts and what they announce when we keep meeting these poor people swallowed up by war, most of them living like animals. Difficult, even impossible, not to hear the echo of that echo when I think again, even today, and in hind-sight, about the confused torpor of those soldiers at the little Rutana checkpoint jammed into a bunker stinking of decaying carcasses; or of those sick people in Bubanza, lying by the side of the road, shivering with fever, their eyes already glassy, who seemed to have nothing more alive, or human, about them, except the gesture of their hands to beg; or of those corpses of children, dead for many days, and thrown, like the carcasses of dogs, into a little streambed, near Tenga.

That the dissolution of the subject, in its traditional form, is not unique to Burundi, that the prosperous and developed West has also progressed some distance along the way of a dehuman-ization that is obviously gentler, that phenomena as diverse as the degeneration of the 'Name of the Father,' in France, or the new legislation on personal names, the desexualization of our societies, the growing non-differentiation of the sexes, animal chatter, pervasive zoophilia, the growing alignment of "animal rights" with the "rights of man," all these bear witness to the fact that we too have surely entered the path of this becoming-animal of neo-humanity. But—how can we deny it?—the phenomenon takes on much more tragic dimensions when one reaches the point of treating the corpses of children like the carcasses of dogs. And if a final example were necessary of this "hard" animalization, if a final proof were necessary of this unprecedented liquidation of the subject-form as such, which we are witnessing in Burundi, I would take the treatment, not of the living, but of the dead in this war.

"*Humare humanum est*," said Vico. To bury, to dig graves, is the characteristic unique to the human being. And it is unique to humanity because it is a wager on the presence of death, hence on its singularity, its history, the system of its ancestry, perhaps the immortality of the soul that was once attached to its buried body. But, thinking it over, I see that it is not so clear as all that, the treatment of the dead in this massively Christian country that Burundi still is. There are graves, of course. Huge cemeteries under the white sky, especially on the road north, towards Rwanda. But desecrated. Devastated. Hundreds and hundreds of gravestones that barbarian hands have overturned but that no one, seemingly, takes care anymore to right. And, in the actual war zones, these mass graves, these ossuaries, these little piles of fresh corpses rotting, as in Tenga, on the edge of a stream, under a vague cover, half devoured by ants and hyenas, that regularly become news items for the international press. Sometimes one finds, as in Japan, scraps of clothing hanging from the branches of trees. Sometimes good-luck crosses, made with two pieces of wood and a shoe nail that the forest and the rain have, after a few days, already begun to swallow up. And my astonishment finally when I discovered that Faustin, the man of the reconstructed Tutsi corpses, the one who travels across Burundi in search of the heads, the limbs, the cut-up bodies of the victims of Hutu barbarism, in other words, the very incarnation of the piety due to the dead of this atrocious war, he himself seems not to know where his own father is buried. Desert of bodies. Desert of souls. Last sign of the End of History.

From these remarks, I draw several conclusions. From this exercise in a historian's phenomenology, I deduce, if not lessons, at least hypotheses: two, in fact—plus a series of questions that I will restrain myself, on the other hand, from answering for the time being.

First hypothesis. Just as Marx and Engels were mistaken when they announced that the world Revolution would begin in Germany, whereas it was in Russia that, against all expectation, it was finally to break out, so Hegel, Kojève, and Fukuyama were perhaps mistaken when they saw the first signs of the End of History, one in Jena, in 1806, the day Napoleon passed under his window; the other in Moscow, 130 years later, when Joseph Stalin achieved socialism; the third, half a century later, at the time of the fall of the Berlin Wall and of the seemingly absolute triumph of liberal capitalism.

You can take hold of the problem from whatever angle you like. You can say: "Here is what the Hegelians say; here is how they describe the entrance into post-historical *durée*; what they announce is, pretty much, the situation in Burundi." Or: "Here is what is happening in Burundi; here is the strange rhythm that History seems to have taken there; it is exactly what, in their improbable prophecy, the holy apostles of the End of History announce." Or again, in the manner of Benjamin in his *Thesis VII* already quoted: "Given Burundi, Angola, black holes, hell; what sort of thing must History be for this hell to be possible? What idea of History should I conceive that corresponds to this irrefutable fact? Well, there it is; the exhaustion of the resources of the negative, the fatigue of dates and of time, the falling back of men into bestiality—in other words the End of History..."

In all the examples, the result is the same. This End of History they have told us about for two centuries, in relation to which everything that counts in philosophy, since Fichte and Schelling, has kept defining itself, this End of History that, since the death of communism, once again animates public debate and that I have challenged, well, here it is, beginning to enter the facts—except that it's not in Jena, or in Moscow, or in New York, but in the outskirts of the world, at the margins of the empire, in the "outmoded civilizations of the peripheral provinces," that it is in the process of occurring.

History has stopped in Burundi. Let's say that I came there, to the end of the world, to see perspective be turned upside-down: an End of History that, not content with being an "End of History in one single country" (or, at least, a few countries, a few black holes, a continent), not content with breaking with the "clause of universality" that seemed coextensive with its concept, not content with saying to us: "We always act as if the End of History, like the Revolution, had to be universal or not be at all; we take it for granted that the End of History must be the human kind or nothing at all; well, that's not true; perhaps not; perhaps we have to renounce this superstition of 'History' with a capital H; perhaps we have to admit that there is, from the point of view of its completion, not one History, but two"— an End of History that will go even further, then, and reverse the conventional division between "historical" and "post-historical" peoples since it describes, not the well-to-do, but the damned... Return of History in Moscow (Post-communism & Co.). Return of History in New York (terrorism, state of war, renewing old ties with the Tragic). End of History in Burundi (and generally, in the black holes).

Second hypothesis. This End of History is, pretty nearly, what the Hegelians had predicted. The same signs. The same traits. It's the same phenomenology of time and space. Except that everything happens as if an evil genius had, at the very instant of implementation, reversed all the reference-points— everything happens as if a devil had disturbed the whole array of a system that was supposed to promise, I repeat, only pleasant and cheerful perspectives.

Did the breakdown of the negative, the end of dialectics, the renunciation of technological labor and its unflagging concern to transform the given, proclaim an idle but happy humanity, almost opulent, that, in exchange for its desire, for its passion for recognition and for all the mimetic competition that went with it, saw itself freed from what Marx called "the realm of necessity" and, thus, from its needs? Here, now, it signifies a fallow land doomed to vermin, rotting harvests, mire in the fields, starving men—it signifies, not idleness any more, but misery; no longer opulence, but destitution; no longer satisfaction, but the absolute empire of need.

The end of dating and of time, the entrance into a slack, almost abstract time, made of a series of juxtaposed instants, fixed in their "now," the establishment of post-historic humanity in an eternal present where Kojève says[24] that subjects (but can one still speak of "subjects"?) "recognize each other mutually without reserve," "no longer fight" and "work as little as possible"—should all that give post-historic existence this smell of eternity that one breathes, they say, only in the streets of paradise? Here, in the black holes, the opposite occurs: time, because it is immobile, is without memory; because it is without memory, it erases first and foremost speech, complaint, the suffering of poor people; because it stifles the speech of poor people, because it bars them access to memory and to time, it reinforces the impunity of others—the killers or even themselves since they too are assassins; and that is how this time without intermittence is the foretaste, not of paradise, but of hell.

Finally, were the end of the individual and the becoming-animal of the subject synonymous with a gentle way of life? Was the "last man" one who, as Max Weber said commenting on Nietzsche, "invented happiness"?[25] Should we at least "take it for granted" (Kojève)[26] that these re-animalized men "will fashion their buildings and artworks as birds construct their nests and as spiders weave their webs, that they will perform musical concerts like the frogs and the crickets, that they'll play like young animals and will indulge in lovemaking like mature animals"? Here again we find the reversal of the program. Now the same animality signifies: massacres; hecatombs; decapitated bodies; faces beaten to a pulp; bloody corpses that totter their last steps; half-corpses that hide themselves, like dogs, to finish dying in peace; dogs, real ones, fat from human meat, enormous, who no longer have enough corpses and who, on the frontlines of rural Bujumbura, as in Gogrial, in the South Sudan, attack the living.

The End of History is not happiness but horror. It is not the first morning but the last. It is not perpetual euphoria but the flames of hell.

My questions start from there. And these, to begin with: What really has happened? Where does this End of History come from? What was its mechanics? Did History, in Burundi, die out, or was it extinguished? Was it a process of the dialectic or of violence? Did it come from within or without? And if it came from without, if it was a sudden and deliberate rupture, what is the name of the alleged guilty party? The first name that comes to mind is, obviously, the West. I don't much like, usually, systematically incriminating the West. I hate to make it—I've said this elsewhere, often—the single, diabolical entity responsible for all the evils on the planet. But how, this time, can we shy away from it? How can we ignore—as Jean-Christophe Rufin has already shown in *L'Empire et les nouveaux barbares*—that these wars had a meaning only insofar as the West gave one to them? How can we not recall the blessed time of the old Angolan musketeer: when the Angolan factions were parties, when these parties were ideas, and when these parties, these ideas, were what they were because they found themselves enrolled in the great global conflict of the East and the West? And if that were the theorem, if the meaning left when the global conflict stopped, if it's really the West that, victorious in its long war against Communism, withdrew from the immense global periphery and also took away with it, by doing so, the meaning it gave to these wars, how can we avoid the logical conclusion? The question, in fact, becomes: What if History departed the way Meaning did? What if History, in the black holes, lasted just as long as the cold war and Communism lasted? What if it was the West that, by withdrawing, had carried History away in its suitcases? What did one call History, in this case? What does History have to be if someone is able to carry it off on the way out, like a suitcase? A pure effect of the West? A graft? An ersatz? Might the Burundians, the Angolans, the Sri Lankans, never have been anything but the auxiliaries in a History that had its center and initiative elsewhere? Were all these countries nothing but secondary stages, theaters of shadows, where nothing would ever be performed except a replica of the only real History that counts, the one of metropolises? In this case, isn't the process even more ancient than that? Didn't the End of History begin with the beginning of representation? Don't we have to suppose a kind of first History, or an arch-History, the kind that, in my youth, following the footsteps of Antonin Artaud, I went to look for among the Tarahumaras and about which I wrote, in the wake of Lévi-Strauss and his *Tristes Tropiques*, that modernity had tragically changed its nature? And, in this case, doesn't the End of History coincide with its beginning? Mightn't it be the other name for this second, almost foreign History, that the West brings in its luggage and that it will carry away when the time comes?

Another question. What begins from that starting-point? What happens after the End of History? Will there even be an after? In this new time without dates or reference-points can we even go on saying, as if nothing had happened, that things "happen" or "take place"? In other words: Is it the End of History just till some moment? Forever or only for a time? I know that the End of History, in principle, is forever. But this one? This End of History in one single country? This End of History in a world that is not unified, but divided in half? This End of History that, above all, has the characteristic of not having eliminated Evil but of having preserved it like a strange accursed share* (triumph of Céline over Sartre... I should add: of Bataille over Hegel and all the Hegelians, including Sartre)? There were three possible configurations, actually, as to the relationship of History and Evil. Configuration No. 1: History as a solution for Evil, Evil soluble in History, the very movement of History as agent of liquidation of Evil and promotion of Good—that was the progressive's system. Configuration No. 2: insoluble Evil, impotent History; Evil that lasts, History that lasts too; this irreducible residue of loss, malevolence, suffering, which is the very definition of the Tragic and whose end cannot be reached by any End of History—that is the theological system. Configuration No. 3: End of History and extinction of Evil; End of History as the finish, both of History, and of the presence of Evil in this world; Evil at that soluble stage in History (configuration No. 1), the existence of History at that stage linked to the existence of Evil (configuration No. 2), so that one cannot be erased without the other being erased along with it—that was Kojève's melancholy arrangement. Well, here is a fourth system: the End of History at the same time as the perseverance of Evil; Evil, in all its states, and especially those of war, in the beating heart of ended History; the death throes of

---

*A reference to Bataille's *La part maudite*—Trans.

dialectics, progressivism, etc., but without the death—quite the contrary!—of the negative—that is the system of the "black hole," or of the "war-damned," as I discovered it during this journey and as I am trying here, after the fact, to deal with theoretically. What are the consequences, then, of this final system? Don't we have to suppose, for this particular system, a particular future? And isn't this insistence of Evil enough to re-launch a form of History inside the End of History? The case of Sri Lanka, for instance. The theory of the cauldron. Can't we imagine the End of History also like a cauldron? Or a soup-stock of culture? Or, conversely, but the result would be the same, a kind of sterile environment where unheard-of modalities of political or meta-political fate would be tested, a unit of unique historical intelligibility, having its present, its past, its future? End of History and ruse of History. The End of History as an unexpected revival of History. Think about this oxymoron.

And then a third series of questions, finally: the relationships with the West. Here, things become complicated. Because of uncertainty about what will take place in the black holes. But uncertainty, too, about the future of a West where, in this beginning of the twenty-first century, two systems of totally antagonistic forces seem to be confronting each other. On one side the feeling that, spurred on by the total war that radical Islamism has declared on it for fifteen or twenty years, forced to face up to it, the West is in the process of rediscovering a taste for the Tragic, the meaning, the torments, and also, perhaps, the drunkenness of History. But, on the other, different signs, older ones, that testified and continue to testify today to an exhausted History, out of breath, in the process of making its way, slowly but surely, towards its end: a slow animalization, a dead time of commemorations, fatigue of the negative and its procedures—are we so sure that the neo-Hegelians were mistaken when they saw dawning there the first symptoms of entrance into post-historic ages? Aren't there excellent minds (Baudrillard, Muray...) to explain to us that we have already become these post-historic animals that Hegel and Kojève prophesied? Can't we imagine, then, two worlds that, each on its own side, one in a harsh version (the damned), the other in a gentle version (the prosperous), would see History shoot its final bolts (even if this were under the terrifying face of terrorism, of total hatred, and of the necessity to reply to this hatred)? Better: don't we have to get used to the idea, even in the West, of cohabitation with these two kinds of seemingly—but only seemingly—antagonistic forces (History *and* End of History, the signs of one *at the same time as* the signs of the other, a world summoned to face up to the return of History at the same time that it presents all the symptoms of departing from History)? From these alternate uncertainties, from this redoubled and seemingly exponential uncertainty, three great hypotheses nonetheless emerge.

Separation, first of all. Radical de-correlation. To each his History or to each his End of History, it matters little—but, between these two "ends," or between the "end" and the "revival," no more communication, interaction, connection, mutual interests. We are almost there. It is global apartheid. It is the "we're locking the door and throwing away the key" syndrome. It is the cancellation of the Sabena flight. It is two, really two, worlds, where one continues while the other is exhausted, or that have their concomitant ways of being exhausted, but that have, in any case, stopped speaking to each other; and their temporalities have given up intersecting.

Contamination next. Death that seizes the living. The black hole absorbing the last light. Anti-matter, matter. The End of History surreptitiously winning the territory of History, or the "harsh end" carrying along the "gentle end" in its logic and its course towards nothingness. The periphery that, according to a classic (too classic?) schema, imperceptibly conquers the center. The damned in the dark vanguard having (as usual? as in the Marxist schema, turned upside-down?) just a bare head-start over a History that finally is one. No one knows, of course, how this contagion would proceed. It is as mysterious, for now, as all viral contagions. But I remember Solzhenitsyn, Vladimir Bukovsky, and Vladimir Maximov, my Russian friends from the 1970's, seeing a watered-down Sovietism winning over people in Europe. I remember, conversely, the strange euphoria that people experienced, just after the fall of the Berlin Wall, when we felt a new wind blowing from East to West, which was revivifying the idea that we had had of freedom; we felt everything was happening as if central Europe, by shaking itself, were pouring out its frail supplies of defrosted freedom onto the world market of rights. Why not a mechanism of the same kind albeit in a sinister version? Why not imagine a sort of evil radiation that, this time, would go from the South to the North? Why couldn't this South in distress give us some of its traits? Tribalism, for instance? The defeat of the Universal? Or, more simply, more concretely, doesn't this world adrift, or fixed in its dereliction, have terrible weapons of its own—the drugs in Colombia, the terrorism of Sri Lanka, the ecological pollution of Burundi, or the illegal immigration in Angola? And isn't it the characteristic of these weapons to act in a silent, latent way, without any declared malign intention?

Finally, *confrontation*. The clash, the collision, the violent conflict of paradigms and worlds. And this, once again, according to two possible modalities. Either a desolate world that, in defiance of all the laws of dialectics, finds in its very desolation a dark energy, a momentum, and which, even in its last gasp, on its knees, mobilizes this last strength to mount an attack on the world of the prosperous: End of History against History; End of History against End of History; war of Histories, of Ends of History, of counter-Ends of History. This is the fantasy of the prosperous, the fantasy that dominates rich nations when they try, in vain, to stretch their *cordon sanitaire* between themselves and the damned; but who knows? Is it really unimaginable that such unhappiness, humiliation, despair, will one day be converted into resentment, into hatred, and find the technical means to express itself? Isn't that the very heart, incidentally, of the entire present-day debate about globalization? And then the other solution, more terrifying but almost more plausible: the recruiting of the forgotten and their brooding forces in the other war, our own, the one that seems, listening to the latest news, to need to give its rhythm to the History of the century that's beginning. It would mean their conscription, direct or indirect, into the great army of those—strong, for now, with an ideology, a faith—who hate the West with all their soul and dream of destroying it. Didn't these forgotten, senseless wars have their heyday, the time of their meaning, during the great confrontation with Communism? Why couldn't they rediscover it, this glory and this meaning, in the time and within the framework of the new confrontations that post-modernity seems to promise? Why shouldn't the black holes serve as a reserve for new armies? as sanctuaries for new sects of assassins? Isn't it clear, moreover, that Africa is today along with China one of the zones most receptive to the influence and penetration of Islamists? Once again, I don't know.

1. Kojève: "democratization" of Germany by means of Hitlerism. What, exactly, did he mean?

2. What is the "opposite" of History? Eternity (that which escapes History)? The event (that which interrupts the course of History, fracture, ruin)? The End of History (that which, strictly speaking, annuls History, that wipes it out as one wipes out a debt)?

3. I had always thought that the same applies to the End of History as to death: it would give a meaning to what had preceded it, it would bestow on it the form of a destiny. Not so. The opposite, actually. If the End of History happens here, in Burundi, in the black holes, that's because it coincides, on the contrary, with the disappearance of meaning.

4. Beethoven, unlike Hegel, his contemporary, did not see Napoleon, hence the End of History, pass on horseback beneath his window. But he was finishing the Third Symphony. His idea was to dedicate it to Napoleon, since he too admired the revolutionary general. But at the very last minute, he learned that the latter had just, after what seemed to him an incredible and shameful conversion, had himself crowned emperor. Cold rage. Rancor. He rips it off his score. And decides to dedicate it, under the name of *The Eroica Symphony*, to Prince Lobkowitz. Political intelligence of an artist.

5. A History or histories? When you don't believe in universal History, how can you not resign yourself to the idea of a piecemeal History? How, when you're no longer either Hegelian or Bergsonian, when you no longer believe either in the *durée* of the one or in the theotelelogy of the other, how can you not consent to pure diversity, to the multiple, and finally to cultural relativism? And how, above all, can you remain faithful to the vital hypothesis (since it's the only serious rampart against the deadly spread of racism) of the unity of the human race? First answer: History does not exist, that's a fact; there have always been many histories, there's no doubt about that; but not existing has never prevented something from being; and there is a way of being, at least, that is perfectly compatible with non-existence and that is the way of the Idea, of what some would call the regulating Idea, others a horizon of intelligibility or demand, others an indeterminate and impossible command—not to believe in History, but to believe, or to want to believe, in a principle of imbricated Universality overlapping, subsuming the scattered Histories, that is the necessity; not to believe in a majestically unified historicity, but to believe in the rights of man, for instance, and in the right that men give themselves to judge what occurs, hence to judge Histories, that is the correlate. Second answer: "plurality" doesn't necessarily mean incommunicability; the fact that there are unique, separate, autonomous Histories doesn't prevent them either from intersecting or from forming one with the other; thus pre-1975 Angola could play its part, via Portugal, in the great European adventure of the struggle against fascism; thus Burundi, in the 1950's, could mingle in the world history of national liberation movements; just so that time, the

period of the "Trotskyite" experiment of the Bandaranaike government, when the Sri Lankan calendar coincided with that of the Fourth Internationale. What do we call "History," after all, if not that very encounter of all these layers of History, and the pattern that emerges from it? What is an event if not the meeting, the short-circuit, between two or more segments of time?

"...the Kojèvian hypothesis of a spectral, absurd confrontation..."

I often speak, in these texts, of specters, ghosts, phantoms. I keep coming back to this idea of a History obsessed by its evil shades. Already in my Angolan narrative, the image of old Holden, certain he was seeing the Cubans returning, some nights, to Luanda, and my feeling that, in this war, it is the dead who command the living, the specters who do the programming, who manufacture corpses. In Sri Lanka, facing the Tamil leader in Batticaloa and his ideological junk yard, the image of all these themes, of all these hiccups of the century, returning to appear together as for a final judgment, ultimate parade of specters in the ruins of an abolished future. And finally Gogrial, the phantom city of the South Sudan, the most phantom-like of all the phantom cities I have known—except that you can no longer tell who, precisely, is the phantom, those who are there no more and for whom it had become a communal grave, or those who wander about in their place and look scarcely more alive...

In a certain sense, this is a mistake. It is not so certain, really, that this state of being haunted by being haunted, this hauntological obsession, is compatible, really, with the Kojèvian hypothesis or, at least, with what I have made of it—it is not certain that it agrees with this landscape of "black holes." For, in the end, what is a specter?[27] It is the shadow of a subject. It is the remnants of an individual, linked to this individual by virtue of a fragile, tenuous, evanescent, but solidly identifiable link. It has a name. A biography. Almost a face. And if it returns, if it wanders amongst the living, if it persists, as they say, to "haunt" us, it is to bear witness, in the present, to that past, dated, and precisely situated personality of whom it is the memory. The specter, in other words, is a witness. A martyr. It is a malignant remanence, but a remanence all the same, of the deceased individual. The very principle, though, of the "End of History in one single country" is that it recognizes neither witnesses nor martyrs, and that it does not consist of the faces of victims, their poor and fragile singularity, that, as I have already said, tend to be erased or have their outlines fade. There is a risk, then, with this story of ghosts, of weakening the impact of that statement. There is a risk, in this hauntomania, of covering up one of the distinctive traits of these wars. There is an inarguable danger of a hauntology that would have the effect of giving an aura of romanticism, a glimmer of lyricism, to an Evil whose charm I have done everything I could to dispel.

In another sense, though, the metaphor is good. Provided you take the measure of the risk, provided you are well aware of the danger of hauntological re-enchantment, it might be a legitimate thing to use it. For, once again, what is a specter? And what did I have in mind each time this phantom-filled imagery came back to me?

This, first of all. More than with us, in the West, in our way of carrying out mourning and its duties, the dead of Burundi inhabit the living, harass them, hound them, torment them, leave them no rest. The characteristic of life, there, is never to be finished with the dead. The proper function of the dead is tirelessly to persecute, to torture the survivors. These dead are no longer a link with life prescribing to us, in this life, our loyalties, our duties—they are a link with death, exclusively with death, snatching up the living into the kingdom of death. The problem of graves, again. When you lack the essential, that is to say honest-to-goodness graves, how can you separate yourself from the dead and hold them at a distance from yourself? I call "phantom" one of those ill-honored, or un-honored, dead, who return to remind us of "our unpaid debts." I call "phantoms," like Baudelaire again, "the dead, the poor dead" and "the living, the poor living" who all have "great sufferings," caused by each other.

And this, too: Contrary to what happens when mourning achieves its purpose, the living, in Burundi, not content with being inhabited, to the point of hypnosis, by their dead, inhabit a world, and the dead inhabit the same world. Is it a world of the dead or of the living? Where is the border? The line of division? Where are the dead and the living, when the cemeteries are destroyed and the world itself is a cemetery? All the civilizations in the world, to make the world viable, begin by marking the frontier where Erebus, Hell, Purgatory, begin. Here there is no limit. No Styx or Acheron. Transparent shades of the living... Resounding, confused commotion of the dead... One foot in the realm of the living for the dead, one foot in the realm of the dead for the living... Last chorus of Brecht's *The Threepenny Opera*: "Think of the night and the cold of the tomb that reign in this universe of the damned"—you can't say it better.

And, finally, this. Not content with sharing the dwelling-place of the dead, not content with being their only abode in this world (Baudelaire, again: "I am the grave of my father"), the living, sometimes, are themselves dead. We think they are alive. On one side there are the dead, we say, and, on the other, them, the living. There was a company of the living, for instance, that the war decimated and turned into a company of the dead: but one of them is left, nonetheless; one living person, truly living, is left, who testifies for life and the living in a world that death has invaded; one "revenant," in the strict sense of the word, remains, a messenger from the other realm, and we must do everything we can to save him from death, everything we can to keep him alive. But it is not so simple. For the living also are dead. They are, literally, the living-dead. What, literally, is a living-dead person? Either a dead soul in a living body. Or a body here, forgotten— and a soul elsewhere, already damned. Or, finally, a body, just a body, but one that is dead in some places, living in others—I have seen those faces that seemed alive while their eyes were already dead! or those half-dead bodies where it's only the gaze that survived! or those bodies in tatters where you had the feeling that the blood was circulating only in certain zones—the rest already had the blue tint that is a sign that death has begun.

What is a specter, then? Are we finally certain that it is still a question of a ghost? hence of a witness of the past? hence of a vestige? Specters like ruins. Specters in the present. I have met them in Burundi.

"... patience of the blind, immobility of corpses..."

The era of the Proletarian (Marx). The era of the Worker (Jünger). The era of the Refugee (Arendt). The era of the Deported (Solzhenitsyn, Primo Levi). Well, perhaps we are present at the arrival of another era, the fifth one, which would be that of the "damned," of the "black holes," and that we could call, for example, the era of the Wreck. What is a "Wreck"? What distinguishes this figure from the first four? It is beyond the known forms of misery, especially that of the Refugee. It is inaccessible to any idea of *Erlösung*, that is to say of "redemption," of "deliverance"—and that distinguishes it from the figure of the Proletarian. It has no function in the structure of Being; its disappearance, as I said in the last line of the Sudanese narrative, would in no way disrupt the world economy—and that is what differentiates it, not just from the Worker, but from the others. And finally, it is incapable of bearing witness and hence, literally, of martyrdom—era of the anti-witness, age of the anti-martyr. In that way it differs, whether you like it or not, from even the most afflicted deportees. It is these four characteristics that give me the feeling of having reached the extremity of the horror. It is these things that make me say, sometimes, that I have seen the worst, during those few months, of what man can do to man.

BERNARD-HENRI LÉVY

248

"…graves overturned, a burned school, burned coffee plantations…"

Walter Benjamin again. Portrayed in the book, not by Löwy, but by Stéphane Mosès, the image of "the angel of History," his "face turned toward the past," seeing in this past, instead of the glorious "chain of events" with which progressive tradition is enchanted, "nothing but a single and unique catastrophe that keeps piling ruins upon ruins" and that "casts them down at his feet."[28] Metaphor for my travels? Distant image of Burundi? Presence, in any case, of Benjamin. A guidebook, more than ever, of this journey into the black holes.

"...not a ruin, but a nothingness..."

Ruins, again. But which ruins, exactly? And what, once again, is a ruin?

There are ruins—the majority of them—that testify to the past: these are ruins that are vestiges; these are witness ruins; this is Chateaubriand, Ossian, Romanticism; the paintings of Hubert Robert; phantom ruins, message of the past for the future—it's the extreme case of the Prince de Ligne who had new ruins built for him so that the past could speak to him.

There are ruins that, on the contrary, speak to us of the future and are like a message from the future coming to act on our present: these are Hegelian ruins; these are the ruins full of meaning that I contrasted, for this reason, with Walter Benjamin's ruins; it's the providentialist idea that there is no ruin without promise, no ash without rebirth, no apocalypse without Annunciation; it's the hypothesis, no less romantic and, at bottom, perfectly symmetrical, of a ruin that is the signature, not of things that have fallen, but of what is yet to come.

What about right here? These villages that are not just ruined, but pillaged, scraped to the bone of the last piece of sheet-metal and cinder-block? What about this literally burned land where I say the war has behaved like forest fires whose incendiary rage finds nothing more, in its passing, than dead spaces and that, still, keep on burning? Certainly not the future—I've said enough about the indecency of that hypothesis. Nor is it really the past. But the present. This present without past and without future, this eternal now, about which a theologian would say that this is the time of hell and perhaps, more simply, this is the End of History.

"...a new kind of bomb that would leave things and even men standing, but would empty them—how to say it?—of their positivity, of their substance..."

Let's recapitulate. What, upon contact with the damned, shatters into pieces, is, in no particular order: the Universal. History. The Human Condition. Meaning and the search for Meaning. The Subject. The self-evidence of the Subject-Being and the known mechanisms of subjectification. The separation between life and death. The idea that it is either one or the other—dead or living, you have to choose: well, no, not at all; the living-dead of Burundi are both at once; they did not have to choose; the choice was imposed on them and the choice is a dead life. Identity. Alterity. Estrangement from oneself. Facing one another. Desire. Evil as a trick of the Good. Good as the opposite of Evil. Being and time. *Durée*. Proofs of the existence of God. Proofs of his non-existence. "The clear night of the nothingness of anguish" (Heidegger). The "miracle of the face" (Levinas). The hypothesis of the world and of reality (all of philosophy). Reality, a given? The world, self-evident? For us, perhaps. For the damned, surely not. The same goes for all the crypto-Heideggerian definitions of Man like being-there, guardian of Being, shepherd of Speech, language incarnate. The same for all the Sartrean concepts of situation, being in the world, a man is what he does more than what he is, existence before essence, and so on. What shatters into pieces, on these Burundian roads, is all the philosophy I have in my head. What disappears into the black hole is the very claim of this philosophy to put the world in perspective, to judge it. Yes, there, on that road, in the middle of burned coffee fields, faced with these poor people lining up, plastic jugs and gourds in hand, in front of a broken fountain, what appears to me like a terrible fact is the necessity of reversing the perspective and letting, not this philosophy judge the world, but the world judge this philosophy and dismantle its systems as one dismantles a bad stage-set. Philosophy lesson. True end of philosophy. Philosophy stripped bare by the damned, even.* The perfect crime.

---

* An allusion to Marcel Duchamp's monumental sculpture *The Bride Stripped Bare by her Bachelors, Even*—Trans.

"We left, early in the morning, in the windowless bus that
makes the journey up to the hydro-electric dam at Frasquillo."

For a long time, I had respect only for ideological journalists endowed with a vision of the world, lovers of general ideas, interested in reality only insofar as it seemed to them to confirm and glorify their prejudices. I admired partisans. Activists. I swore only by Edgar Snow's account of the "Long March" because he had been a companion of Mao's. I venerated Wilfred Burchett, the other American journalist who had known how to tone down the pseudo-imperative of objectivity in order the better to serve the holy cause of Ho Chi Minh and North Vietnam. I didn't believe in information. I didn't understand how one could pay so much attention to the course of things and events as they occurred in their coarse and stupid materiality. I scorned Gaston Leroux. I was unacquainted with either Joseph Kessel or Albert Londres. Malraux, I was sure, followed, day to day, the news of the Spanish War only insofar as it was a pretext for him, either for novels, or for resounding press conferences where, great with the authority acquired by an alleged contact with the terrain, he would collect a lot of money for a lot of weapons for the Reds. But someone like Lucien Bodard (with whom I would, much later, become linked in a lively friendship) seemed to me to be, with his taste for the epic, the very image of what a journalist-writer should above all not be.

I had a friend at the time. His name was Jean Vincent. He looked like Clappique in *Man's Fate* and had the soul of Casanova. A character with a ruddy complexion, tempestuous, utterly legendary among professional journalists. He was the bureau chief of the Agence France-Presse in New Delhi when I arrived there. And he had, among other merits, that of having directed the agency's office in Beijing during the first years of the Cultural Revolution and of having been expelled himself, four years later, for ultra-Left deviation. The question I asked myself was very simple. How, when one had done that, when one had been a witness to that great moment of the history of the century and of the mind, when one had known Mao and Lin Biao, when one had seen them, as Hegel saw Napoleon, pass under one's windows, when one had, moreover, winning at both casino tables, succeeded in overtaking them on their left and in getting oneself kicked out for that reason, how, when, on top of all that, despite an old badly treated hemiplegia that gave him a lame leg and a face, at certain moments, convulsed with pain, when one had this impudent charm, those incredible storytelling gifts, that supreme elegance, that unstoppable seductiveness with women and colleagues, how, when one was all that, when one was Jean Vincent, could one accept being just a humble "bureau chief," madly in love with "info," spending your days and nights, a bottle of whisky within reach, lying in wait for news from the BBC and Radio Free Europe?

Today it's just the opposite. Time has passed, and the opposite is the case. Now my admiration goes out, from here on, to the other kind instead, to the very ones I used so to look down on, the storytellers, the narrators, the lovers of things and facts—and, among these, in the very heart of the family of Bodards and

Vincents, the ones curious about details and the trivial, the exegetes of minute particulars, the explorers of the commonplace, this journalism of investigation or inquiry that refuses to see more than things in things, and that on the whole would prefer to see even a little less in them: impressions, sensations, irregularities of the story, colors, smells, portrayals, little true facts, rough sketches, chances, atmospheres. From among the dead: Albert Londres, whom I ended up reading; Kessel; Bodard; but also *Les Notes et reportages d'un vagabond du monde** by Panait Istrati; Herbart's reportage from Indochina; *Cacaouettes et bananes*** by Jean-Richard Bloch, then his Spanish chronicles published in 1936 in *Europe*; Sartre's article on liberated Paris; the war reports by Vailland in *Action* and then in *Libération*; the masters, in a word, of that literary journalism I had so long considered with disdain and that I read and re-read, now, with a constant delight. From among the living: the journalists, the real ones, the ones I think are ready to stake their reputation, their talent, sometimes their lives, on the question of knowing what really happened, down to the smallest detail, in some village near Kigali; if the front line, northeast of Freetown, in the Sierra Leone, had advanced, in the last few weeks, by a hundred or two hundred meters; what was the exact trajectory of the bullet that killed, in Gaza, the little Mohamed el-Dura; how many died, exactly, during the capture of Cazombo in Moxico, then of Samba Lucala in Cuanza-Norte; how many Taliban bombs, in one hour, exploded in Taloqan; the relative weight, in the South Sudan, of Riek Machar, Lam Akol, Kerubino Kuanyin Bol, William Nyuon, Paulino Matiep, all the warlords rivaling Garang; I won't name them, the living ones; whoever cares to will recognize them.

---

* Notes and Articles by a World Wanderer
** Peanuts and Bananas

What has changed, then? What made me change and convert in this way? Time, first of all. The maturity that comes. A little less romanticism. A little more humility. The era, too. The end of the great narratives. The suspicion that strikes what we usually call ideologies or systems. This renewed "perspectivity" that is, in my mind today, our best inheritance from Nietzsche, and it has—need I say it?—absolutely nothing in common with that sinister relativism, culturalism, differentialism, that they foist on us again, in general, to justify the sexual mutilations of young women in certain regions of Africa or the mass murder, in Beijing, of dissidents, democrats, and other supporters of the "Fifth Modernization." If I had to designate this whole collection with one word, if I had to quote an individual, one single person, who summarizes this "Nietzschean" conversion of our viewpoints and, in any case, of my own, if I had to give the name of the one who, by both his public and behind-the-scenes influence, by the concepts he has produced and also by his example, has undoubtedly made us move furthest on this terrain, if I had to name the master, in a word, of this new journalism of which *The Damned* is the fruit, it would not be Kessel, or Malraux, or Bodard, or any of the ones I cited, none of whom had, probably, as much theoretical authority: it would be yet another name, seemingly quite distant from theirs, incongruous in this landscape, a philosopher in fact, a very, very great philosopher to whom I have already had, in this book, many occasions to pay homage but whom his reputation of hyper-theoreticism seemed a priori to keep as far as possible from these questions—Michel Foucault.

What does Michel Foucault say? And what is the relationship with this question of reportage, of information, of journalism? There are of course several Foucaults. Foucault was, more than anyone else, intent on dispersing, dismantling, what he always refused to call his oeuvre. He was, par excellence, a nomad philosopher, in perpetual transit between several identities and writing in order, he said, above all not to have a face: "Do not ask who I am and do not ask me to remain the same: leave it to our bureaucrats and our police to see that our papers are in order. At least spare us their morality when we write."[29] But in the end there is one Foucault, the one of post-May 1968, of the "Groupe Information sur les Prisons" and of the "intolerance-investigations" of the beginning of the 70's, the political, militant, activist, leftist Foucault, the Foucault of the *Corriere della sera*, author, notably, of the famous series of articles on the "Iranian spiritual revolution"—there is a Foucault whose theoretical positions remained, over ten or fifteen years, unusually constant and around whom a sort of *doxa* has crystallized that I regard as an essential component of this new journalism.

Proposition one of this *doxa*: Philosophy is History. Philosophy has no meaning, henceforth, after Nietzsche and

Heidegger, unless it takes on the face of History. It has served its time, this "pompous" philosophy that told us that Man is the shepherd of Being and History is the field of operation of the Spirit. It has served its time, this "vague little university discipline in which people speak of totality, entity, scripture, the materiality of the signifier, and other such things" that we call "Philosophy" and that has so little to do, in any case, with the great thinking of the "establishers of discourse," the "founders of discursivity" of previous times. It has served its time, this hollow and pretentious philosophy, and so it must cede its place, therefore, to history.

Proposition two: History is the event. The History that Foucault wants, this History to which philosophy, according to him, cedes its place, has no meaning or interest unless it breaks with the old discourse of continuous History whose facts are supposed to follow each other in an uninterrupted series of neat causalities. The philosopher has no interest in turning himself into this historian unless he begins by substituting, for the old stubborn History, "striving to exist and to reach completion at the very outset,"[30] an entirely different History, taking its inspiration more from Husserl than from Hegel, more from Nietzsche and his "positive History" than from Husserl himself and his transcendental idealism—a History that is centered on surges and differences, discontinuities, discordances, transformations, bristlings of time, a history that breaks with belief in the eminent reality of "universals," rehabilitates the idea of a reality composed of pure "*res singulares*," and draws all attention to the noble, the enduring, the beautiful event. Better than History, genealogy. And, instead of the "chimera of origins," the reality of today.

For—proposition three—the event is the present. The event interests Foucault's historian only inasmuch as it refers to an actuality and, in this actuality, in the "conflicting imminence" that constitutes it, insofar as the archival role ("what we are in the process of ceasing to be," said Deleuze in his text on Foucault) gives way to that of the actual ("what we are in the process of becoming"). There is present and present. There is the present of Augustine, which will remain that of Vico, and which we examine only in the hope of discerning signs in it, either of a hidden origin, or of a glorious advent. But there is the pure present, without end or goal, without promise or retrospection—there is this present conceived as a "philosophical event to which belongs the philosopher who speaks of it," about which Foucault credited the Kant of *Was ist Aufklärung* with having known how to pose the question. "What is happening now? What is this 'now' inside of which we all are?" And again (about a book by Jean Daniel): "Who are we at the present time? What is this so fragile moment from which we cannot detach our identity and which will carry our identity with it when it goes?" And again (further on, in the same text): What is hiding beneath "this precise, floating, mysterious, absolutely simple word, 'Today'?" These, according to Foucault the reader of Kant, are the only questions that count. Here, he says, is "the heart of the profession of the journalist" who is explicitly defined as "diagnostician of the present."[31] And that, in effect, according to me, according to a Foucaldian chronicler, is the kind of journalism we should know how to practice.

Proposition four, finally. This actuality, this present, these conflicting imminences, are expressed in texts we call reportage or investigative reporting. But watch out! These texts have, in turn, three characteristics that distinguish them.

1. They no longer have to be submitted to the synthesizing activity of a founding, constituting, meaning-giving awareness— they have parted company with what the author of *The Archaeology of Knowledge* called, in the last few pages of the book, the "transcendental narcissism" of the modern subject.

2. Their aim is neither to say what must be done, nor to pronounce, in the manner of Sartre, the great principles to which the actual speech of men should conform, but instead to produce information, to diffuse it, to revive new "circuits of knowledge and capability"—there are, Foucault said, in 1978, in the little programmatic text that the *Corriere della sera* had asked him to write as a preface to the series of articles by young intellectuals that he was supposed to coordinate,[32] "there are more ideas on earth than intellectuals often imagine," and the task of the transcendental journalist, far from assertion, demonstration, and preaching, is to "witness the birth of these ideas and the explosion of their force."

3. These texts are gestures; just as these ideas in all their variety are found, "not in the books that utter them," but "in the events in which they manifest their power," just as these texts are, as I myself wrote in *Comédie*, mixtures of texts and gestures that one can, by common agreement, call "gexts"; these "gexts" are not the preliminary step to an action, an intervention (Foucault said a struggle)—they are the struggle itself; they are the action as such; they are, "at the point of intersection of ideas and events," political acts in their own right that have all the weight of politics; "when information is a struggle," wrote Daniel Defert, a Foucaldian if ever there was one, on May 24, 1971, about the birth of the GIP (Groupe Information sur les Prisons)—and what he meant by that was

the constitution, by means of investigation, of the prison as an object of thought, ergo of combat...

I am not an unquestioning admirer of Foucault. Even less do I adhere to an explicit Foucaldian politics whose last word might have been, in the dialogue with Benny Lévy in *Les Temps modernes*, the praise of popular justice ("Why not just carry out arbitrary punishments and parade their heads on stakes") or, in the 1971 dialogue with Noam Chomsky, the evocation of a time when "the proletariat," victorious, could easily (and Foucault points out that he does not see "what objection one can make to this") "wield a violent, dictatorial, and even bloody power against the classes over which it has just triumphed." But there it is. That is my history. It's from that, too, that I am made. I would not, without Foucault's lesson, have embarked on writing adventures of this kind.

Anti-intellectualism, in France, has two preferred targets. Sartre —I've spoken of that elsewhere; I have refuted, at least I hope I have, the incredible calumny that made him out, for fifty years, to be the incarnation, among intellectuals, of compromise with Vichy. Foucault—he is the second target; it is hardly less obsessive; the relevant thing here, this time, are his famous texts supporting the Iranian Islamic revolution that have remained in the annals as "the" final recorded error of French intellectuals. What is there, exactly, in these texts? What precisely do they say? They'll call it an obsession. But since anti-intellectualism disgusts me and always seems to me to be (along with a few others) one of the surest signs of advancing stupidity or fascism, I proposed to do what people never do (if only because the main part of the corpus was for a long time available only in Italian, in the archives of the *Corriere della sera*): to go look at them.[33]

When you go look at them, then, what do you discover?

First surprise. They are not, as people still believe, just two or three texts (the ones published in *Le Nouvel Observateur* and for "Inutile de se soulever?" already cited, in *Le Monde*), but eleven, or even twelve if you count the great interview with Claire Brière and Pierre Blanchet published in *La Révolution au nom de Dieu*.

It is, in other words, a lengthy and sustained intellectual adventure, complex, intense, with advances, retreats, painful questions, doubts, personal and philosophical emotions, many journeys, encounters, contradictory portrayals, things seen. We are far, in any case, from the cliché of the scatterbrained intellectual, spinning in place, seized by militant fever and, from the height of his authority, blessing God's madmen.

Second surprise. These texts, or in any case the reports themselves, are spread out from the Fall of 1978 to the beginning of 1979. The first, "The Army, When the Earth Trembles," published in September, during the first prohibited demonstrations in Tehran, when the army shot at the crowd and caused between three and four hundred deaths on the Djaleh square. The last one, "A Powder Keg Called Islam," is dated February 13, that's to say (in the history of revolutions, every day counts!) the day after "*les trois glorieuses* of Tehran"* and twelve days after the triumphant return of Khomeini. Which means that the main body of reportage (eight out of nine articles) is concentrated on a short period of time and was published before the fall of the Shah, before the coming into power of the Islamist republic and at the time when the Ayatollah was still an obscure opponent, a refugee in Neauphle-le-Château with the blessing of the French powers that be and distributing, through his cassettes, the image of the "great joust" between "two characters with traditional coats of arms," the king and the saint, the armed sovereign and the exile—the "despot" and, opposing him, the insurgent with bare hands "cheered by the people." We are far from the conventional picture of the philosopher beneath the heel of Islamic dictatorship.

---

*An allusion to the French three-day July revolution of 1830—Trans.

Thirdly, these texts are on the whole enthusiastic and fully of sympathy. But sympathy for what, exactly? For precisely what aspect of the spiritual and political tidal wave that is carrying the country away? "I feel embarrassed," Foucault explicitly says in "What Do the Iranians Dream About," one of the two articles that were quickly published in France and that everyone could read, "I feel embarrassed to speak of the Islamic government as 'idea' (or even as 'ideal'), but, as 'political will,' it has impressed me." His way of saying this, when he speaks of "political spirituality," when he is moved by crowds that rise up and "open up a spiritual dimension in politics," when he "hears the French laughing" and reminds them that they are "in a poor position" to give advice about revolution, his main concern is less the revolution as such, its conformity or non-conformity to known precedents, the birth of a new power, the establishment of a new state or new institutions—it's not even a question of Islam as such, about which he no doubt knows and understands little; it's "the very enigma of uprising"; it's the mystery of this "naked will that says 'no' to a sovereign"; it's this moment, so strange, and, for a philosopher haunted by the question of power and social cohesion, so fascinating to observe, in which "men with bare hands" undertake to "lift off the massive weight" that weighs them down, and in the course of which the cement of what political philosophy since La Boétie has called "voluntary servitude" becomes undone—Foucault's interest, in these texts, is in the formation of this bizarre entity that no one has ever seen, about which he himself thought it was, "like God," or "like the soul," a sort of "myth," "idea," "artifact," "theoretical instrument," which is called a "collective will." A collective will, a real one—

"you don't encounter that every day," he confides to Brière and Blanchet—and so "you welcome it." A philosopher's reasoning. An engaged philosopher, to be sure. Passionate. But a philosopher first of all, posing philosophical questions.

All the more so since, fourthly, the texts, the same texts, do not hesitate to emphasize everything that, in this nascent movement, makes for anxiety, or terrifies, or perhaps announces the worst. On this Iranian stage, he will say in a text in *Le Monde*— the very last one, the one that will summarize the final lessons and will bring an end to the adventure, as far as he is concerned— on this Iranian stage "the most important and the most atrocious" are mixed. And, clarifying what he means by "the most atrocious," he will cite "xenophobia" on one hand, the "subjection of women" on the other (in the dialogue with Claire Brière and Pierre Blanchet, he will again evoke—once again, he's right on the mark—the demonstrations of "virulent anti-Semitism" that are the "counterpart" to the "uniqueness" of the uprising). But already, in the "open letter" addressed to Mehdi Bazargan a few days after the first executions of opponents by the Khomeini commandos, he worries about the "trials that are unfolding today in Iran," emphasizing that "political trials are always touchstones" and insisting that if "nothing is more important in a history of a people than the rare moments when it rises up together to bring down the regime that it no longer supports," nothing is more important, "in its daily life," than the moments, "so frequent on the other hand," when "public power is turned against an individual, proclaims him its enemy and decides to bring him down." And before that, in October, he evoked "the risk of a bloodbath" as well as "the definitions" of a "scarcely reassuring" clarity of the Islamic government that was taking shape. And even before that, in the very beginning, in his meeting, in Qom, with the Ayatollah Chariat Madari, an opponent of Khomeini, who was, let it be said in passing, his true great man in this affair, he posed the question of the terrible fascination with death in a religion "more preoccupied" (this is Foucault speaking) "with martyrdom than with victory." As examples of blind enthusiasm, unconditional belief, and happy complacency go, one could find better. Shouldn't we be obliged to him, rather, for having pointed out the symptom? Shouldn't we, instead of this interminable posthumous trial, credit him with the merit of having been one of the very first observers to see this morbid, martyrological, sacrificial dimension, which is the mark of radical Islam?

And then, one last word, finally. These texts, as we always forget to say, are also very beautiful texts. They are not just carefully written, but precise. Not just inspired, but rigorous. And the Foucault who tells us day by day, sometimes hour by hour, about the Shah's last calculations, the maneuvers of auto and copper manufacturers, the hesitations of the generals, the states of soul of the personnel flying Air Iran or of the strikers in Abadan, the Foucault who portrays this little mullah, "leaning against a bookcase of religious books," facing "an old telephone that keeps ringing," the Foucault who tells about the demonstration in the Tehran cemetery, the crowd behind its banners and laurel branches, the machine guns that block the gates, the crowd surging back in disorder, the Foucault who tells about the transistor radios and the cassettes in the mosques, the Foucault capable of writing about those who died in the Tabass earthquake that "they're still stretching out their arms to hold up walls that no longer exist" or the one who measures the power of "the biggest refinery in the world," that of Abadan, against "the stupendous misery it created all around it," these landscapes of "subtropical mining villages," these "hovels where kids crawl between truck chassis and pieces of scrap iron," these "dens of dried mud, bathed in refuse," where "squatting children neither cry out nor move," this Foucault—what can one say?—is an exemplary journalist.

"...the assassination, in Tierra Alta, in the middle of the
street, of José Angel Domico..."

Jerusalem. Yad Vashem. That room where, twenty-four hours a
day, in absolute darkness, children take turns speaking the names
of the victims of the Shoah. Just the names. Just the voices. Real
voices, clumsy and shy, that stumble over certain names, go on,
run out of breath, go on again. And that till the end of time.

Sobibor, Claude Lanzmann's fourth film. At the end of the
film, a blank screen. And another. And yet another. And so on for
ten minutes. And, in these screens, black on white, a hallucinating
succession of names and, opposite the names, numbers. These are
the names of the villages the Nazis emptied of their Jews. This is
the number of Jews who, each time, were deported. Beautiful film.
Long litany without words.

Is it naming, or counting? It's praying.

"...why, asks Manolo..."

I listen to Manolo. I listen to Juan and Carlito. I leave them, especially on the last night, in the warm night, lying on the ground of the hut where they set up our camp, telling me about the good life of Quebrada Naïn before that fateful day when the paramilitaries arrived. The surprising thing, though, in their account, is that they speak to me less about the past than about the future. They bewail their dead, of course. They bemoan that little girl—Castaño's men had begun by gouging out her eyes, then sent her out to run, blind, on the path, and shot at her like a rabbit. But I have the bizarre impression that the essential part of their sorrow has less to do with this, with the very scene of horror (and I am the one, after all, who's pushing them to tell it, to go into the details—they would have kept their distance from what had been glimpsed that night), than with the interruption that this scene has made in their existence, on the portion of life that, when all is said and done, it has stolen from them. We would have done this, they say... We would have done that... Manuela had saved a thousand pesos... She had hardly any gray hair... That night Pilar was supposed to make the marrow-bone soup I liked so much... Pablo was supposed to go to the water-fall... And cockfights were planned for the next month... And the sombrero that Andres was supposed to buy from the Indians in the neighboring village... A whole catalogue of little actions, so many little happinesses, that death deprived them of. A kind of optimism of the virtual, or a melancholy for the nevermore, almost more poignant than the account of the tortures themselves. What do we mourn for? For what has happened or for what did not have time to happen? For what was done or what was left undone? For what you did with your beloved or for what you did not have the time to do and now will never do again? Important, for me, these questions. Extremely important, at this moment. For I know, in the end, why I am there—for what intimate, inexpressible mourning, this sharing of mournings and sufferings.

"...this humble life petrified by the double savagery..."

To take the point of view of Manolo, Juan, Carlito.

To tell the whole story, this and all the others, not from the point of view of the leaders, the great ones, the usual speakers, those who hold the floor of History and claim to pronounce its meaning, but of the others, the nobodies, the ones forbidden to speak, or, when you get down to it, the conquered.

That is a most difficult task, I know. That is a most demanding feat for a philosopher—or (but it amounts to the same thing) a journalist stoned on Hegel. And it's clear that I am not, myself, by temperament or biography, by my mode of life or my usual preoccupations, at all the one in the best position to accept this challenge. But in the end I tried. With varying degrees of success, of course. With, especially here, in Colombia, huge infractions of the rules. Carlos Castaño, for instance... Ivan Rios... I am well aware that Carlos Castaño or Ivan Rios are not exactly what we usually call "nobodies"... But that at least was my ambition. My aim. With, in my mind's eye, in the guise of a guidebook, two or three great philosophical tutors.

Walter Benjamin, again. The critical Walter Benjamin (in *The Origin of German Tragic Drama*, then in the "Thesis VII" of *Theses on the Philosophy of History*) of that "laziness of the heart" that he calls "acedia" and that he defines as the melancholy feeling of the omnipotence of fate. The Walter Benjamin who denounces the metaphysical figure of a "courtier" whose distinctive traits are "empathy" for the "conquerors," mute and terrible attraction to the retinue of the powerful, total submission to an order of things whose sole virtue is to be imposed against other plausible orders, thus to exist. The Benjamin who, in a word, urges the "chronicler" to rely on this double refusal in order to resist the temptation of "stroking in the right direction" the "too-gleaming coat" of History.

Nietzsche. The Nietzsche of *Unmodern Observations*[34] and especially of the second observation, "History in the Service and Disservice of Life," (which, according to Löwy, Benjamin had probably read). Against the "*faitalistes*" "swimming and drowning in the river of becoming," against the pseudo-intellectuals who practice "naked admiration of success" and "idolatry of the fact," against the Hegelians who, in a word, always "bow and scrape before the 'power of history'... like a Chinese puppet," Nietzsche advocated a *gai savoir* of which one of the first principles was to swim "against the tide of history" or "to stroke it the wrong way." The literally "unmodern" Nietzsche, the philosopher "with the hammer," who remains one of the best adversaries of servile historicism and of its philosophy of conquerors systematically associating success with morality.

Levinas, finally. The Levinas who never stopped, from his first Jewish texts onward, talking about the "trap of the *fait accompli*" and of "prophecies after the event." The Levinas for whom Judaism in its essence is nothing other, at bottom, than the capacity to "point out good and evil without worrying about the meaning of History." The "Sunday Talmudist" was faithful to a Law that, far from being "subject to the implacable course of events," is the only authority that, on the contrary, can "denounce" the course in question "as a misinterpretation or madness." The political Levinas, who defined freedom as the "fortunate possibility" to "judge History instead of letting oneself be judged by it" and dictatorship, that is, totalitarianism, as a confusion of what is with what should be, of what occurs with what is right, in short, of "victory" with "truth." Levinas never stopped fighting against those who want to prophesy "in the wake or expectation of the conquerors" and thus gave us the means, against all the realpolitiks of all periods, to take the side of the conquered.

Levinas, Benjamin, Nietzsche: the sacred triad of this book; the three good masters of humility.

"...those contented lives broken, those almost silent despairs..."

Everything is in that "almost." Everything is in the "almost silent," which we can easily see the chronicler overusing. Break the silence, he says. Help these poor people break their poor silence. And, for that, his language, his noble writer's language placed at the service of the damned to relay, at least, their inaudible murmuring. Generous intention. Laudable course of action. Except that he clearly sees, at the same time, the rest of the set. He is up there, at the end of the world, in that loop of the Rio Sinu that leads to Quebrada Naïn, and he sees, because he is honest, the comic aspect that, when the time comes, when he's returned to Paris and to writing, will be the counterpart to his wonderful unselfishness. The clamor around these texts. The radios. The rumors. Congratulations from friends. Television appearances. Translations that proliferate. The publisher who will flatter him. The questions they'll press on him. The modest demeanor he'll take on. You, really? Under gunfire in Tenga? In the flat-bottomed barge in the bend of the Rio Sinu? And the risks? And the mosquitoes? How can you go, with no transition, from the Café de Flore to the flat-bottomed barge, to the mountains infested by the FARC, to Carlito wandering in what had been his street, hugging the walls, his arm half-raised as if he were trying to protect himself from another blow? And the writer, modest, yes, keeping a low profile: he knows that the real heroes are the ones who don't lay it on too thick; he has a friend who calls that "the Malraux trick": the dividends of a noble nature at the same time as those of modesty, being in the Spanish War and saying immediately afterwards, "Oh! Spain... we know, the ones who were in Spain, that it's not such a big thing, either, to have fought in Spain." The writer, then, with an expression fitting the occasion, with a suffering look, allowing himself the luxury of replying: "Oh! The Rio Sinu, it's not such a big thing, either, to have gone down it..." And so on. In short. In vain has he decided to distinguish, as he says, faces. In vain does he say: "Names! names! oh damned ones, I write your names!" He knows it's his own, his own face, that they'll see the most, at the end of the day. He knows that it's his own, his own name, that will be on top of the newspaper page and, when the time comes, on the cover of the book he'll extract from all that. In vain is he sincere when, in the bottom of his barge, he tells himself: "I am there for them, only for them, I have only one allegiance, to the mourners," he knows the tune too well, he is too used to the devilish tricks of self-forgetting, to create for himself the least illusion about the tainted, absurd quality of the system: when the chronicler shows horror, Paris looks at his pen; when he says, "Look at these conquered people," he is the one who emerges as conqueror. And then the style, finally... The comedy of style... "A horse sweating, that is gleaming," the poet said... What about when it's a man sweating? And when it's a sweat of blood? And when what's at stake in the style is to make even garbage shine and, even more than garbage, crime? In vain the chronicler protests that he has no style but breath. In vain does he repeat: "Writing, real writing, is not a matter of style but of rhythm, that is to say, at bottom, of physiology—what harm is there in having a physiology? Am I going to prohibit myself from having a body? Isn't a body the exact opposite of playacting?" In vain does he say all that. In vain does he protest his innocence. In a certain way, he is innocent in vain. In vain has he read, for the occasion, some books and been warned off pitfalls to be avoided (Apollinaire again; *Calligrammes*; the "splendid sky" of battle; "*tir amour des batteries*"[35]; bombs "the color of the moon"; the pious peal "of bursting shells"; how beautiful the missiles are, above a city, at night; Cocteau's *The Impostor*; the war painted by him, Cocteau, like Watteau's "Gilles"; Apollinaire, again: "Our invisible army is a beautiful starry night and each of our men is a wonderful star..."). There will always be something indecent in the act of turning horror into fine phrases. "Troubadour of sepulchers," said Céline. "To use men," said Garine (and perhaps it's about him, Garine, that Céline is thinking), to use, not only men, but their "revolutionary mythology," in order "to accomplish one's will," one's "destiny." Kundera's "dancer," this "intellectual" (who?), adept of "moral judo" and expert in "mass media," actor and martyred king of telegenic showing-off, "did you see me," "exhibitionist of public life," who, one day, leaves for Africa to have himself photographed next to "a dying little girl with her face covered with flies," another one "flies off to an Asian country where the people are rebelling" and where he will "cry out his support for the oppressed loud and strong." And then, once again, Foucault (or rather Deleuze commenting on Foucault, in the text already mentioned) dreaded extorting a kind of voice-over from prisoners, madmen, and various misfits in the same way others are wary of extorting overwork from the proletariat; so he was careful not to establish himself as their herald, their spokesperson: "It's up to them to take the floor," he cried, "it's up to them to take it from us! And, in the meantime, shame on those who claim to speak in their place." God knows I am far, today, from this Foucaldian "leftism." God knows if this form of bad conscience—"sad passion," if ever there was one—has become foreign to me, and if I have resigned myself, in the name of effectiveness, to these inevitable perverted effects. And as to Kundera... oh! Kundera... I clearly see the coarse comic side, the Poujadism* in his portrayal of Berck the dancer. But there it is. I am in Quebrada Naïn. And all this stuff is spinning in my head.

---

* A reactionary movement to protect the business interests of small traders—Trans.

"...these men, these shadows of men..."

Then why the victims, after all? Why this absolute privilege? This sacerdotal prescription? Are the conquered always right? Necessarily? Is it all that impossible to be conquered and still be a bastard? Defeated by history and yet barbaric? Isn't it just as possible, even common, to accumulate the double disgrace of being historically and morally wrong, of being conquered by History and, despite that, not being in accord with the Just, the True, the Good? The Kurd terrorists, for instance... The Hamas Palestinians... The kamikaze in Gaza, certainly a victim, damned of the damned, and yet a killer... The Hutu assassins, defeated by the RPF (Rwandan Patriotic Front), thrown onto the roads of Rwanda, poor emaciated shadows, pathetic, but who nonetheless remained the despicable ethnic cleansers they were before... Is being conquered enough to be sanctified? Do we, since conquerors are conquerors, take it for granted that what they have to say is wrong? And if I do that, if I am content with reversing Levinas' argument, if my entire gesture is reduced to changing "it's not because one has won that one is right" into "all you have to do to be wrong is win—and to be right, you just have to be defeated," what, for example, becomes of the Jews? What of the victims who are no more? Must we, because the

Jews have become Israeli, because they have equipped themselves with a state and because this state is confronted with all the moral, political, even police problems that have been, from time immemorial, the problems of all states, conclude that the inheritors of the Shoah have moved to the other side? If we did so, wouldn't we be granting the main part of what's being asked by those who, in the name of a rivalry of victims, transform Zionism into racism, Jews into the new executioners? Without going as far as that, wouldn't we run the risk of feeding a kind of chic populism renewing, but with the colors of this time and its love of misery, all the old Hegelian, Marxist, para-Marxist systems? In dolore veritas... Aristocracy of suffering, of unhappiness... The defeated as the new hero... The pariah in his glory... The victim, new chosen subject—sinister choice, a backwards choice, but a choice all the same—of universal History in its twenty-first century version (Pascal Bruckner)... It's no longer the Proletarian, the Worker, the Refugee, the Deportee and, now, the Wreck. But: the Proletarian, the Palestinian, the Immigrant and, now, the "war damned" taking up the fallen scepter of the only monarchy that counts, that of dereliction... The original title of this book (*Les Damnés de la guerre*, The wretched of the war)... The subconscious of the language to which, whatever I say, I claim to adhere by adopting this title... Can one, when one has done what I have done, written what I have written, write a pastiche, at the finish, of a title by Frantz Fanon?[36] Hegelianism backwards? Is that my last superstition? How, and why, I am still devout.

"Before, in 1969, I went, not exactly to Colombia, but to Mexico, to villages in Chiapas that were like Quebrada Naïn..."

My first Mexico.

There will be others, of course.

There will be many other encounters with this Mexico that will turn out to be, in the end, at all, or almost all, the crossroads in my life.

There will be the Mexico of "Le Jour et la Nuit," unforgettable—see *Comédie*.* The Mexico of A., the woman of my life, woven from so many novels, hers, mine, her secret, her purloined letter, perfectly exposed and, yet, absolutely secret—and then, also, Malcolm Lowry's *Under the Volcano*, which I think she made me read, here, for the first time, in a little hotel in Cuernavaca, behind the Borda gardens.

There will be, in the spring of 1978, with S., the mother of my son Antonin, the Mexico of that famous philosophical tour, organized by the Televisa network, who gathered us—Guy Lardreau, Jean-Paul Dollé, Françoise Lévy, André Glucksmann, myself—shown around by a surprisingly political, combative Octavio Paz: tumultuous crowded amphitheaters; tomatoes; rotten eggs; half-rinds of oranges steeped in ammonia they threw in our faces; projectiles of excrement in paper bags that exploded when they reached their target; bomb scares; uproars;

---

*"Le Jour et la Nuit" is a film BHL directed in Mexico; *Comédie* is a commentary on the film he wrote later—Trans.

hisses; it was ill-advised, at the time, to say that Castro was another Pinochet or that Marxism-Leninism was the opium of the people of the Third World.

So there will be all those Mexicos.

But in March 1969, a few months after the October that was their May '68, after the student demonstrations that had the bloody face of the massacre in the Plaza of the Three Cultures, it's then that I discover Mexico in general, and Chiapas in particular—and also, by the way, the enchanting status of author, since it's when I returned from this first journey that I gave Jean Puillon, for *Les Temps modernes*, the very first text I had ever written for publication: "Mexique: Nationalisation de l'impérialisme."

It's another Mexico, obviously. Almost still the post-war Mexico. Ramon Mercader has just died, but one can still meet, at a barber's in Polanco, an old hoodlum who passes himself off as him. There still are, between the Lomas and Coyoacan, people who say they knew Trotsky. Others, who guided Breton or Eluard into the seediest parts of Tepito, the neighborhood of Oscar Lewis's *Children of Sanchez*. And I spent many weeks, in Mexico City—Paseo de Lomas Altas, I still remember the address—at the home of Dominique, Eluard's last wife, whose glamour was augmented, in my eyes then, from the fact that she had married (as his second wife) a gorgeous specimen named Aurélien Griffouilhères, the head of Renault in Mexico, not just whose name, but also whose bearing, whose haughty nonchalance, high indolent profile, seem to me straight out of a novel from the period between the world wars.

It's another Chiapas, not yet the one of the Zapatistas, even less of sub-commandant Marcos and his photogenic balaclava.

We are in 1969, I repeat; the sub-commandant has, no doubt, at that date, not yet been born; the only Westerners one meets in San Cristobal are two old German women, dressed like nuns, but who are not nuns, and who run a boarding house, behind the cathedral, where chance has it that I read, for the first time, Sartre's *The Words*; and the main difference is above all that between Zinacantan and Tenejapa, by the shore of the Agua Azul, further on, in Chamula and San Andres, in the Tzotzil villages in the mountain where the great scholar of the native culture Pablo Gonzalez Casanova brought me, no one has ever heard of any of these "friends" who, thirty years later, in Paris, will make the "Zapatistas" a new holy cause.

It's another me, finally: another wife, I., the first one, mother of Justine-Juliette; another, more irregular, perhaps coarser, way of living the adventure of my freedom; other books too; Artaud more than Althusser; the Tarahumaras more than the Marxism-Leninism of my future Bengali stint; or rather no; both of them; the lived unity of Artaud and Althusser, of the Tarahumaras and the Marxists; the impossible synthesis, in the manner of early surrealism, of poetry and politics, of changing one's life and changing the world—that's maybe why when I'd barely entered the Ecole Normale I dashed off to Mexico; it's perhaps that gold that I was going to try to extract from my first Mexican time.

But that said, I find that the big difference, the real flip-side between these times, is in my own text.

I have in front of me that issue of *Les Temps modernes*. That famous white cover, almost unchanged after thirty years. The double colors of the lettering, black and wine-colored, which has disappeared. My name, Bernard-Henri Lévy—yes,

"Bernard-Henri," my full name and not my abbreviated name as I talked about it, for fun, and provocation, in *Comédie*—plainly printed (but this sobriety seemed to me the height of the conspicuous) under the heading "Mexico." And then the text itself, hyper-theoretical, dogmatic, overwritten (however much I say "Artaud, Tarahumaras, poetry," etc., I know I was, at that time, closer to Bonnie and Clyde than to Malraux, I must at that period have done a lot of stupid things that I had to get excused for, I must have had a lot of unpaid hotel bills and flights between the states of Morelos and Guerrero, for it's difficult to imagine a more stilted, constrained style, or one more in keeping with the political correctness of the time), the text, then, which consisted, for the main part, of a critique of the concept of a "country in the process of development." People talk about "development," I explained. Country "in the process of" development. But what else is it, this "process of development," but integration into the great chain of oppression that encircles the globe? What does that mean, if not the replication, within a country, or within a region of this country, or within a sub-region of this region, of the relationship of exploitation that functions on a planetary scale?

Everything is there. The real taste, again, of the passage of time. In that period, the great reproach I made against the system was trying to integrate the damned. Whereas, today, what overwhelms me is, on the contrary, their expulsion from the system and from History—their disintegration.

"…small people, minuscule existences…"

All the same.

I who love only the heroes, who was fed on Malraux and who spent my childhood and my adolescence dreaming about Jean Moulin and Colonel Berger, the fact is I have devoted days and days, between a windowless bus, a flat-bottomed barge, and a bivouac infested with insects, to taking an interest in the minuscule lives of Juan, Manolo, and Carlito.

If I try to find out why, if I try, setting aside the narcissistic self-justifications and the traditional humanist explanations, to justify this inclination, and to get to the bottom of the "change in my point of view" that made me go from the salt of the earth to the scum of the earth, from the infinitely great of the marble men of years gone by and their dazzling biographical careers to the infinitely small of this living but tiny humanity, I see, in fact, three reasons.

Kleist, first of all. Kleist the journalist. We know Kleist the poet and playwright. We know the author of *Das Käthchen von Heilbronn* and *The Marquise of O*. But we are less familiar with the surprising journalist, the resolute opponent of the person he called "the Corsican emperor." For six months, from October 1810 to March 1811—while an epic wind was blowing over the intelligentsia of Europe and while Hegel, at the same time, was seeing in Napoleon the architect, even the messiah, of a dreamed-of and revealed Europe—Kleist ran the *Berliner Abdendblätter*, a tiny daily newspaper made up of short news items, miscellaneous news briefs mixed with gossip, rumors, police reports published as such, laughable or purposely ridiculous paragraphs, in which the spirit of the time was, however, meant to be distilled.[37] One is reminded, except for the addition of the police reports, of Mallarmé's *Le Journal de la Dernière Mode*. One finds, too, with the possible exception of irony (for the chronicles in the *Berliner Abendblätter* are masterpieces of humor, facetiousness, derision, and diversion), the spirit of the Soviet samizdats from the grand era, where one had to know how to read between the lines. What interests me is the reversal of the hierarchy of the essential and the futile; it's this idea that, in the anecdote, the dross of time, its dregs, in these stories of "vicious dogs"—one step further and Kleist would say "crushed dogs"—told on a measly "quarter-page" and treated with the art of ellipsis, of innuendo and some-times of provocation, the salt of actuality can be found; what fascinates me is this confrontation between Kleist and Hegel, and the decision to contrast the great adventure of *The Phenomenology*, with its prosopopeia of the "Universal" and the "Concept," to the humble stories of a cloth-maker organizing, in order to celebrate the birthday of "His Royal Highness," a bal-loon trip into the Berlin sky (and we learn some fine things, in passing, about the winds, the apparatus, the art of introducing the latter to the former, and the holy terror this art inspires in the imperial police) or about "pieces of information about an incendiary named Schwarz and the band of thieves he belonged to" (a text that, at first sight, has no meaning either, but that, re-read with the third eye, that of derision and cunning, said much about the methods of the "soldiers of the guard at the gates of Berlin"). That this decision is dictated by necessity, that police censorship was, in this case, the muse for the *Catechism of the Germans established in accord with that of the Spanish, for the use of children and old people, in sixteen chapters*, doesn't prevent one from seeing in it rather a good metaphor for what one can expect, today, from journalism. Greatness of rumors. Nobility of the minute. Truth, no longer of History, but of sub-history.

Secondly, Benjamin. The Benjamin, once again, of the *Theses on the Philosophy of History*. And the portrait, in "Thesis IX," of the one he calls "the chronicler," whose characteristic is that he "narrates events without distinction between the great and the small" (nothing, from the viewpoint of the chronicler, "nothing of all that has ever happened" can or should be considered "of no use to History"). There is a political logic to this bias: a mechanical effect of the decision to unearth the history of the excluded and, systematically, to take the point of the view of the defeated and the rejected—does one choose from among the conquered? Are there good and bad rejects? How, when you opt for the nameless, can you tell some to enter the house of History, and others to stay outside? A philosophical logic: an effect, no less mechanical, of the deconstruction, following Franz Rosenzweig, of the concept of universal History and the great signifying scenes summoned up—to say that History, as such, does not exist, is to admit that there is no longer, anywhere, an authority or a judgment upon which one can determine the meaning that should be accorded events. If there is no more meaning, if there is no longer a keystone or a great transcendental signifier allowing us to impose an order on the pure disorder of what happens, that's because there is no longer any real criterion allowing us to distinguish between the central and the peripheral, the essential and the derisory, what has to do with world-history and what does not have to do with it; an event is an event; all events are valid. If the perverse effects of this change in perspective are obvious (insipid parrotings of *droidlommisme plat*—"Rights-of-Man-ism"—the worst versions of humanism), the advances are no less so (starting with some concern for what is happening in the black holes of the planet). But the most interesting thing is obviously, beyond politics and philosophy, the theological concern shown in the same "Thesis IX," in the next sentence, when the author of the *The Arcades Project* adds that "it is only to redeemed humanity that its past fully belongs": he does say "redeemed"; he will say, elsewhere, "delivered"; and it's a way of saying, firstly, that no one can say, before the Redemption, what fully belongs to the past and what does not belong to it; but, secondly, that this Redemption, this Deliverance, are themselves not possible unless there is invited (Benjamin says "summoned") to the order of the day the memory of all events without distinction, great and little, noble and humble. This Redemption will occur only if one proceeds, in the manner of those historians of the lives of princes who, not knowing what, when the time comes, will be retained to the credit of their examples, unable to foresee upon which incident of their existence the mercy of God will rest, preferred, in their uncertainty, to write everything down, to record everything, to register the everyday as well as the grandiose or the monstrous; it will occur only if the chronicler, too, anticipates the Last Judgment by absolutely forbidding himself to make a choice between souls. Löwy notes that Benjamin came close, by doing this, to Origen's speculations about the apocatastasis, with which he was familiar enough to have mentioned them in his essay on Leskov, and according to which all souls without exception will go to paradise.[38] I mostly think of the old Jewish speculations, analyzed by one of Benjamin's great interlocutors, Gershom Scholem, who acted as guide to me during the time of my *Testament de Dieu*, and according to whom the Messiah would not come to this world with the traits of one particular man, of a prophet, speaking at a given moment in time to imprint his definitive form on this time—but with the face of any man whatsoever, this one as well as that one, working at each instant of time by making himself the witness of Justice and of the Law. This is Messianism as I, following and accompanying Scholem, understand it. My way of believing in the Messiah is to give a voice to Manolo, Juan, Carlito.

And then I have a third reason to proceed in this way. It's this business, again, of the End of History. It's this night of the world that I have called the End of History, even if it didn't have much to do, in the last analysis, with the literal interpretation of Kojève's hypotheses. It's this space-time of the "black holes," this "hell" on earth, this "ruin," the characteristic of which I have shown is not just that the victims of it no longer have a name, that they scarcely have a face, that the very idea of a biography has become almost unthinkable to them, but that the events themselves of which they are the witnesses or victims seem to have been carried off in the whirlwind and have ceased being registered on the tablets of History. How can we struggle against that, then? How can we come to the aid of the inhabitants of such a hell? By taking hell at its word. By forcing what is not spoken to be spoken. By causing what is erased as it occurs to be recorded. By restoring their status as a fact of History, of event, to the improbable dust of the crimes and misdeeds collapsing into the black hole, the forgetting of which itself ends up being forgotten. In short, by doing all that we can do to restore to these peoples, not memory, but history, almost the archive, the meaning of historicity of which they have been deprived. I have said that naming, in these zones, was already an act of resistance. I have said—and, moreover, there are, in Benjamin's work again, in his 1916 essay for instance, many notations on the virtue of the name and the faculty each person has to forge his own destiny from the name that was given to him or that he has decided to inhabit—I have said that the fact of returning their names to people, of identifying their lives, their faces, was already a way of coming to their aid. Now I say that, beyond names and faces, there are events; that to record an event, to re-inscribe it into a system of previous or concomitant events, is also a political act; that to distinguish events, to break the false temporal unities, the ready-made unities of time, to return its dignity to the event, is an act of resistance. We send doctors to Colombia. I almost want to say, half in provocation but half in earnest, that it would be almost as useful to send NGO's of archivists and historians there. To save the past and the present, that's what's urgent. To save the events snapped up by the black hole, swallowed up by the whirlwind, that's the idea. The event is a new idea in Colombia, in Burundi, in the South Sudan, in Angola, in Sri Lanka. The event is a revolutionary idea for two-thirds of humanity.

Hegel, in *Lessons on the Philosophy of History*—an echo, and an encouragement, of this mission that should be entrusted to archivists and historians: "History is made less by those who make it than by those who tell about it..."

So, obviously, the problem is Stendhal. Stendhal's theorem. Namely the fact that Fabrice sees nothing, understands nothing, has access to none of the keys that would allow him to understand the logic of the battle at Waterloo that occupies the early pages of *The Charterhouse of Parma* and that he lived through without really experiencing it. The problem is this old idea that, for convenience, I date back to him, Stendhal, but that all the witnesses of all the wars had more or less felt—namely that the point of view of the minute, of the minuscule, which is to say, at bottom, of the fighter in his hole, of the French infantryman in his trench, or of the observer in his barge headed for Quebrada Naïn, is a particular, local, partial point of view, "idiotic" in the etymological sense: a point of view that sees nothing, hears nothing, says nothing, serves no purpose. Doesn't Homer himself express the inevitable "limit" of the point of view of Achilles and Hector? Doesn't the bard, in order to tell about the capture of Troy, have to transport himself, in thought, to the clouds where the Olympians sit? And as for me... I talk big. Brag. I cradle pious phrases like "grandeur of murmurs," "nobility of the infinitesimal," etc. But what is the first thing I did when, after diving into the Gehenna of Bangladesh, I returned to breathe a little, in the other Bengal, in Calcutta? I charged into the offices of the *Times of India* to check, in the issues I had missed, the maps showing the troop movements, and thus the meaning of the battle I had just experienced from within, and about which I had the impression, while it was happening, of understanding nothing.

Three possible attitudes towards this theorem:

The first. Stendhal's theorem is false. I believed in it, that's true. I was the first, at the time of Bangladesh, to fall into the trap and to wait to get outside in order to find the true point of view. But it was false. I discovered, with time, that it was false. For the eye of the fighter does see true, after all. Even if he is local, enclosed in his singularity, bogged down, he still has access, very quickly, to the profound truth of the battle. Fabrice? Fabrice is special. A foreigner, first of all. Ignorant of military matters. Dropped as if by parachute onto a battlefield about which he couldn't give a damn. Indifferent. His head elsewhere. Give me a Fabrice who's a little forewarned. Give me a Fabrice concerned with the "war damned," the "humanism of the other man," the "Messianism of the quotidian," Scholem. Give me a Pierre Bezukhov climbing, in civilian clothes, up to the front lines of the battle of Borodino, or a special correspondent in Bangladesh more awakened than the man from '68 who, in Jessore, looked first to a mirror to learn his moods and emotions. And then see what you see! You'll see that, in five minutes, he'll notice the nobility of the minute, the profundity of the most minuscule incident—in five minutes, he'll discover that it's starting from the local that one arrives at the general, and that extreme singularity is a good way to reach the universal. That was surely Kleist's conviction. Or Karl Kraus's, polemicist and journalist, seeing—once again it's Benjamin speaking—"in the least element of one single local piece of news, of one single sentence, of one single announcement, all of world history building upon it." Or even, who knows? of Leibnitz distinguishing in each monad a miniature of the world, a presentiment of the whole, a *pars totalis*. That's the conviction of all those who think that, not just the devil, but the truth is in the details.

The second. Stendhal was right. Fabrice's point of view is in fact a partial point of view. Obtuse. Unintelligent. But there it is. It's the only one. There is no other. There is nothing more to see in the reality of wars than this absurd hell where one continuously wonders where one is, where one is going, where the shells are coming from, who is firing them and what have become of the fine heroic virtues chanted by the literature of war. Perhaps Fabrice has understood nothing at all. But that's all there was to understand. That's the very essence of war, to yield this feeling of incomprehensible chaos, of absurdity, of a juxtaposition of idiotic, blind viewpoints closed off from each other. The *Times of India* business, for instance... What, frankly, did the big black arrows on the *Times of India* maps give me? What more did they teach me about the reality of the battles of Jessore or Khulna in which I had been involved and about which I thought, at the time, that their essence had escaped me? Nothing, in fact. For the battles of Jessore and Khulna, as I know today, did not exist. They were chimeras. Creatures born of reason. They were abstractions that had to be surpassed, pulverized, yes, literally pulverized, reduced to dust, in order to rediscover, beneath the chimera, in the fascinating but idiotic shadow of "the" great unique battle, the grit of the micro-battles or micro-destinies that were its truth, its prime number, its reality. What exists is Fabrice in Jessore. Fabrice in Khulna. What exists, what counts, is that all of us—infantrymen, of course; but also humanitarians, reporters, witnesses, and even, if they are honest, leaders, officers—all of us are Fabrices in Jessore and Khulna, overwhelmed by the war that they're waging and that is waged through them. And those who tell you the contrary, those who come to say to you: "There is another point of view, there is, somewhere, a vantage point from which you can see what the fighter is doing but doesn't comprehend," are either fools, or cheats, or professional sugar-coaters who just want to create a diversion and delude us about the depths of aberration that are the truth of wars. Bardamu would say that, I think. And the Sartre of the *Carnets de la drôle de guerre.** That's the conviction most compatible with my hypothesis of wars which meaning has deserted.

And then the third attitude, finally. Stendhal was right, yes. Perhaps he was even completely right and there in fact exists, somewhere, another point of view that is not that of Fabrice but of an omniscient observer, a general for instance, or, what amounts to the same thing, a novelist. The problem is that I couldn't care less. That's not what interests me. This grand point of view, if it exists, is absolutely not the one I'm looking for. There is "the" battle of Khulna, on one hand, which had nothing to tell me; and there is the little Mukti Bahini, on the other, who preferred to kill himself rather than have to fight—and he is the one that haunts me. There is the strategy of Ivan Rios, the head of the FARC, which makes me yawn with boredom; and there is Quebrada Naïn, its survivors, its twenty forgotten dead about whose existence even Rios was unaware—and even if I've served

---

*"Notebooks of this Joke of a War," translated as *War Diaries*

just for that purpose, even if I've made this entire journey just to learn that and draw the attention of the Marxist-Leninists of the FARC to the fact that their units, on the field, are acting like fascists, then I won't have wasted my time. There is, in a word, what a character in Jules Romains' *Men of Good Will* calls "general staff strategy." There is this "specialist" tone that Malraux easily adopts, and that I still find a little ridiculous, when he tells about the attack on the Colon hotel, the armored trains of Siberia, or the technical and logistical problems of the squadron in *Sierra de Teruel*. There is Proust, of course, devouring the chronicles of Henry Bidou and putting them in the mouths of the two rival strategists, Charlus and Saint-Loup. There is that interview from June 1941, in *PM*,[39] where Ernest Hemingway is proud to allow the interviewer to disclose that "long before he was a novelist," he was a "war correspondent," and that, before he was a "war correspondent," he was a "military expert" who "was a student of war in its totality"—"its totality," he insists: "Everything about war, from the machine-gun emplacements to tactics and maneuvers"; and adds, to show his expertise, "to civilian morale and industrial organization for war." In short, there is a whole tradition of war writers, curious about war as such, passionate about weapons, armies, the games and goings-on of war. That tradition is not my own. Those centers of interest are not my own. The knowing airs that armchair warriors assume (more Proust's Norpois than Bidou!) as they evoke the global chess games to which, by their lights, the confrontations between peoples are reduced, have always seemed grotesque to me. Because my problem is not the warriors but the victims. Not the strategists but the civilians. In the phrase "war damned," the important word is "damned," not "war."

The Communism of the Stalinist doctors of law for whom ideology was just a knout for the purpose of taming human cattle? Malraux, in *The Royal Way*, had already understood and expressed the essential thing: "Garine believes in nothing but energy. He is not anti-Marxist, but Marxism is by no means a scientific socialism for him; it's a method to organize workers' passions, a means to recruit shock troops from the workers."

"...naked, unadorned violence, reduced to the bone of its
bloody truth..."

*In bello veritas?** Perhaps after all. Maybe I have to reconsider the
idea, revise my stubborn refusal to consider it. Perhaps we should
restore to war this role of human observatory that the writers of
the 1930's gave it. But be careful. It's true in Céline's sense, not
Drieu's. Because it would be an image, not of grandeur, but of
filth. Because it would in fact be a magnifying glass, a mirror—
but of the worst. Exaltation of the human? No. Debasement.
Degradation. The Freudian veneer cracking. The solidarities, fra-
ternities, communal ties, exploding and leaving behind them an
immense field of naked hatred, furious resentments, deliberate or
tolerated torture, barbarisms. The inhuman, not the human. The
face, rather, of the human when the inhuman works through it
and occupies it. Everything we had suspected about the most
inhuman within the human. The whole abjection that rose to the
surface, that we had guessed at, but that, like a domesticated animal, had been kept on a leash, that whole dark ground that makes
everyone the worst enemy of everyone else—that is what war lays
bare. That, in fact, is the truth of war.

"Without war, Joan of Arc would have died a shepherd
girl and Marshall Hoche an ostler," Dorgelès marveled. True
enough. But we must immediately turn the comment around

---

* In war there is truth.

(and this is no longer the exception but the rule): without war, Carlos Castaño would die as an inoffensive and weak psychopath; without war, all those guys who were gathered around him, in the conference-tent, and whose horrible crimes we know from the reports of the UN and the big NGO's, would die as *finqueros*, farm workers; it is the function of war, in other words, to create the exceptional state that has made these farmhands, these decent guys with the slow gestures of peasants, full of prudence and self-control, into appalling killers. Pepe, the man who serves coffee to the leader, his eyes stuck together from sleep, shaving cream in his moustache... That officer, with a childlike and guileless smile, who seems, at times, to escape into daydreams... The other one, who looks at me with kind, gentle eyes and who urges me to take fewer notes and to eat: "You don't like *huevos revueltos*, Professor? Do you want something else? Green beans? Rice? Grilled meat? Tell me, Professor, tell me; we are yours to command; you've made such a long journey..." It's war, yes, that has established the exceptional state in response to which these men calmly, without betraying or disowning themselves, without ceasing to be what they had been, honest farmhands, have been able to make themselves guilty of a massacre, the one at Quebrada Naïn, a few of whose scenes I have already described (a peasant woman with her throat cut; another, crucified in her barn; the little girl whose eyes they gouged out before they sent her running, blind, and shot at her like a rabbit) and the rest of whose scenes must be spoken, all the others, as Carlito, Juan, and Manolo told me (breaking the bones of a man, one by one, methodically, before finishing him off with a bullet in the head;

cutting up the face of another man with a razor; forcing a third, with a rifle to his temple, to tear apart with his teeth the balls of a companion chained to a bench; destroying a mother with a flamethrower in front of her child). War, truth of farmhands?

Return to Bogota. Last day. Some excitement, in the local press, at the idea that a foreigner could have gotten as far as the country's invisible man and extracted an interview from him. And a meeting with a French-Colombian journalist who asks me the question that Mufid Memija asked me, the director of the Bosnian radio-television, the first time he saw me in Paris, at home, then in a restaurant where I was a regular: "Why do you do this? Why does a philosopher, a successful writer, seemingly spoiled by life, probably content, do such things? Why, if you are not a journalist, when it's not your profession and when you don't make your living from journalism, why do you take such reckless risks? Why do what you have no reason to do?" My answer (a little "official," no doubt; but why shouldn't it also be,—though official and acceptable—sincere? Why shouldn't it deliver—as does my confession of the sort of pleasure a plunge into the situations of war produces—another portion of the truth?)—my answer, then, in a tone which, looking back, I judge a little grandiloquent, but oh well, that's how it was: Proust and Mallarmé had no "reason," relatively speaking, to become involved in favor of Dreyfus; Mauriac and Bernanos were the last people, in the spring of 1936, you would expect to side with Republican Spain, against Franco. Marc Bloch took arms against Vichy while everything, in the way he had, in the *Annales*, conceived of history, in the "inherent fatalism"—this is Marc Bloch speaking—in the practice of his discipline, in the emphasis placed on "the long run," in the insistence on the "play of massive forces" that give structure to society—all of that should have "turned him away from individual action." And are we, in fact, sufficiently surprised at how the prophet of the death of man, Michel Foucault, could establish himself as a defender of the rights of man! Have we gone on enough about the so-called paradox of this "structuralist" philosopher, master of "archeology" and "epistemic regularities," who had denied himself, for the sake of principle, the ease of the idealism of consciousness and who took it upon himself to speak of asylums, prisons, rebellions, the ethics of liberation, the subject's resistances to modern scenarios of subjection, strategies! Well, it's just this paradox that I like. Foucault is the one who, in my opinion, takes the prize for his characteristic gesture. I have often expressed my admiration, among scholars, for these traitors to their own family, their tribe, their class, their supposed or required solidarities (the red bishops and marquesses of 1789, the French bearers of portfolios in the FLN, the great revolutionary or third-world members of the middle class, Feltrinelli, etc.). Even more interesting is the act of becoming involved against what, not just your class, but the inclination of your own thinking seemed to compel you to do and think. More admirable, more exemplary, are the absolutely paradoxical ones, the one who contradict themselves, the ones engaged, not just without compulsion, but without logic—the ones who have, in effect, no reason for doing what they do.

"As if, in the Sudan, even Good had been placed in the service of Evil."

The years pass. The setting changes. But, each time, the same uneasiness confronts humanitarian ideology. Each time the same malaise. And, each time, the same litany of objections.

The people, first of all. Often they are generous. Courageous. They are the honor of a world without honor. The soul of a planet without soul. They have the merit of being the last European representatives, whether we like it or not, of the Universal, in a world that Europe has abandoned. But beside them are the others. The bureaucrats of misfortune. The functionaries of horror and assistance. Those folks who in Addis-Ababa ran after the refugees and lined up at the ministry of "Solidarity" in order to obtain the right to sell their "humanitarian" merchandise. Those others—maybe the same ones—who, already in Cambodia, then in the so-called "safe" zone in Iraqi Kurdistan that, after the war in Kuwait, the UN forces occupied, reasoned only according to the "market share" they needed to satisfy their shareholders, sorry, their donors. In short, that whole humanitarian population that makes aid into an end in itself and refuses to mix it with any kind of economic, political, or moral consideration. It's the "Don't touch my well" syndrome. It's aid for aid's sake, which has become a crazy machine, dedicated to its own self-nourishment. It's the ridiculous Princesse de Bormes who, in Cocteau's *Thomas the Impostor*, "is forced to turn away the wounded whom she needs to keep her role in the war." Or it's that page in Gide's *Journal* where we see a lady of good works, probably the model for the Princess and for all those men and women who resemble her, shouting to the company at large, on the stairway of the Red Cross building (we're in the middle of war, August 20, 1914): "They promised me fifty wounded for this morning; I want my fifty wounded."[40] I found a little of all of that in Barnum in Lokichokio, on the South Sudan border. I heard the old music again in the discourse of this American who, when I told him they had found his aid packages in the black market, in the villages on the Kenyan border, shrugged his shoulders and replied: "What do you want me to do? My job is to transport aid to the scene of the action... to pass it out to the recipients... afterwards, what the recipients do with it, if they want to sell it in the Kenyan markets... what do you want me to do about it?" The Princesse de Bormes, plus some cynicism.

The war. The place, in the war economy, for humanitarian logic and procedures. My concern, here, in Alek, stems not from the fact that an NGO could, in good conscience, decide to mobilize in the service of one of the opposing parties—in this instance, John Garang's: what else did I expect, after all, during my years in Bosnia? Isn't that what I demanded (although in a different ideological and political context) from the over-timid organizations who were afraid of their shadow and recoiled at the mere idea of assuming the political responsibilities that the madness of the world was imposing on them? But it certainly stems, on the other hand, from the fact that the whole system could, thoughtlessly, mechanically, without trying to think the thing through, sign up for the game of war and its economy. There too, everything began in Addis-Ababa, in 1986, during the great population displacements from the North to the South that were decreed, in a fit of Sovietized madness, by Mengistu, the red Negus. The operation, insofar as it ripped almost all the Ethiopian farmers from their land and thus paralyzed the harvest cycle, was technically possible only if an influx of food resources came, from outside, to fill the gap—which, in a fine spirit, without reflection, most of the big NGO's did, participating in that way in this immense reshaping of human geography, and of the geography of the country itself. Well, it's the same thing here. The same exploitation of pity. The same inscription of good feelings in a game that gets out of the hands of the actors. And the same macro-economic contribution of aid to an overall strategy that is nothing but war against civilians. What are our aid packages used for? To feed civilians or to allow the warlords to continue in their warring existence? To save children or to allow some killer to expropriate the peasants, burn their fields, destroy the entire country?

The economy in general. The place of humanitarian aid in the economy, not just of the war, or even of the region, but of the world. Generosity, actually? Compassion? That does exist, of course. And far be it from me to come down hard on the simple people who, at each catastrophe, with an admirable regularity, take action and contribute—far be it from me to deny that the NGO's, when they send food supplies or doctors to populations deprived of everything, when they give supplies to stave off death to men and women who, like the Nuba, have been feeding themselves now, for a long time, on nothing but bark and roots, earn the incalculable merit of saving bodies from an agonizing death. But at the same time... Those poorly freeze-dried foodstuffs. Those sometimes expired canned foods. Those tins of stewed fruit, stored in a warehouse in Lokki. Those military rations. Those crates of condensed milk. That silo of sugar. That coffee in bulk. What if Lokki also happened to be a dumping ground for products the West no longer wanted? What if the Third World in general were also serving as a trash-bin, not just for our nuclear waste and our pollution, but also for the surplus of an economy of overabundance? In short, what if, by receiving our donations, by getting parachuted, as, previously, the Bosnians of Gorazde or the Kurds of the operation "Provide Comfort" did, tons and tons of products or inferior products, in fact the living-dead of the region of Gogrial, and the war damned in general, also helped us to absorb our economic surpluses, which are the toxic wastes of our economies? There was the time of pillaging the Third World. There was the great era when the Marxist economists (Pierre Jalée, André Gunder Frank, Baran, Sweezy) took apart the mechanism of the extortion of excess labor, of excess value, in the Third World. Times have changed. Perhaps even the prevailing trend has ended up by being reversed. Extortion certainly continues. And the servicing of debt, the unending negotiation of new loans intended to finance the repayment of interest on the old ones, can certainly be considered, in the poorest countries, as another way of wringing dry already bloodless economies. But the new element is elsewhere: a Third World that has become, no longer the reservoir, but the dumping-ground for the developed world; no longer a mine for profit but a trash-bin for refuse; no longer the function of surplus-value, but the old potlatch function about which we have known, since Marcel Mauss, that it is one more function essential to the functioning of the system.

Politics. Or, more precisely, forgetting politics. And the confusion of humanitarianism with the politics whose place it is taking more and more. How can you avoid the political and make it seem you're not avoiding it? How can you abandon the disinherited populations of the Third World to their fate and prevent public opinion, whose emotionalism is familiar to us, from having a sudden awakening of conscience and reproaching their governments? By humanitarianism. A strong presence of humanitarian aid. The transformation of the government itself into a giant humanitarian aid agency. And a media/humanitarian frenzy that will at least have the effect of masking the absence of vision, of aim, of will. Sometimes, though, it's not so bad; sometimes the humanitarians are the last ones, as I said, to carry the colors of Europe, to defend a certain idea of humanity and human honor and to remember, consequently, the time when it was through politics that one resisted oppression; I have known these kinds of humanitarians; I have seen them at work, here, in the Sudan, torn between rival warlords and refusing to give in to the commands of either side; I have seen them, in Angola, refusing to serve as auxiliaries for the army of the MPLA in order to hold for the MPLA the zones it had conquered; I have seen them fighting, in a word, so some remnant of unbroken universality can, I don't dare say live, but at least survive in countries that have, with our help, abandoned them. But sometimes aid is catastrophic; and, without giving in to the temptation of pessimism, it is difficult not to reflect that the whole humanitarian apparatus serves to anaesthetize public opinion, to disarm its protests, and above all to discourage the initiative of those who could be tempted to do more; this was the case in Bosnia where the presence, on the field, of forces of humanitarian intervention capable of becoming the target for a potential Serb reprisal quickly became the sledgehammer argument of the non-interventionists; this is the case in Afghanistan, where the safety of the teams present in Kabul, in Taliban territory, served as a pretext for the President of the French Republic to refuse to receive the leader Massoud when he came to Paris. That is the case here in the Sudan, where the humanitarian machinery has as its prime effect the prolonging of a war that the West has, if it wanted, the financial, hence political, means to stop.

The ideology, finally. This mixture of vitalism and knee-jerk *droidlommisme*—Rights-of-Man-ism—that is the spontaneous ideology of the humanitarian party. What is *droidlommisme*? It's a discourse of leveling out, of banalization, of Evil which, starting from the right idea that every victim deserves sympathy and help, ends up with the false idea that all victims are worthy, that there are no grounds for distinguishing either between the types of sympathy they should inspire in us or between the reasons that induced or precipitated their suffering—a *droidlommiste* is one who tells us that a death in Auschwitz is equal to a death in a demonstration that went awry; a *droidlommiste* is one who, to use a case already cited, refuses to distinguish, with the excuse that they are all equally victims, between the Rwandan Tutsis genocided by the Hutus and the Hutu genociders then driven from Kigali and threatened with famine in the Goma camps. What is vitalism? It's the spontaneous philosophy of the *droidlommistes*; it's the metaphysics that *droidlommisme* needs to base its claims on; it's a metaphysics that, roughly speaking, comes down to saying that men are only bodies, that these bodies are only matter, and that, since nothing resembles a heap of matter more than another heap of matter, it is not just absurd, illegitimate, and scandalous, but also impossible, to distinguish between victims and to confer a privileged status, for instance, on the Shoah; a vitalist is one who denies the soul (that is the high, noble form of the system); vitalism is the elision, or foreclosure, of politics (that is its trivial version). A vitalist, thus, is one, since neither the soul nor politics exists, who prohibits himself from entering even a little bit into the reasonings of the Devil.

The years pass, yes. Situations change. But what neither passes nor changes is the unease I feel faced with this Red Cross discourse. Stefan Zweig: "Beware of pity." Nietzsche, *The Gay Science*: love also must be "learned." Brecht, *The Caucasian Chalk Circle*—it's Grisha, the kitchen girl, speaking: "Great is the temptation to be good." But what, truly, is this temptation? What is the nature of this goodness, this pity, this compassion? Is it a virtue, really? Or a passion? Or a vice like the others? Or a neurosis?

"...devastated amphitheater of an ancient city, witness to a disappeared civilization..."

Usually, apocalypse threatens. Here, in the Sudan, it has taken place. Usually, hell is beneath the earth; here, it is on the earth, visible to the naked eye, it can be visited; a few hours in a Beechcraft and you're there. Usually, hell is invisible; here, there it is, testimonies are available, you just have to lean forward to hear, open your eyes to see, you just have to take a Beechcraft in order, three or four hours later, to land in the Nuba mountains and plunge into the heart of the night—I've done it, why shouldn't the UN people do it? And the people from NATO? And the various and diverse ministers, the important ones, the masters of the world, all those people who have nothing on their lips but the charter of the Rights of Man, the merits of globalization? But no. No one wants to see; no one wants to hear; as in the time of the dissidents, as in the time of Bosnia, as in Chechnya, as always in the twentieth century, this terrible desire to escape horror, to keep from being exposed to it—until the day, of course, when it catches up to you and strikes you in turn... Nietzsche and the Nietzschians believed we take refuge in nothingness out of hatred and fear of life. The truth is that we take refuge in life out of fear and hatred of nothingness—the truth is that we cling to life, we drown our sorrows with diversions and life, most of all in order not to have to think about death and nothingness. We have to force them to see it, then. There has to be a terrorism of the gaze. We'll have to do what the American soldiers did in 1944 after the liberation of the camps, when they forced the German city dwellers to file past the corpses. Innocent, the ordinary German citizens? Never, ever lent a hand to the crematoriums of Bergen-Belsen? Maybe. If you like. But that's not the question now. The gesture, all the same, of the Americans forcing them just to file by, to look, to keep their eyes open, above all not to go back to sleep. A good metaphor, in short, for the role of intellectuals.

"...Responsibility for responsibility, a suggestion."

Optimism is not dead. Return of activist instincts. I am ready, at this moment, to mount a crusade against the oil companies, guilty of all the evils in the Sudan. But a crusade for what, exactly? For the eradication of war? To convince my contemporaries, oil companies or not, that it would be so easy to be good, to renounce killing, etc.? I don't believe in that. I believe, in my innermost being, that war is, like sex, and death, a given of the human condition. I believe that man, just as he is the only animal able to love just to love, out of pure pleasure, without procreating, is also the only one able to kill just to kill, without necessity, also out of pleasure. I believe Clausewitz is right when, well before his *On War*, in the polemics of his youth with the von Bülow of *Geist des neuern Kriegssystems**, he hacks to pieces the idea that the technical progress of weaponry, and even progress just by itself, can lead us one day to perpetual peace. I think his later famous definition is perennially valid, often quoted in an abbreviated version ("War is not just a political act but an actual instrument of politics, a pursuit of political relations, a realization of these by other means..."). Against the same von Bülow, against his illusion of postmodern states, based on "justice and liberty," against his dream of states which, having ended up

---

* "Spirit of the Modern System of War," written by Adam Heinrich Dietrich von Bülow in 1798.

extending "to their natural limits," would one day find it "useless and dangerous" to operate beyond these "borders that nature has prescribed for them," Clausewitz predicates the perpetuity of war on that of the nature of the state. I believe, more precisely, that the only way of overcoming the definition is, as Foucault has already done, to reverse it by saying "No! it's the opposite! Politics is war continued by other means! It's the system of war that functions as an analyzer of relationships of power and not the relationships of power as analyzers of the war"—and I believe that, by proceeding in that way, by reversing the definition, one only generalizes it and gives it even more force, more range. Even if there is still a lot to say—Raymond Aron has done so—about the illusion of a Hegel-Clausewitz rapprochement and an identification of the two concepts of "dialectics" at work in *The Science of Logic* and in the *Notes on Prussia in its Great Catastrophe*, I finally believe that it is not just the followers of Clausewitz but also the Hegelians, who, on this point, were right, and that we'll be done with the desire for war only when we're done with History, Evil, or that elementary form of History and Evil we call Politics. Death wish (Freud). Man cursed by man (Bataille). Trans-historicity of the desire for war.

One can always dream, of course, of an era that would do away with History, Politics, and thus war. We can always tell ourselves the same eternal fable of post-historical times when humans, freed from the fatal cycle that these games of History, Evil, and Politics lead them, will live the happy, almost vegetative life that Kojève ascribed to animals. And surely the fear we experienced when we saw the specter of war return to Bosnia and Kosovo, our reluctance to get involved in it, our laissez-faire attitude of let-the-UN-do-it, our cowardliness, the transformation of our soldiers into blue-helmets and of the blue-helmets into bureaucrats of humanitarianism, clerks of the deaths of others, Kafka-like accountants of tears and horror, perhaps all that, this myth of a war with zero dead, testified to the mad, pathetic desire we had to see von Bülow still wind up, one day, being right, and Clausewitz wrong. For now, we haven't reached that point. The least one can say is that History is still here. War, whether we wanted it or not, prospers, knocks at our doors even now, right at the heart of the Western capitals. And there is, for a democrat, only one obligation, arising from this, one task, and only one. Not: "to have done " with war—pious wish! absurdity! and, like any time we act as if we could dispense with Evil, like all the times we play with crossing out Evil, there are inevitably the opposite effects, starting with the return of actual wars! But the rhythm of human affairs being what it is, wars dragging along on one hand (forgotten wars), and coming back again on the other (the shock of terrorism), our obligation is to force ourselves, on the contrary, to confront this double reality head-on and deal with it.

Faced with international terrorism and the terrible threat it imposes on democracies, there is one single objective: to stop closing our eyes, to stop burying our heads in the sand, to take the responsibility of naming the adversary and provide ourselves with the means—at once military, political, and moral—to conquer him.

On the other front, that of the forgotten wars and of the second evil, dependent on the first, its counterpart, its mirror-image, perhaps even the obscure hearth from which it draws part of its energy, there are three simple, clear, minimal tasks, but which, if we really take them seriously, they too force us to break with the stupidity of pacifist visions of the world.

To defend civilians, first of all. Since these wars are wars where one can scarcely distinguish civilians from the mass of combatants, since these wars' very principle is to erase the border that, from time immemorial and as long as the world has been a theater for wars, implemented this distinction, we must do everything we can to overcome this—do everything, mobilize all the resources of the laws of media hype, so that civilians, at the very least, are protected.

To penalize war crimes, next. To judge them. To remind people that there are laws of war and that it is up to us—to public opinion, to the international judicial institutions that are forming—to see to it that these laws are respected and, when they are not, that the guilty parties, all the guilty parties, the soldiers of Khartoum of course, but also, when the facts indicate, the Nuers, and the Dinkas too, are implacably condemned. How, without so doing, can we prevent people from saying Good when they mean Evil, and by doing that, entering the eternal road of the Devil?

War for war's sake, finally; war being what it is, we must try to conduct ourselves, in these wars, as warriors of thought—to try to think as war does, that's to say to take the side, or even the point of view, not just of groups alone, but of the ideas that wage war through people. Are these wars without meaning? Is it their whole principle no longer to implement ideas or values? First of all that's not always true and, when that isn't true, in Bosnia for instance, the task of thought is to refuse the comfort of neutrality,

to break the terrible logic that dismissed victims and executioners alike and instead take a stand with the—mainly Bosnian—
camp of Justice and Law. And then when that is true, when it is
impossible, in fact, to choose one camp over another, when the
cause of the Hutus in Burundi seems no more just than that of
the Tutsis, or that of the Sri Lankan army no more righteous
than that of the Tamil kamikazes, when one can scarcely discern,
in the Sudan or in Angola, any place where the ideas of liberty,
right, universality, have found to lodge, it's still the fact that
these ideas exist; the fact remains that they continue to live the
eternal life of ideas. The fact remains too that we should bear
witness to this life—the fact remains, to continue in the
language of the Bible, that, of this (metaphysical) "remnant," we
should be the (prophetic) "remnant" and that, if we can neither
stop these wars nor make them disappear, we can at least, in the
war itself, be witnesses, the only and final witnesses, of what they
are trying to eliminate. That is what the best humanitarians do.
That is what war reporters do. That task is the responsibility of a
writer traveling through the black holes.

September 10-11. Death of Massoud. I met him, for the first time, in 1980, right after the Soviet occupation of Afghanistan. Then, eighteen years later, still in the Panjshir, when I was doing a report for *Le Monde* (see the note linked to this). Now how can I not be tempted to connect the two threads of the sequence? How can I not imagine that the false journalist who trapped him was actually just the first in a chain of kamikazes whose final objective was the Twin Towers in Manhattan? As if the barbarians were intent on doing things in order. As if, anticipating an American reprisal, they had wanted first to make a clean sweep and rid the country of the only credible alternative to the Taliban. As if they had wanted, too, to inaugurate a new era by the elimination of the one leader who embodied, not just in Afghanistan but in the world, democratic and tolerant Islam. Grief. Infinite sadness. Presentiment of a catastrophe that already wears the face of the killers of Massoud.

Here, then, is this legendary commander, at war for almost twenty years—first against the Soviets, and now against the Taliban.

We met again in Dushanbe, capital of Tajikistan, that Muslim republic, outcome of the ex-USSR, which itself is scarcely over its own civil war but where he has established his rear bases.

And we are in one of those big combat helicopters, completely dilapidated, which, when weather permits, make the connection with his stronghold in the Panjshir and which are, in a way, his last link with the outside world.

He is wearing a khaki tunic and beige trousers.

On his head is his traditional Afghan cap with the edges rolled up; with his fine beard, his pointed face, his long eyelashes, the hat makes him resemble Che Guevara in his final days.

He is smaller than I had thought. Almost frail. He has a look of extreme pallor that contrasts with the black of his hair and makes him seem younger than his almost fifty years.

He spent the beginning of the journey among his men: about twenty fighters, very lightly armed, wearing uniforms that don't match, or no uniforms at all, and sitting on two metal benches, on either side of the cabin. Then he went to sit in the cockpit, on a wooden jump seat, gently towering above the two pilots, silent, strangely stiff: doing nothing but, in mid-flight, above the summits of the Hindu Kush, the traveler's prayer and then, the rest of the time, a funny swaying motion of his shoulders, down to up, back to front, as if he had to unburden himself of an invisible load.

What is Commander Massoud thinking about, on his child-size seat, his face turned to the sky, his gaze on the horizon?

The scene at boarding, just now, at the military airport in Dushanbe, with its Russian customs inspectors, at the foot of the gangway, who called the names of his soldiers and verified their passports... that air of arrogance... The Russians' way of making them feel they were at their mercy! Could anyone be more humiliating?

These strange relationships he has with his Russian "protectors": adversaries yesterday, allies today? How can one be the ally of people whom one has battled for so long? What confidence can one feel in enemies who declare themselves your friends only because you have become the enemy of their enemy—Pakistan, Saudi Arabia, Muslim fundamentalists...? And how could he help but see that these "experts" they're sending him, these so-called "specialists" supposed to help him take up arms and resist, are the ones who knew him the best, that is, who fought him the hardest?

Or is he still thinking about this desolate immensity he sees going by beneath him: his beloved country, his land that he loves and for which he has been fighting for almost twenty years— Yangi Qala... Rostaq... Ab Bazan... the foothills of the Hindu Kush... a village, to the east, that we avoid since it is held by the Taliban... another, a little more to the south, where their anti-aircraft defense, this winter, shot at an aircraft… the circle of mountains, opposite us, with their wall of snow… the Taloqan mountains… the Farkhar river… he knows the names of these summits and passes… he knows the least trail and streambed… he knows everything about the epic of Alexander coming back up the Panjshir valley to conquer his Bactria and crossing the Amu Darya here, at the very place we're flying over… but is it still his country? About this lost and dreamed-of land, these magnificent landscapes he can no longer contemplate except from above, can he still say: "That is mine, that is my country"?

The flight lasts a little over two hours—zigzagging between peaks, colossal barriers the aircraft swerves around as if it didn't have enough power to fly over them, valleys. And when, at nightfall, we finally land in his region, in Jengalak, in a stone amphitheater, wedged between the mountains, where we wait for the village elders, a few soldiers, a bunch of children, he slips, still without a word, into a car—leaving it up to another Toyota to drive us, Gilles Hertzog and me, to the "tea-house" at the river's edge which serves as a guest house. He goes to his house. I to mine. And an old Mujahaddin welcomes me in his name: a cool room, a rug and a bedspread, a storm lantern, a pitcher of water changed every morning—royal treatment in this besieged Panjshir, which lacks everything…

In two hours he had said nothing. A sentence of welcome, on the tarmac. Another to say—but this was simple courtesy— that he remembered my first journey, eighteen years ago, via Peshawar, when, with Marek Halter, Renzo Rossellini and others, we had launched a campaign for "free radios for the Panjshir." Rarely, though, has a man who says nothing made such an impression on me—rarely has a silence seemed so charged with meaning, promise, mystery. His beauty, perhaps. This Christ-like leanness that in the West contributes to his legend and that, from close up, strikes one even more. But also this air of mingled sadness and serenity that he did not lose during the trip—a sovereign without a kingdom who, alone in his cabin, his gaze lost in dreams, flies over a territory over which I have the feeling, for the moment, that he has lost control. Pale shadows, names of countries, quavering narratives, memories. Massoud has lost everything; but, with his soul and his dreams, he resists; what a symbol!

But where has Massoud gone?

They tell us he left for Golbahar, in the extreme south of the valley, to visit a soldier who had just been brought home, his leg severed by a mine: time to arrive in Golbahar, time, with Hertzog and an interpreter, to travel in our turn these 80 kilometers of bad road littered with potholes and, on the embankments, carcasses of Soviet tanks that haven't been cleared away for ten years. He has gone.

They tell us he's in Bagram, further south, about forty kilometers from Kabul, where his troops have regained control of the air base: we go to Bagram; we note, in passing, that it has at its disposal two fighter planes seemingly in good flying condition, another being repaired, and a helicopter like the one yesterday; but in the time it takes to make ourselves understood and then for the patrol to clear away the barricade of anti-tank boulders—he has again disappeared.

They tell us again: "He is further off, in the plains, on the Charikar front, where an offensive is being prepared"—so we set a course for Charikar; the atmosphere is characteristic of the outskirts of a front line, with empty houses, razed villages that no one has rebuilt, abandoned dogs, buried artillery, and, on top of that, a company of children who make us get out of the car and ask us for our passes: here again, in the time it takes to explain ourselves, for their little commander to confer with the outpost and announce our arrival—Massoud has again taken off.

Chance, or is this on purpose? A series of mishaps, or is it the cunning of an actor directing the scene, one who is cleverer than he seemed? We will have spent this first day inside Afghanistan running after the most elusive of war leaders if, as evening fell, we hadn't stumbled on this scene—strange, magnificent, that erases whatever disappointment this pursuit could have left us with.

We are very close to the Salang pass, the same place where, a year ago, the opposition, using heavy weaponry, fought one of its most decisive battles.

A mosque, on the side of the mountain, overhanging the gorges.

Parked on the slope, in front of the mosque, an immense traffic jam of Toyotas surrounded by a swarm of armed teenagers.

And, inside the mosque, sitting on the ground, their faces lit by flashlights held like torches above their heads, here are two, maybe three hundred men, some in the djellaba over which they've slipped a jacket, others in camouflage combat gear, still others wearing the silk skullcap or the large rolled-up turban of traditional Afghan leaders: those often ageless men who are probably very young, fighters who have walked for many days to reach this place and who have, most of them, kept their weapons with them in this sacred place, men exhausted by the journey if not by war, food shortages, bitterness, these are the faithful commanders from the provinces of Parvan and Kapisa—and the man standing, facing them, to whom they are listening with a composed silence, is obviously Massoud.

"We did not lose Mazar-i-Sharif," he explains to them. "Mazar gave itself up. The leader of Mazar did what Bassir Salangi's officers did here, last year, when they went over to the Taliban, or what Abdul Malek did, in the North, in the province of Faryab. He betrayed. He sold himself. He handed over his city for a handful of dollars. Listen..."

For it's Massoud the orator, this time. He's a storyteller who can't be silenced, who, with a gentle voice, walking back and forth on his improvised platform, tells his warriors about the good and bad fortunes of Mazar, the criminal and honest commanders, the heroes and the bastards—how the Taliban are, at bottom, nothing at all but the playthings of the Pakistanis... how, wherever they triumph, they make Afghani civilization fall back "five centuries"... the obscurantism of their Islam... the fact that they are, not the friends, but the enemies of the true faith... the fate they have inflicted on the women of Kabul, which is an offense to God... and then his certainty, too, that there is, in this mosque, enough spirit and heart to liberate the country, sooner or later, from this dismal spell...

Sometimes he makes them laugh. Sometimes he makes them shudder. Sometimes, trembling with a contained fury, he lowers his voice even more—a muted voice, almost whispering, and then the leaders are quiet, hold their breath: their faces turned towards him, utterly concentrated.

At the end of the meeting, he yields the floor to an old leader who gets up, bent over his cane, to say that the Taliban are perhaps the "enemies of God," but that they are above all the "friends of the Communists"—and it's Massoud now who listens: seated in his turn, looking suddenly very youthful opposite this older man who corrects him; he has an enigmatic smile on his lips.

Then he makes room for another old man, a mullah, perhaps of this mosque, who intones, at the top of his voice, the muezzin's chant: and now all the commanders, along with him, having put down their weapons, their foreheads in the dust, begin to pray—and, outside, around the Toyotas, the men of his escort do likewise.

Is it the solemnity of the place? The somber brilliance of the faces? Is it his "oriental storyteller" side, and the contrast it makes with yesterday's strange silence? Whatever the case, this second Massoud radiates an even greater force—all the greater, perhaps, since it seems torn from the depths of poignant melancholy. We are conscious of him transmitting this force. We are conscious of the men, exhausted, who, listening to him, regain their courage. Massoud the war leader, inspiring his army of shadows. Massoud, the Commander, awakening his "epic tramps." For a resistance movement, it's fortunate to have a Massoud. This other mystery of iniquity that offers to one people, and not to another, the remarkable privilege of being embodied in a Massoud.

Yet another Massoud. Relaxed. Almost jovial. We are—it's the same evening—in Jabul Saraj, not far from the front lines, in an old military base that serves him as a local HQ, and where he likes to stop over, on evenings like this one, when the situation at the front is too tense for him to return to his house in the Panjshir.

The room is modest. The light, poor. His dinner consists of an apple, a little watermelon, a cup of tea, a few almonds.

"Why," I asked him, "did you insist, just now, at the Salang pass, on the role of the Pakistanis?"

"Because they are at the heart of this war. They are financing it. They are fomenting it. They have a vital interest in making Afghanistan into a kind of protectorate that would double the depth of their strategic territory, in case of a confrontation with India—and it's for this reason they invented the Taliban."

"Isn't it a little simple to reduce a phenomenon of this magnitude purely to foreign manipulation?"

"It's the reality. There are Pakistani instructors in Kabul. Pakistani officers on the field. In Mazar-i-Sharif, we even picked up conversations in Urdu on the radio, on the eve of its surrender. And the million dollars given to the commander of the city in exchange for this surrender, where do you think it came from, if not, yet again, from the Pakistani secret service—maybe, it's true, working with the Saudi secret services?"

"Haven't you committed mistakes too? Isn't it true that, if Afghanistan has reached this condition, it's also the fault of the leaders of the resistance in the red Army who, once they came into power, fought among themselves and discredited each other?"

Massoud gets ready to answer: but without spirit—I can see that he's exhausted and that these kinds of questions, tonight, weigh heavily on him. Then there appears, brought in by his aide-de-camp, a large turbaned character who presents himself as a merchant who, that very morning, had taken a bus out of Kabul and come to bring him fresh news of the city.

Massoud knows this man.

He is even, if I understand correctly, a sort of family friend whom he hasn't seen for a long time, but with whom he feels at ease.

The family friend takes off his turban.

They bring him tea, a plate of dried fruit and candies.

And now, taking out of his pocket a wad of scribbled-on pieces of paper, he launches, half-reading, half-improvising, into a long narrative, colorful and full of action, in which he figures first of all, along with the seventeen children he left there, his four wives, the fourth especially, the youngest, and the way in which, despite his 77 years, he is still capable of honoring her— and then especially about Kabul, about daily life in the occupied city, the weariness of the inhabitants, the stupidity of the Taliban: "Do you know that they forbid kites? And caged birds? And free doves? And the representations of the Buddhas in Bamayan? Do you know they're hunting down radios and televisions? And as soon as they discovered that ingenious people were managing to piece together antennas from bicycle wheels, they began to search everywhere, in caves, in courtyards, on terraces, to confiscate bicycles?"

Then stopping for a second to mop his forehead, breathe, and measure the effect he's produced:

"And the Koran! Ah, the Koran! I met, the other day, one of these 'theology students' who had just condemned a guy suspected of having his beard trimmed to forty lashes of the whip. I acted the imbecile. I said 'I am an old illiterate merchant and I'd just like to ask you the exact meaning of this prohibition from trimming one's beard.' Well do you know what he told me? Nothing! He looked panic-stricken and he stammered that he didn't know anything, I'd have to ask Mullah Omar! Ah! Ah! Ah! These students are ignoramuses—my youngest wife, at 25 years of age, knows more than they do about the holy commandments..."

The scene delights Massoud.

The merchant, it seems, has other stories in his bag—beginning with a matter of Taliban commanders on the point of betraying Kabul and defecting to his side. But either because he didn't have confidence in the reliability of the informant, or because he suspects a trap and doesn't want to show his interest too much, or because, once again, he first of all wants, tonight, to relax and laugh, Massoud makes him repeat the names of the three commanders, asks if they had any ties, in the past, with his old adversary Gulbuddin—but only to return, very quickly, to the rest of the narrative: the clownishness of the Taliban, which fills him with joy.

Another Massoud, yes, an unexpected one—the opposite of the stereotype, the other side of the official image: happy as a child, his eyes shining, punctuating the most comical moments of the merchant's story with "ha!" and "ho!".

Another image altogether of the Taliban: a terrible regime indeed, but also a ludicrous one; what can one say about a dictatorship that makes you laugh as well as tremble? And isn't this the first good news of the trip—a fascism that, for once, could stop exercising its troubling fascination over its victims since it gives them, in the same narrative, its tragic version and its farce together? Malaparte's "Hitler Was a Woman." This "comedy of the Taliban" according to Massoud...

I waited for him at the guest house.

But as time was getting on, since he didn't seem to be coming and I felt he was, when it came down to it, not anxious to answer me about the "mistakes" committed, by him and his people, in the years that followed the defeat of the Soviets, I convinced the "engineer Ishak," my old accomplice from the time of the "free radios for the Panjshir," to take me here, to his home, in this village house, nestled in the valley, where he lives, in principle, with his family, but where I find him, once again, surrounded by mujahaddins.

These are the commanders from the Panjshir, this time.

They come from the neighboring mountains, these hundred war leaders who, at the darkest hours of the two wars—the war against the Soviets, then against the Taliban—helped him stand fast.

And, from afar, seeing them all standing in the garden, pressing around him, greeting each other, placing their right hands over their hearts in a sign of respect, embracing each other in silence, bowing, you'd think it was a ballet, or a royal court, or even a celebration—except that instead of glasses in hand everyone is holding out pieces of paper they're submitting for the signature of the "leader": one is asking for new shoes for the soldiers; another wants a relief guard; another has had enough of being in the mountains and wants to see his unit advance to the front line; yet another is seeking permission for one of his artillerymen to go visit his family in Iran; a fifth wants to be assured that the Koranic code prescribes stoning of thieves—Massoud, this time, does not sign—this Muslim of the Enlightenment, this democrat, maintains that stoning is an archaic and barbaric form of judicial punishment. Finally another complains he doesn't have enough artillery and Massoud, as a military professional, suggests an arrangement of the existing weapons that would increase their firepower without needing to add more. As for me, since it seems that, to approach him, you must have a paper to sign, I scribble my own: "An answer... I ask the Commander Ahmed Shah Massoud for an answer, just a brief answer, as to the mistakes committed during the years of government in Kabul, etc." Massoud laughs, asks for a few minutes of patience. And, when the commanders have left, resumes the conversation.

"My mistakes, then? The first is to have been mistaken on the political evolution of Pakistan: I thought the military would hand over power, that civilians would resume permanent authority, and I'd come to an understanding with them."

Still the obsession with Pakistan...

"And then I committed a second mistake, probably more serious..."

He says it regretfully; I feel him hesitating.

"It was a 'democratic' mistake. It's the mistake of too scrupulously respecting, after victory, the equilibrium of the movements that had made up the resistance. But imagine for an instant that I hadn't done so. Imagine, since I'm the one, after all, who liberated Kabul from the Communists, then barred the road for Gulbuddin Hekmatyar's fundamentalists, that I had taken power alone. War would have started up again. Bloodbaths would have followed."

I think of the very beautiful image, in Christophe de Ponfilly's film, *Massoud, The Afghan* where we see him, minister of the Armies—a foreigner among the other ministers, his mind obviously on other things, and, yet, sharing power with them, making deals.

"And today? What proves you wouldn't do the same thing today and that, if you chased the Taliban out of Kabul, you wouldn't associate again with those politicians without souls, without morality?"

He smiles.

"The situation has changed. Gulbuddin is in exile in Tehran. Rabbani—whom I respect—is old and no longer interested in power. So..."

He gestures with his hand, as if to say: "I'm the last one, no one's left but me." And I think of de Gaulle, whom I know he admires—I think of that moment, still so beautiful, in the biography of a Resistance fighter, where he tells himself: "There, I'm alone now, I am responsible for my own actions; it is I who elected myself, I who chose to be de Gaulle..." Is Massoud at that point? Has he experienced his inner June 18th? Has he resolved, whatever the cost, to stop compromising with anyone at all? As if he guessed my thoughts, he continues.

"The real question is the Taliban. Total war or not total war against the Taliban? I'm going to tell you a story..."

A late commander arrives, carrying new bad news from the Northern fronts: troop movements in Mohammadabad; the Iranians are getting stirred up and risk complicating matters. I fear the interruption will make him lose his thread, or change his mind. But no. He resumes.

"A few months ago, I spoke by satellite telephone to their leader, Mullah Omar, the self-proclaimed 'emir of the believers.' I told him: 'Let's organize a meeting of *ulemas* to decide between us, and then let's have elections; I'll accept the verdict in advance.' On the subject of elections, Mullah Omar immediately said 'No, elections aren't part of Islam.' The meeting of *ulemas*, though, took place in Pakistan—but, after a few days, he recalled his people on a specious pretext. So it's complicated, isn't it? What should we have wanted, when it comes down to it? Not to make deals. I don't want to make any more deals or consent to compromises. But to have discussions, to try to stop massacres by entering into dialogue—that's not such a laughable aim..."

Evening falls on the Panjshir. Outside, we hear nothing but the sound of dogs fighting, amplified by the mountain. It's cold. Massoud dreams and is silent. A little boy comes out of the house to pick a petunia, and plays near his father. Warlord, really? In love with war and its rites? De Gaulle again. I quote Malraux to him and his famous phrase on the art of "waging war without loving it."

"That's my case," he replies, a touch of nostalgia in his voice. "I do not love war either. I've been waging it for twenty years, but I can't say that I like it."

I point out to him that he's done nothing but that all his life—hasn't this war changed him, by necessity? Irremediably transformed him? Is he certain he knows, when the time comes, how to work at something else?

"Do you want to know my most cherished dream? It would be to rediscover, in a peaceful Afghanistan, the engineer's profession that I never really exercised. These people are so extraordinary! So courageous! Have these twenty years of war changed me? It's my people they have transformed. But for the good. The years have hauled them above themselves. They've allowed them, through suffering and resistance, to transcend themselves. I loved my people, before. Now, I admire them. And my most cherished dream would be to contribute, with the people, for them, to the reconstruction of a free Afghanistan."

A people ennobled by History? Yes, he says. The Afghani people. The proof by means of the Afghani people. The other lesson, again, of Commander Massoud.

Indefatigable Massoud. Yesterday that meeting with the commanders of the Panjshir... The day before yesterday the Salang meeting... Today, early in the morning, a meeting of the council of elders he is presiding over, in a section of Bosorak, in the very heart of the Panjshir, ten minutes by foot from the bazaar—a landscape of shrubs and reeds, clay houses, bridge over the stream made from the debris of tank treads, cow pats drying in the courtyards of houses, and then, at the end of the path, in the middle of a field, a little mosque, recent, with a jumble of shoes in front of its door.

He looks, at first glance, a little more tired than the day before. Less present. I have the feeling of an imperceptible distance when the old men of the valley come to greet him, one by one, in great ceremony, before entering the mosque. But when the time comes for him to enter in turn and take the floor, when the time comes for the sermon before this new assembly of people who, this time, represent the civilian and political authorities of the region, then his voice is raised once again, melodious, clear, as in Salang: this bard's voice that will captivate for four hours the audience of white beards—four hours! the art of time as the sinews of war, with Massoud!

"The worst is behind us," he explains to them. "The traitors have betrayed. The corrupt have led their war of corruption. A purified army remains. A fine army that will now mount a counter-attack, I promise you."

Then, to the *malek* of a neighboring village, a hero in the war against the Soviets, who gets up to say he wants to return to the front but that his sons forbid him from doing so:

"Stay where you are, *malek*. We have enough commanders. We even have enough weapons. What we need, now, is materiel. Do you know that it's because of lack of supplies that, two years ago, we had to beat a retreat from Kabul?"

Then again, in reply to the few words he did me the honor of asking me to utter, and in which I said of course how much I admired his heroism and that of his fighters—but also that only a unified resistance, surmounting divisions of tribes or people, would perhaps, one day, have the support of the West:

"That time, too, has passed. Those divisions are finished. Do you know that the other night, in Salang, in the assembly, a third of the Pashtun commanders had come to listen to me— me, a Tajik? Isn't that the proof that we have overcome this inevitability of division?"

And, to the assembly of white beards again:

"Our commanders are the heroes of Afghanistan. They bear its name. They will make its unity. Tell them—this is your role— that a divided Afghanistan is like a mule with stiff legs. Divided, we will die. United, we will win—and the world, mark my words, will fly to our aid."

Does he believe what he says? And what is the role, in his self-assurance, of his anxiety—always the same—to feed the faith of his partisans? On the wish for unity, yes, of course, he is sincere: Massoud is, today, the only statesman worthy of this name in Afghanistan. When it comes to his confidence in the resolution of other nations to support him, things are, on the other hand, not so clear: and that's what emerges from the continuation of our conversation when, the meeting over, we return together to Bosorak.

He: much less optimistic than he wanted to say in public, as to the "virtue" of the West.

Me: a feeling that America is nonetheless in the process of sizing up the danger of the Taliban.

He: of what America are we speaking? The one of the rights of man or the one of oil companies that think only of their pipeline bringing Turkmenian oil to Pakistan?

Me: difficult to imagine the world letting the matter of a pipeline decide the fate of a country; didn't they, moreover, prove otherwise by bombing the hiding-place of the terrorist Bin Laden, in the heart of Taliban territory?

He: who knows what is weightier, oil or democratic values? And as to Bin Laden, do you want another piece of information? He is living in Kandahar, on the same street—the Americans know this—as Mullah Omar, the supreme leader of the Taliban; so that when they bomb, a hundred kilometers further away, a refugee camp where he may never have set foot, they're making fun of the world in general and of us, the Afghans, in particular. . .

So, is he an optimist or a pessimist? Hard to tell. I think of Alija Izetbegovic, whom he resembles in so many ways, and one of whose main convictions I wonder if he shares: the West never comes to the aid of anyone except conquerors; the victims have to help themselves, break the silence of the lambs—only then will the West realize that they were defending its values.

"We will win this war," the Bosnian President had told us, one night in Sarajevo, while the Serbian shells landed like never before on the city. Isn't that also what Massoud is saying? Isn't that the meaning, against all expectations, of all that I've seen and heard since I've been here? And isn't that the main teaching of a journey begun to the tune of prejudice—"Massoud the melancholy one, cornered in his Panjshir hideout, at bay, already dead..."?

That Massoud can win this war, that he is perhaps readying himself, all alone, without our aid, to make the Taliban withdraw—the next day, on the front line, above the plain of Kuhestan, I had the most intense intuition of this.

We left, again, from Jengalak.

We took that famous Panjshir route which the partisans like to say is like a salient bound straight for Kabul, in the heart of Afghanistan.

Having arrived at the end of the valley, we took another road, or I should say a track, whose existence I never would have suspected; hollowed out between rock and ravine, it climbs alongside the mountain up to the plateau.

And, on the plateau, in the place where the track stops to give way to the trench, on this vast naked stretch, beaten by the wind and the whirlwinds of earth and dust, we found Massoud one last time.

He is wearing a large, immaculate white sari over which he has slipped a navy blue blazer with gold buttons.

He runs from one trench to another, from one group of soldiers to the next, with a rather mad energy, as if he were dancing.

"Ah, you're there? Come with me."

To one of the units, he says its anti-aircraft artillery are aiming too low.

To another unit he thought was too exposed, he demonstrates, shovel in hand, how to free the entrance to a bunker and especially how to keep covered the slope that Taliban will have to climb, if they attack.

To a third, the one posted farthest in front at the tip of the spur, he gives an actual lecture on the placement and concealment of mines in rocky terrain.

With all of them, in fact, he gives himself over to this surprising exercise that reveals the great chess player as well as the poet or, if you like, the strategist combined with a tactician of genius: imagining the enemy's attack, almost playing it in its place—preventing the worst by simulating it.

"For the enemy is there," he says, handing me a pair of binoculars. "Look. On the mountainside. Beyond the plain. They tried, last year, to retake the position. They stayed there for eight days. Since then, we have held it."

And, seeing that I'm surprised by such an advanced, and solid, position, beyond this "stronghold" of the Panjshir to which he is supposed, in the eyes of the Western press, to have withdrawn and is supposed to be strangled, he jokes:

"That's your illusion. The reality is that we haven't been there for a long time. For many months now, we've gone out of our fortress. You don't see? You don't believe? Hold on. Lend me your map..."

He unfolds the map on the bottom of the trench, kneels down.

"Look. We are there. This entire zone, there, is ours..."

He points out the east of the country, from Badakhshan in the north to Kapisa in the south.

"This zone too..."

He outlines the central part, west of Bamayan.

"Here are the Shiites, but they are with us. There (he points to Nouristan) is Haji Qadir and his Pashtuns—with us, too. There again (the axis that goes from Kunar to Jalalabad) we cut off the road when we want to. And as to the rest (vague gesture), the Taliban are, of course, at home in the regions of Kandahar, Paktia, Zabul, Helmand and Wardak. But, elsewhere, they are in a situation like that of the Soviets before: they occupy the roads, the communication centers, the cities—but leave that zone, go into the heart of the country, and you'll see they no longer have control over the villages, or the support of the populations."

Over there, on the other mountain, the brief glimmer of a machine gun. Further on, in the sky, the drone of a plane's motor, which puts the men on the alert. Massoud straightens up. Listens. He gives his artilleryman a wink, as if to say: "That gun that was aiming too low—it was the right time to correct it, wasn't it?" He knows that his fate is being played here, these days, in this trench or in another one, but that, morally, he has won. He shrugs his shoulders. He smiles. Then he dusts off his sari and, standing on the deserted plateau, stares at the clouds—and waits.

"...Mujibur Rahman and his free Bengal..."

I see him again, thirty years ago, in Bangladesh. I see him, in Dhaka, in the temporary office, set up in a straw hut, where the President, Mujibur Rahman, receives him. There reigns, in the city, a feverish atmosphere of victory. It is hot. The crowd, in jubilation, shouts: "Jay Hind! Jay Hind!"—Long live India! Long live India! And he is almost as happy as the people of Dhaka.

"I am not a journalist, Mr. President," begins this young man who resembles me, as is his wont at a first meeting, perched on his readings of Aragon and Malraux. "I am an engaged intellectual. *En-ga-gé*. I am a French student of the Marxist economist Charles Bettelheim: a specialist in unequal development in post-colonial societies; unbeatable in Chinese people's communes, proletarian and peasant sciences, the art of war, internal colonialism. I haven't come here to be a witness but to act. I have participated in your struggle. I place myself at your service."

The President contemplates him with a little surprise. They had announced the special correspondent for the French paper

Combat. And here he has in front of him an excited youth who is explaining to him that he couldn't give a damn about *Combat*; that he scorns journalism; that he respects journalists only when they defend, under cover of objectivity, a great cause that, etc., etc. He has spent three months, this young man explains, with a battalion of his Mukti Bahini; he entered the capital of his country with them, and with the victorious Indian army; and he can, if he wishes it, tell him the true story of the war he has won. President Rahman smiles. Thanks him. Makes a little speech, also, on the necessary solidarity of the West with his newborn government. And since the young man calls himself a "specialist in unequal development in postcolonial societies," he appoints him, quite randomly, as his Adviser for Affairs of Industrial Planning and Development—nothing less!

The adventure will last for three months. Just three months. Almost right away, the time of suspicions and complications came (too much China... too much about people's communes and proletarian science... too many contacts with too many Naxalites in a country that was under the Soviets' heel...). And, since the commands of Brezhnev reigned over Dhaka, they came, one fine morning, to collect this unsatisfactory subject in the little office he occupied at the Presidential Palace and put him on the first plane for Calcutta, on the way to Paris. But the scene had been set. He remained, for a very long time, this character I describe, who would rather have himself chopped in pieces than admit he was "only" a journalist. He was that "journalist-who-made-history" and who, I've also said, would have felt dishonored to be confused with the horde of great reporters— Oulman and Garofalo of *Paris Match*, but also

Jean Vincent, Lucien Bodard —whom he happened to cross paths with in the jungles of occupied Bengal but who, once the war was over, went home, and were, in his eyes, only mercenaries of the event. So lively was his passion to serve, so great his conviction that intellectuals had for too long interpreted the world and that the time had come to change it, that the idea didn't even enter his head that the real mercenary could be him...

A little later he saw Bodard again. He became his friend. Real cooperation became possible between them, sometimes literary, often ordinary life: a summer in Carros... private confidences exchanged... a portrayal of the younger by the elder, which he had to negotiate line by line, with a scalpel, since undisclosable episodes of his life were revealed in it... the affair of Ludmilla X. with whom Bodard was in love and who had said: "All right! But only on condition that you get that 'journalist-who-makes-history' (promoted, now, to the status of 'new philosopher,' and in vogue) to write about my work as a painter"—and the young man complied, he did that for his friend, and it's one of the rare texts of his life that he regretted a little having written... But the only thing that truly separated him from Bodard is that, despite the writer, and even the great writer, that Bodard was in the process of becoming, Bodard still believed in journalism, whereas the young man believed only in adventure and action.

And today? Where do I stand, today, with this young man and his "activist" fantasies? He is still there, of course. He was there, in Afghanistan, eight years later, when I went to bring Massoud the first transmitters of "Radio Free Kabul." He was there, in Bosnia, twelve years after that, during the entire duration of that war where, as in Afghanistan, as in Bangladesh, as I did at the age of twenty and again at thirty, I devoted myself body and soul to a cause that surpassed me. And he is still there, after fifty years, in the heart of this South Sudanese jungle, face to face with Garang.

No matter what I do, no matter what I say, no matter if I have only Foucault, Walter Benjamin, the windowless bus in Frasquillo, the flat-bottomed barge, the minuscule lives, on my lips—I am well aware that there is a corner of my head where the same little voice still breathes, the same crafty spirit, I almost want to say, like in the Jewish fairytales, the same dybbuk: "You're not a journalist... you're not a journalist... the intellectuals have interpreted the world too much... the honor of an intellectual, here, in the South Sudan, as before in Bangladesh, is to help this man, to give him advice, to tell him the right strategy—isn't that precisely what you did, last night, in the Alek camp, with Deng Alor and his gathering of commanders, in that Malraux-like scene, beneath the stars, around the fire?..." Except here, for the first time, I manage to correct myself, and to the question of the mistrustful leader of the SPLA—"What are you doing? Who are you?", I knew how to answer wisely, stifling the voice of the dybbuk: "I am French, a French journalist, I'm preparing an article for the French paper *Le Monde*..."

What has happened? Where did this come from, this new wisdom, and how did it come? I have said: from time, which still wound up passing. From Foucault, the new journalism, the work of thought. But also, from Garang himself who, since he's no Mujibur Rahman, or Izetbegovic, or Massoud, didn't "deserve" this status of a "knight on horseback" that I was tempted to offer him, as I did the others. But there's something else. One doesn't rid oneself just like that of one's dybbuk, and so there is something else. Romain Gary, grand master of the dybbuks, said that dybbuks never die. They are there, he explained in *The Dance of Genghis Cohn*, his best novel, whose main character was a dybbuk. Still there. They do not die. They don't even get old. It just sometimes happens that they've had enough of the soul that they're dybbukizing (unless it's the soul that's had enough). Then they go out for a little fresh air. They take a vacation. They go to squat in another unknown soul, for a little while. And then, one fine day, either because they've really had enough, or because the dybbukized subject is dying and they no longer have a choice, they fly off for good and go make their nest in a replacement soul.

The dybbuk of Barrès in the soul of Aragon and Malraux. The dybbuk of Malraux in the soul of Régis Debray. Of Drieu in Tillinac and Rouart. Of Marc Bloch in Colombani. Of Fitzgerald in Enthoven. Of Péguy in Bensaïd and Plenel. Of Camus in Jean Daniel. Of Sartre in Bourdieu, for lack of anything better. The mad dybbuk of Céline alternatively succubusing the souls of Nimier or de Roux. The dybbuk of Debord in Sollers. Of Bernanos in Clavel. Of Clavel in Glucksmann and me, around 1977—or not just "around" 1977! I can more precisely name the day, almost the instant, of the flight of the Bernanos dybbuk coming, with the consent of Clavel, to besiege the soul of his two "heirs"! I was there... I saw it... I saw, with my own eyes, on the set of Bernard Pivot's TV program, the flight and landing of the little migrating Clavel dybbuk...

Where are the dybbuks? Where are we all, with our dybbuk? Who has taken good care of his dybbuk? Who has let it escape?

Who has chased it away? This would be a good question to ask not of the dead, but of the living. This would be one way to classify the members of a generation—friend, where is your dybbuk? What have you done with it? Kouchner, the other day, back from his mission to Kosovo: wound up, possessed by his mission, enraged, the eternal apostle of the empire of the Good—dybbuk intact. Benny Lévy, in Jerusalem, a new man in black, headed towards sainthood: the same powerful influence, the same reflexes of a leader, the same relationships with his disciples as with his troop of Maoists from before—dybbuk still green. Friend Sollers, fighting, in *Le Monde*, against a left of the left that will serve no purpose but to elect Chirac: Guy Debord's dybbuk, the old denunciation of moldy France given a new look: nothing to report, everything working smoothly. And then, on the other hand, Colonel Debray: surly, stodgy, his new "I'm done! I'm turning in my weapons... you won't catch me at it again" side—maybe the dybbuk actually has left him; and perhaps it's gone to take up residence in the head of Chevènement or Védrine... Or even Deniau: he seems tired, too, of his dybbuk; one feels he'd like nothing more than to hand it over to someone else and just concern himself with his solitary journeys. But to whom could he give it? What soul for the old dybbuk of Major Deniau? Given (theorem) that dybbuks never die, given (corollary) that dybbuks travel but don't give up, it's not enough to be bitter, grumpy, tired; you still need to find a welcoming soul, and there are dybbuks who don't find any—there are dybbuks who are looking desperately for souls.

That's perhaps my problem, at bottom. Tired of my dybbuk. Asking only to disburden myself of it and to be finished with my old lyrical neurosis, my wish for epics, my man-of-action side disguised as a journalist and almost ready, again, to provide John Garang with a ready-made plan to recapture power in Khartoum. But where would he go, this dybbuk of mine? Where would it reincarnate, my inner child? Among those fighting the greenhouse effect? The anti-GMO activists? *Attac**? Not very likely...

---

* *Action pour une Taxation des Transactions financiéres pour l'Aide aux Citoyens,* an international anti-globalization organization.

As a child, I admired fighter pilots. The great ones in the RAF, of course. The American pilots who, after Pearl Harbor, left to bomb Japan without knowing if they'd come back. A friend of my father's about whom it was murmured in my family that, having voluntarily enlisted in the English army, he had been one of the bomber pilots over Dresden. Romain Gary whose *Promise at Dawn* they made me read, at the age of twelve. Malraux, a little, but not much, later: too young to read *Man's Hope,* I knew the great and petty deeds of the España squadron, as well as that magnificent story, which was not a war story, but which fascinated me just as much, of the intrepid explorer leaving, with Corniglion-Molinier, on board Paul-Louis Weiler's Farman 190, to search, in the sands of Yemen, for the remains of the temples and palaces of the legendary Queen of Sheba. And then, long before all that, Antoine de Saint-Exupéry's *Night Flight* and *Southern Mail,* and the illustrations of Hélène Boucher, "the Amazon of the air," cut out from an old *Paris Match,* and especially, especially, a big book of photographs whose name I am incapable of remembering—something like *Les As,** or *Les Conquérants du ciel,*** I just remember a big sepia-tinted cover, like a fake newspaper cover, with a photo of Guynemer standing

---

* *The Aces*
** *Conquerors of the Sky*

next to his fuselage, and, inside, a series of portraits of pilots from the other war, photos and texts, presented like young heroes, the knights of modern times, heroic lives, archangels of the sky, halfway between the spirit of modern war and of the medieval tournament: Guynemer was there, and his squadron of Cigognes; Navarre and his red airplane; Dorme, the aviator with the wooden leg; Nungesser, and his artificial jaw; Noguès; Mermoz; Védrines, the ace of "special missions" sent to gather information inside enemy lines; a certain Romanet; Roland Garros, the elite marksman, inventor of machine-gun firing between the blades of the propeller; I have all these names, and also the names of the great "grease monkeys," engraved in my memory with an incredible precision; they live there along with the characters of Joseph Kessel's *L'Equipage**, or the ones in Malraux's *Man's Hope*, read much later (but I also fell for the gallant, very "virile war" style of Drieu and Montherlant, those souls so distressed by the idea of dropping their bombs over Alicante from the shelter of the clouds that they forced themselves to fly low, very low, to give the enemy anti-aircraft guns a chance!); or even, much later still, in the mannered pages of Proust's *Time Regained*, those almost living planes that soared into the purity of the sky like modern Valkyries and there, lost in the immensity, became like stars of fire and sword.

To be brief. Mixed memories of all those as I watch the pilot of the old Beechcraft play with the clouds and then, lower, approaching the Nuba mountains, with the sandy wind blowing in gusts and slightly destabilizing the machine. Impression of *déjà lu*—already read—as in Colombia, approaching Bogota, when the little plane scarcely cleared the barrier of mountains,

---

* The first novel of aviation, written in 1923—Trans.

or as in Angola, when we descended over Lobito, when Joe, the pilot, under pretext that UNITA wasn't far away and that its guns were aimed at the sky, set about taking aim, reeling, throttling the engines, diving, gliding, straightening up, descending vertically, then in loops, beautiful curt circles, well-drawn, which were like the rings of an impeccable spiral. Impression of *déjà lu*, when I find myself, here too, paying attention to the rumble of the motor: now strong, or soothing, and I'm reassured—the wonderful gentleness of flight above the sand; now a suspicious spluttering and coughing, the sound of a large unstable insect, and I can't keep from scrutinizing the pilot's face, or that of Ostrowski—those faces are my real instrument panel, my compasses, my only way, since the altimeter is broken, to guess if a mechanical disturbance or failure, a total collapse, are looming. And then the approach itself, finally: the Nuba mountains below us; the hills alternating with stretches of sand and rock as far as the eye can see; but the pilot doesn't know the zone; the runway is invisible; so he searches, hesitates, gains altitude a little, comes back, scrutinizes again, almost bends over—this time just like the aviators of my childhood photo album, muffled in their bomber jackets, helmet and goggles flattened on their heads, their scarves streaming in the propeller's wind, without a windshield. But where is the damned runway? In what fold of the terrain? What valley? What sheet of stone or greenery? Half an hour of fuel is left, not enough to return to Loki or any other known base. We have to find it, then; despite the sun, despite the powdery sand that blinds us, despite the total absence of landmarks, we absolutely have to find it; here? No, not here; there? No, still not there, the pilot has descended even further, it was only a dried-out wadi, or a goat path, or the shadow of the plane on the sand; time passes; the fuel is running out; I have the impression that the motor is making a weird sound and that his hand on the stick trembles a little; now's the time for all the superstitions, for childish wagers, now's the time when I really have the feeling of coming to the end of my hallucination—in Joseph Kessel's plane, above Nouakchott or Villa Cisneros, or even in Yemen, with Corniglion and Malraux.

Last trip. Last article. Rereading the book, I'm surprised at the energy that I seem to have put into differentiating, not just these five texts, but the systems of impressions that ordered and inspired them. For I could have done the opposite, after all. I could have, I now realize, given the impression that nothing resembles extreme distress more than another extreme distress and that, in the night of these wars, on the scale of hell of which they are just so many modalities, one of the damned is worth as much as another of the damned, and resembles him like a brother. And I can easily imagine a very last essay or, on the contrary, a very first one, which, instead of distinguishing the situations as I have done, instead of insisting on revealing one from many, and many from one, instead of spending such effort in pointing out the thousand and one little differences whose effect is perhaps, in the end, only to dissolve the monotony of a nameless suffering in local color, my unwritten essay could have expressed the uchronia of a world randomly taking its characteristics from Angola, from Sri Lanka, from Burundi, from Colombia, from the South Sudan. What's the use of "local color" when one is dealing with radical Evil? What's the use of "things seen" when it's the Devil that's pulling the strings and when the

Devil has no face? And isn't the highlighted, and thus theatrically manipulated, thing seen the very definition of the obscene? I had the temptation. I rejected it, but I had it. And a part of me tells myself that it would have been another way to remain faithful in this night without a night that is the realm of the victims. Buzzati. Jünger's *On the Marble Cliffs*. The great parable-figures in Guyotat, or in Genet's *The Screens*...

"...hamlets where, in the dry season, they're reduced to digging in the sand, with their bare hands, to find water..."

I have seen dead men, I mean men who died in war: Sarajevo;
the scene, especially, in the morgue, at the end of *Bosna!*; a
seemingly peaceful, or pacified, scene, but which I had to bend
over backwards to film. I've seen men dying: in Bangladesh, on
the night of the capture of Jessore, those bleeding, but still
living, bodies in the midst of the chaos; or that Eritrean, his arm
torn off by a bomb, who emptied himself of his blood in the
time it took to transport him to the Asmara hospital. What I
hadn't yet seen was men in the process of dying of hunger, really
dying, really of hunger—and it's horrible.

First, I thought it was a house. But it was a makeshift
dispensary, made up of sheet metal, logs, and bales of hay
assembled beneath a large tree with, as its only medical equipment, the base of a rusty IV machine that must have stopped
being usable a long time ago. Inside there were three men and a
child, black masses, bony, half-naked shapes, lying on the
ground, over whom a fourth man was watching, scarcely more
vigorous, also very thin, tousled, with an eight-days' growth of
beard, his complexion waxy, his gaze confused, his speech
almost inaudible, fanning himself with tamarind leaves. "It's
over," he whispers to the unit leader who is accompanying me

and who is trying to organize a transport to Kawdah by radio, but halfheartedly, without believing in it. "For those three, it's over. There's nothing left to eat, so it's over."

One of them has his mouth half-open and breathes in little gasps, from time to time thrashing his arms like a fish fanning its fins. The other has his shoulders and belly hollowed out, gathered together in a final effort to retain what's left of life; sometimes his nails scrape his shirt as if he wanted to tear it off; sometimes his over-elongated, emaciated hands, with their large protruding veins and spots of dark blue, stretch out as if they were looking for contact with other hands. The third, who seems to be gathering his last strength to watch over the child, who is also dying, clinging to him, has a translucent face, his feet and wrists strangely swollen—from time to time, he emits a little groan; murmurs something in the ear of the child who doesn't reply; he has crusts of earth around his mouth, dampened by a rivulet of sweat that is the last thing, along with a green fly on his chin, that makes him look a little alive; sometimes he imperceptibly shifts his eyes and looks at me, but I'd swear it was without seeing me.

They have not been hit, these men. They have not been wounded. There's no trace, around the hut, of the slightest recent bombardment. The weather outside is fine. And, yet, it's over. They are going to die, there, of nothing but lack of nourishment, nothing but hunger. They are going, in a few days, perhaps a few hours, to stop breathing because they no longer have the strength to go scrape the earth and suck on a root. The most passive of deaths. The most submissive. In a certain way, the most indifferent, the most absurd and so the most terrifying.

And, for me standing there, powerless, petrified, daring neither to touch them nor to move, scarcely able to breathe, for me reduced to watching the officer fiddle with his walkie-talkie and ask for help in which he does not believe, it's one of the most terrible images of this journey.

1. Sometimes, I think: it's novels that should be written. As a novelist, one should enter the head of the damned at the moment when, at the door of his hut, the killer arrives. One should also be in the head (the body?) of the kamikaze at the moment when he knows, suddenly, he no longer has any choice.

2. A world that tolerates that, a world that takes the risk, as if at the day of reckoning, of being judged about the scandal of these men dying of hunger, a world that cares so little about being ready for a judgment about which the ancient wisdoms teach that we should learn to live as if it might come at any moment—that world is a dead world.

3. Regrets and stammerings. This double quavering of the text. These two ways of making it vacillate: upstream (what breathed it into me, what I try to remember); downstream (what it floods me with today, my regrets). I had never done that. If there's one action to which I implicitly swore, for thirty years, that I'd never yield, it's just this kind of twofold reworking. Fantasy of control... Dream of a completed work, closed in on itself, with no confessions... Let there be Text, and the Text is... That's how I thought. I was like the killer who never revisits the scene of his crime. And now, these notes that do just the opposite

and turn the plot over to grasp the other pattern of the weave, the one I usually don't want to know anything about. The only freedom I still permit myself, in this action of bringing things into the open: never to say what, in these notes, hints at their beginning or end; it's up to the reader to figure it out.

These things are obvious: that the language of the genocide must never, at any price, be trivialized; that watching over the integrity of words in general and of this word in particular is an intellectual and political task that should be given priority; that there occurred, in Auschwitz, an event without precedent, incomparable to any other, and that the struggle against the banalization, both of the thing, and of the word that designates it, is an imperative, not just for the Jews, but for all those wronged by this crime (in other words, the human as such; the human in each man and each woman today); that the Shoah is the absolute genocide, the standard of the genre, the very measure of the non-human; that this singularity stems as much from the terrifying rationality of the methods (bureaucracy, industry of cadavers, gas chamber) as from its no less terrible portion of irrationality (the often noted insane account of how the trains of deportees had, till the last day, priority over convoys of weapons and troops), from its systematization (armies of killers let loose, all through Europe, in pursuit of Jews who had to be tracked down and tirelessly exterminated, to the last one) or from its metaphysical dimension and aim (beyond bodies and souls and, beyond souls, the very memory of Jewish texts and law)—all that is obvious. It is and will be increasingly difficult to make people understand all this, yet it is established and evident. . .

BERNARD-HENRI LÉVY

356

The fact remains that there's no point in laying down a rule if it's only so as not to have to use it. There's no point in saying, "Here is the standard" if it's only so that the standard remains, like a precious relic, in some kind of museum of memory and horror. So the lesson of the Shoah, for me, is also a constant vigilance over all contemporary fronts of misfortune. Far from this lesson anaesthetizing my sensibility, paralyzing my intelligence, and fixing both of them on tragedies in the past, it calls upon me, makes me take action, and makes me be here, today, in the Nuba mountains, in the process of gathering testimonies of what, as in Burundi, looks like an impending genocide. I had a prime reason, till this point, for wanting to remain faithful to the memory of the Shoah: the dead themselves; the homage due to the dead, to the poor dead, to their great sufferings; the idea, as, once again, Benjamin said (Thesis VI), that "before the enemy, if he conquers, even the dead will not be safe"; the idea, in other words, that the risk, for the unhonored dead, is to die a second time and that, for this second death, the survivors, the children of the survivors, would this time be responsible. I had another reason: the living; a demand for the living; a protection for the living; doesn't the modern form of anti-Semitism consist exactly in the denial of evidence? Almost the first article of faith of the modern anti-Semite is this terrible statement to the living: "The Shoah was not what you say; it was not, by any means, this extravagant crime in the long history of crimes. In fact, you wouldn't cling to this counter-truth, you wouldn't tirelessly plead for the centrality of Jewish suffering, if you weren't using it to pursue unspoken ulterior goals." Isn't it essential, right away, isn't it vital to stand fast, not to give in, to plead, more than ever, for the truth, in other words for the uniqueness? Well here's a third reason not to make any compromise about the evidence of this uniqueness: to give us a real chance, if, in some part of the globe, for instance here, in the South Sudan, the smell, recognizable from among a thousand others, of genocide comes floating back, not to brush it aside; to do everything, to give ourselves all the possible means, so that, on that day, we won't have to say: "We didn't know; I didn't know"; a keen memory, in other words; a memory on the alert, at work, which gives weapons to those who need them; a memory that makes one, not deaf, but attentive to the first notes of the fatal music—surely it's never the same music? Or the same smell? History has more imagination than men do? The Devil more than History? And he's not the type, the Devil, to commit the amateurish error of serving us up a genocide similar in all points to the standard of the genre? True; but you didn't have to be a prophet, in Rwanda, to understand what was coming; you didn't have to be very clever, in Bosnia, when the siege of Sarajevo began, then when the first pictures from the camps of Prjedor and Omarska came in, then when we knew there were villages, in central Bosnia, where men were being forced to lower their pants to see if they were circumcised, thus Muslim, you didn't have to be particularly clever to understand what it was all about—you just had, like Hatzfeld in Rwanda, to have the Shoah in your heart and in your head; you just had, like most of those who took action against ethnic purification in Bosnia, to remember that, previously, in a time both very distant and very close, there were millions of men and women who were, not strangers in Egypt, but deported in the heart of Europe. All you needed was to have a memory that was up to date; it's the same, here, with the Nuba.

"...that is and will be increasingly difficult to make people understand..."

September 2001, again. Another accident of my schedule. The Durban conference, in South Africa, where I finished this book. The bigwigs of the NGO's gathered together for, in principle, a big UN conference, sponsored by the governments, on "racism" and "intolerance." Will they finally talk about the anti-Tutsi racism of the Hutus? About the genocide with which this racism is menacing devastated Burundi? About the millions of dead in the Angolan war? About the fanaticism of the Tamil Tigers? About Rwanda? The South Sudan? Will it be a question, since one of the themes of the conference is the struggle against slavery, of those thousands of Dinka slaves abducted, in the South Sudan, in the provinces of Bahr el-Ghazal, Darfur, and Kordofan, by the mounted militiamen of the Forces for Popular Defence, in the pay of Khartoum? Will they profit from the circumstance and the formidable sounding-board it constitutes, to evoke those caravans of women and children, led like cattle, over hundreds of miles, to be sold to Arab families in the North—as servants, beasts of burden, sexual slaves branded with iron, like animals? Will they grasp the occasion, finally, to break the silence and intrude on the world scene the problem of these forgotten wars? (There are only a few of us to say to whoever will listen, not many, that this is the major problem of the century that's beginning. It is by our capacity to confront it or not that we will one day be judged.) None of all this. Instead, the occasion is devoted to the question of Israel. For eight days, we hear nothing but the crimes against humanity of which Israel is supposedly guilty in respect to the Palestinians. And everything unfolds as if everyone had chosen to agree that there's only one racist state in the world, and that this state is Israel, so it's neither urgent nor even useful to lift the leaden sheet that weighs over these lands of desolation and crime that are Angola, Burundi, Sri Lanka, Colombia, the Sudan.

In my secret calendar, it's a date that stands out.

First of all, of course, because of the unbelievable tone of verbal assault against a Zionism that's being linked with the worst the world could produce in terms of humiliation and crime. Has anyone ever gone so far in vehemence? Did the famous 1975 resolution* likening Zionism to a form of racism speak so explicitly about "acts of genocide," about "crimes against humanity"? Wasn't it tragically imbecilic that the very word "apartheid" was uttered there, in the country of Nelson Mandela, with the support of the UN, when they were talking about a country where, as everyone knows, all minorities, Arabs included, actually enjoy the same civil rights, exactly, as the Jewish majority?

Then because the prosecutors, having had the effrontery to conduct their offensive under the sign of anti-racism, and since all the proceedings take their lead from the same words, the same concepts, the weapon of Jewish memory turned against the Jews (and especially, of course, the philosophical-juridical weapon of the notion, born at Nuremberg, in explicit reference to the

---

* UN Resolution 3379, passed on 10 November 1975—ironically, the 37th anniversary of Kristallnacht. The resolution was repealed in 1991.

Shoah, of "crime against humanity"), it's the whole theory of living memory that is suddenly shattered. Memory—remembrance of past offenses, a weapon in future combats—is the very principle of the theorem of Auschwitz. (If Auschwitz, then Rwanda; if Auschwitz, then the Nuba; Auschwitz, the possibility of Auschwitz, as an argument—not, of course, unanswerable! If it were unanswerable, people would know it, and the damned wouldn't be there. In the end the Auschwitz argument is better than no argument at all, we don't have so many others—to draw the world's attention to what, perhaps, is being prepared in Burundi.) The uniqueness of Auschwitz? The standard of the inhuman? Can we take support from this uniqueness, this measure of potential horror, to give ourselves one more chance to intervene, before the irreparable occurs, in the chain of causes that we know will lead to the extermination of others? Maybe I'm wrong. But I have the feeling that in Durban there is finally being put in place the setting for an era in which when the Jews speak in this way, when they evoke the uniqueness of their suffering and when, not content to evoke it in secret, in the silence of recollection and piety, they urge the world not to abandon a principle that guarantees protection for everyone, they will be listened to at best with a polite but weary indifference, vaguely tinted with incredulity, indulgent (yes, yes... since you insist... if that makes you happy... victims have their reasons that reason doesn't know...), at worst with impatience, rage, abusive wrath full of hatred (when will this monomania end? Where do they get the right to a monarchy of suffering, of memory? Isn't one victim as good as another, it doesn't matter what victim, isn't one victim made of all victims, aren't they all worth each other and any other?)—I have the feeling that we are entering a world where this kind of discourse will be more and more difficult to understand.

And then I mark this date in black because of what it tells us, finally, about the stubborn determination of our era to say nothing, nothing at all, about these black holes where the worst is brewing and where History itself seems (according to your preference, according to the perspective you adopt) either suspended or seized with madness. Once again, wasn't Durban the ideal echo chamber? Wasn't it the place above all others for these voices of the other world to be heard? Would another chance come along? When? And did anyone take note of the immense failure—moral, political—committed by choosing once more to be silent, to yawn, to write off the suffering of the "damned"? As to the moral fault, things were clear enough from the start: it was enough to glimpse, on television, the stupefied face of the Rwandan delegate when the crusaders for anti-globalization had just informed him that his genocide did not have the good fortune to interest the new "historic" peoples of whom they claimed to be the representatives; remarkable nuance, unheard-of pronouncement, it was no longer only, or perhaps mainly, the West that was throwing the Rwandan devastation into the void, but the others, all the others, that whole collection of the southern nations for whom anti-Westernism is the cement—and that intensified its own damnation by anointing itself a right-thinking third-worldism....

As to the other failure, the political one, a few days were necessary so that on 9/11, an entirely different event, this one cataclysmic, and seemingly unrelated to Durban, prompted the hypothesis I had had on my lips, but without daring to utter it, all through these journeys: black holes and apocalypse; darkness and fire; imagine for an instant that, in the economy of this beginning of the century, each were the counterpart of the other, and were like the double mode of one single nihilism. Imagine a geography of disaster, finally globalized, where Durban wouldn't be so far from Manhattan, or Manhattan from Khartoum, Colombo, Bogota, Bujumbura, Luanda; imagine a world stampeded, chaotic, already half split up by named and unnamed wars, declared and undeclared, where entire peoples would be denied, ignored, thrown back into the night of non-History, under the combined pressure of the historic peoples of yesterday and tomorrow, of the North and the South, of the prosperous world and its mimetic adversaries. I close these "Reflections" with the same question with which I had begun them: What unheard-of tragic forms will their despair take then?

Endnotes

1. *Remembrance of Things Past*, Vol. III, *Time Regained*, New York: Vintage, p. 778.

2. André Gide, *Journal (1889-1939)*, Paris: Gallimard, Pléiade, 1951, p. 473. Translated as *The Journals of André Gide (1889-1949)* by Justin O'Brien. Chicago: Northwestern University Press, 1988, p.69.

3. Cited, along with the excerpts by Walter Benjamin, by Michael Löwy, in *Walter Benjamin: Avertissement d'incendie*, Paris: Presses Universitaires de France, 2001, pp. 75-76. See Hegel, *La Raison dans l'Histoire. Introduction à la philosophie de l'histoire*, 10/18, 1968, p. 103. Translated as *Reason in History: A General Introduction to the Philosophy of History*, by Robert S. Hartman. New York: Prentice Hall, 1953.

4. Henry de Montherlant, *Le Songe*, Paris: Grasset, 1922, pp. 124-125. Translated as *The Dream* by Terence Kilmartin, New York: Macmillan, 1963. [Translator's Note: The passage Lévy cites does not exist in the English edition; in fact two entire pages of the French edition, pp. 124-126, have been left out of the English. The passage Lévy refers to is this:

"[Alban] saw him raise his arms for mercy, his face ashen. The thought flashed into his mind: "Unarmed... prisoner..." Then, at point-blank range, full in the face, he shot him.

"He was so close that the body fell onto him. He instinctively clung to him; they rolled over; limitless embrace. Alban felt the thing stiffen against him, become larger, take on superhuman proportions, like a woman at the height of her spasm. Extricating himself with a frenzied heave, he slipped on top of the creature; and he put his hands on his throat, while with his right knee, with all his strength, he rammed him in the belly and genitals. Then he saw he was dead."]

5. Frédéric de Towarnicki, *Ernst Jünger, récits d'un passeur du siècle*. Paris: Editions du Rocher, 2000, p. 78.

6. Ernst Jünger, *The Storm of Steel*, translated by Michael Hoffman. London: Allen Lane, 2003.

7. Ernst Jünger, *Feuer und Blut: Werke*, Stuttgart: Klett-Cotta, Vol. 1, p. 481.

8. Pierre Drieu La Rochelle, *La Comédie de Charleroi*, Paris: Gallimard, 1934, pgs. 61 and 190. Translated as *The Comedy of Charleroi, and Other Stories* by Douglas Gallagher. Cambridge: Rivers Press, 1973. [Very useful to the English reader is Alastair Hamilton's introduction to his translation of Drieu's *Secret Journal* (New York: Howard Fertig, 1973), especially pages xii ff. —Trans.]

9. Kant, *The Idea of a Universal History in a Cosmopolitical Plan*. Hanover, New Hampshire: The Sociological Press, 1927. French version: *La Philosophie de l'Histoire*, Paris: Aubier, 1947, reprinted by Gonthier, p. 27.

10. G.W. Leibniz, *Monadology*, p. 57.

11. Quoted in Maurice Rieuneau, *Guerre et revolution dans le roman français, de 1919 à 1939*, Geneva: Slatkine Reprints, 2000, p. 542.

12. Régis Debray, *Les Masques*, Paris: Gallimard/Folio, 1992, p. 166.

13. Pierre Drieu La Rochelle, *Gilles*, Paris: Gallimard, 1942, p. 48.

14. Maurice Blanchot, *L'Ecriture du désastre*, Paris: Gallimard, p. 71. Translated as *The Writing of the Disaster* by Ann Smock, University of Nebraska Press, 1986, p. 41.

15. Ernst Jünger, in *Werke*, Stuttgart: Klett-Cotta, Vol. 1, p. 374. Translated as *Copse*.

16. Hannah Arendt, *Men in Dark Times*, New York: Harcourt, 1968, p. 92

17. Michel Foucault, *Dits et Ecrits II, 1976-1988*, Paris: Gallimard/Quarto, p. 709.

18. Michael Löwy, *Walter Benjamin: Avertissement d'incendie, op. cit.*, p. 38.

19. *Ibid*.

20. Alexandre Kojève, *Introduction à la lecture de Hegel*, Paris: Gallimard, 1947, pp. 434-435. An abridged version is available in English: *Introduction to the Reading of Hegel: Lectures on the Phenomonology of Spirit*, translated by James H. Nicholas, Ithaca: Cornell University Press, 1980.

21. Francis Fukuyama, *The End of History and the Last Man*, New York: Macmillan, 1992, pp. xxii-xxiii.

22. Nietzsche, *Thus Spake Zarathustra*, translated by Thomas Common. Prologue, Section 5.

23. F. Fukuyama, *op. cit.*, p.311.

24. A. Kojève, *op. cit.*, p. 435 of the French.

25. Max Weber, *Essays in Sociology*, Oxford University Press, 1946, p. 143.

26. A. Kojève, *op. cit.*, p. 436 of the French.

27. Françoise Proust, *L'Histoire à contretemps*, Paris: Le Livre de Poche/Biblio, 1999, pp. 59 ff.

28. Stéphane Mosès, *L'Ange de l'Histoire (Rosenzweig, Benjamin, Scholem)*, Paris: Seuil, 1992.

29. Michel Foucault, *The Archaeology of Knowledge*, translated by A.M. Sheridan Smith, New York: Pantheon Books, 1972, p. 17.

30. *Ibid.*, p. 4.

31. Foucault, *Dits et Ecrits, op. cit.*, p. 594.

32. *Ibid.*, p. 707.

33. Michel Foucault, *Dits et Ecrits II, 1976-1988*, Quarto, Paris: Gallimard, 2001, pp. 662-669, 679-694, 701-707, 709-716, 743-755, 759-761, 780-782, 790-794.

34. Nietzsche, "History in the Service and Disservice of Life," trans. Gary Brown, in *Unmodern Observations*, ed. William Arrowsmith, New Haven: Yale University Press, 1990, pp. 87-145. (*Faitalistes* is a play on words, referring to Nietzsche's "men of action," who behave unthinkingly, like animals, and fatalists, who are content with how things are instead of how they should be. —Trans.)

35. From "Fusée (Flare)": "The megaphone cries/ Lengthen the range//Lengthen the range love of your guns"—from Apollinaire's *Calligrammes*, trans. Anne Hyde Greet, Berkeley: University of California Press,1980, p. 241.

36. Frantz Fanon, born in Martinique, is the author of *Les Damnés de la terre*, translated as *The Wretched of the Earth*, a powerful statement of anti-colonial revolutionary thought.—Trans.

37. Heinrich von Kleist, *Anecdotes et petits récits*, Paris: Payot, 1981, with a preface by J. Ruffet.

38. Michael Löwy, *Walter Benjamin: Avertissement d'incendie, op. cit.*, pp. 41-42.

39. Ernest Hemingway, *By-Line*, ed. William White, New York: Scribners, 1967, p. 304.

40. Quoted in Maurice Rieuneau, *Guerre et revolution dans le roman français, de 1919 à 1939, op. cit.*, p. 103.

Translator's Acknowledgements

My thanks to Odile Chilton, for her expert guidance, and to Esther Allen, for her friendship and support. I am also grateful to Marina van Zuylen and Jennifer Cazenave for their help and counsel. I am especially grateful to Jane Hryshko of the Bard College Library and to the staff of the Starr Library in Rhinebeck for procuring various arcane and elusive books for me. And to my husband, Robert Kelly, for his invaluable advice.